THE SKY IS NOT THE LIMIT

THE SKY IS NOT THE LIMIT

Building a Flight Legacy

JAMES WESLEY ETCHISON

REVISED EDITION

Produced by Virtus Publishing LLC, Coeur d'Alene, ID
www.virtuspublishing.com

Book interior and cover design by Marta Samsel
Copyediting and proofreading by Paul Nicolas Baena

Publisher's Cataloging-in-Publication
(Provided by Cassidy Cataloguing Services, Inc.).

Names: Etchison, James Wesley, author.

Title: The sky is not the limit: building a flight legacy / James Wesley Etchison.

Description: Revised edition. | [Middle Village, New York]: [James Wesley Etchison]; produced by Virtus Publishing, [2025] | Revision of the December 2014 edition. | Includes index.

Identifiers: ISBN: 979-8-9912547-0-0 (print) | 979-8-9912547-1-7 (eBook) | 979-8-9912547-2-4 (audiobook)

Subjects: LCSH: Etchison, James Wesley. | Air pilots – Biography. | Vietnam War, 1961-1975 –Veterans – United States – Biography. | Vietnam War, 1961-1975 – Personal narratives, American. | Pan American World Airways, Inc. – Officials and employees – Biography. | Academics of Flight – History. | Flight schools. | Air pilots – Training of. | Flight engineers – Training of. | BISAC: BIOGRAPHY & AUTOBIOGRAPHY / General. | BIOGRAPHY & AUTOBIOGRAPHY / Aviation & Nautical.

Classification: LCC: TL540.E83 E83 2024 | DDC: 629.13092–dc23

For photographs of the people and places that illustrate the story told in this book, please visit the Academics of Flight website home page:

http://academicsofflight.com/

Comments and feedback are welcome. Feel free to contact the author at this address:

jimofaof@aol.com

"What you leave behind is not what is engraved in stone monuments, but what is woven into the lives of others."

—Pericles (495–429 BC)

Dedicated to all those I have met along the way.

—J. W. E.

CONTENTS

PART TWO

FOREWORD

My good friend Jim asked me to write the foreword to his book, which is good because I really want to talk about him!

I met Jim for the first time in 1986, when a call to the dispatch office came in, and the gentleman on the other side asked whether I (or anyone for that matter) was interested in teaching for him! He had an ATP class scheduled in a very short time hence, and it was full of customers who had already paid, most of them line-pilots from Europe who had been flying for years for companies such as Sabena and KLM. I happily accepted, and went to his office at the appointed date and hour, and met "The Man!" Instead of a detailed rundown on what I was supposed to teach, this tall, thin man dedicated a few minutes, and returned to what he did best: Juggling a myriad of balls, smiling all the while, and knowing exactly what he expected of each and every one.

The reason people working with him put up with this chaos—albeit not in Jim's eyes since he knew which arm would catch the 5th ball—was quite simple: He was a fundamentally decent man, looking at the world through a unique prism, and a great sense of humor.

He offered whatever a customer wanted: Flight training, Flight Engineer training, Flight Attendant training, Dispatch training, and if you wanted a class to start tomorrow, Jim would have no trouble committing to it without having arranged for any resources: And, yet, by the next day he would have all assembled, his Rolodex ensuring that people would provide what he had promised.

He was a habitual globe-trotter before that became a cliché. He served in Asia, attended Grad school in Germany, traveled extensively in Central and South America, the Caribbean, and Africa, and no matter where he went, he made friends! His secret? He was a friend to other people, first.

While being a good friend, he can be profane, politically so incorrect that longshoremen would blush, but you would always know that he has your back.

While Jim's professional life was four appointments in 10 minutes, the quiet center was his home, where his beloved wife and daughter shared in, and were the recipients of, a dedicated man creating a beautiful home.

Jim has a story to tell, and he tells it well.

After all these years I think it was not Jim who was "crazy," but it was us: He was the one who kept the show going, and kept all commitments in the best possible way.

Thank you, Jim.

Michael A.N. Winkler
Baldwin, NY
January 2014

ACKNOWLEDGMENTS

I would sincerely like to thank the following people for without their assistance, I could never have completed such an undertaking. My family, Rita and Karina, for their continual support to "keep going." My sister, Dahlgren, along with Irene Liao and Zahra Patterson, for help through the early editing stages.

Special thanks to those who contributed to this revised edition: Paul Nicolas Baena (the copy editor), and Marta Samsel (the cover and interior designer). Special thanks are also due to David George. David took a "mess" and, through many grunts and groans, provided an unmeasurable amount of talent and patience through all the facets required for the story to be published.

PROLOGUE

Many acquaintances have often suggested that I write a book on my life. I never gave it much thought, since there are certainly others who have had more noteworthy experiences to record. One day, my daughter, Karina, made a similar statement that made me consider my family's history. I only really knew one of my grandparents: my maternal grandmother. She was the inspiration of my life, as grandmothers often are, yet I knew very little about her. Once in a while, distant kin would be mentioned; however, the story would soon be forgotten. Each generation is part of a family's building block, and the idea started to have some validity.

Recently, the family buried my dad, James Walter Etchison, in a small country cemetery in Cana, North Carolina. He was a man who left the farm and through his journeys became a true pioneer in aviation from the 1930s after joining Pan Am as a flight engineer when the company began to circle the globe to Africa, Asia, Europe, South America, and other points in between.

As a young boy, I used to sit at the top of the stairs in our Westbury, New York, home in my one-piece pajama, absorbing the tales of my dad's flight crewmember friends as he and my mom entertained them. I listened to their exploits, such as searching the African jungle for an airplane that crashed, which was described by a native as "heap big tin can crashing into mountain" and about a layover somewhere in Latin America, where a fight erupted in a bar between a Pan Am crew and German spies during World War II.

To me, the stories were incredible. Throughout his career, my dad was acquainted with all the historical names in aviation: Charles Lindbergh, Billy Mitchell, Will Rogers, and Amelia Earhart, to mention just a few. World diplomats and leaders of countries were not excluded in his stories since aviation was their primary mode of travel. Although the dates of historic aviation events are recorded in various places, it was the toil, smell, conversations, and atmosphere shared among my dad's companions that made many feats possible. Unfortunately, his adventures were never committed to paper.

In the beginning, I envisioned this book as a weekend project. However, after several years, I am still writing and have no idea when it will come to an end. It has been one of the most challenging undertakings I have attempted: going back and putting the events of my life in chronological order. I started asking myself which experiences and facts were worth sharing with the reader. The reality is that it's not really about me but also mostly about the people I met along the way. I wish I could include everyone, for there isn't a person living who can't teach you something, and everyone I have met has done that. This endeavor has taken me through every emotion, from tears to laughter, and it forced me to look at "yesterdays" from a different perspective.

I wonder why I survived Vietnam when so many didn't. Was it my destiny to teach? After all, prior to attending college through the GI Bill, I was a terrible student, probably the last person one would think would devote his life to an educational endeavor. I always think of the following quote from the movie *Platoon*:

> *For those of us who did make it,*
> *We have an obligation to*
> *build again, To teach the*
> *others what we know, And to*
> *try what is left of our lives,*
> *To find the goodness and meaning to this life.*

I've attempted to abide by that quote, and whether it was destiny or a draw of the cards, I have been privileged to have people come from around the world, preparing them for a future life in aviation. Due to the longevity of Academics of Flight, I have been reunited with many past students from the 1970s and 1980s, now flying as captains and holding other high corporate-level positions. I received the following e-mail from a previous graduate, and it allowed me to realize the true purpose of the school's existence:

> *I came across the school's website and*
> *thought I would send you a hello from the*
> *West Coast. What an influence you had on*

me back in '86—It's been a wonderful career and worth every moment I've been in the business—I've done it all, and in all four corners of the world thanks to you.

Looking back, probably the most important reward of Academics of Flight was the opportunity for Karina to experience the world from an extremely early age. She became aware that there was not one race, color, religion, trend of thought, or financial status. She was surrounded by people representing probably almost every country in the world and gained an education that could not be equaled by formal schooling. This, coupled with her mother's upbringing, along with the assistance of Esther and Nestora (extended members of our family) in raising her, helped mold Karina to become a very successful international executive who travels the world. She has not forgotten her roots and never will.

I was coming out of Tegucigalpa, Honduras, on a flight, and a little boy sitting behind me—we'll call him Johnny—stuck his head over my seat and watched me doing paperwork for a few minutes. He leaned back and asked his mother, "Mommy, is that a businessman?" In my mind, I silently answered him, "Johnny, I don't know what my legacy will be or how I will be judged by those I leave behind. In reality, a legacy is only as valid as the individual speaking."

It is not the critic who counts, not the man who points out how the strong man stumbled, or where the doer of deeds could have done better. The credit belongs to the man who is actually in the arena, whose face is marred by dust and sweat and blood, who strives valiantly . . . his place shall never be with those cold and timid souls who know neither victory nor defeat.

—Theodore Roosevelt
26th President of the United States (1901–1909)
Excerpt from the speech "Citizenship in a Republic"
delivered at the Sorbonne, in Paris, France
April 23, 1910

With the "bumps along the way," I have no complaints. I lived long enough to see my daughter grow and dance with her at her wedding, welcome my granddaughters into this world, own a business and home, and have good health. Many people do not have any of these fortunes. I have all of them, for which I am very grateful. I heard a song the other day by a country singer, which states, "Life is just a temporary stop along the way." I am very happy that I had the chance to make the "stop."

In 2011, my sister Dahl sent me letters I had written that were saved by my mom over the years. They have been of great assistance in compiling this book and refreshing my memory. Below is an excerpt from one while stationed at Loring AFB, Maine, which includes a principle to which I've attempted to adhere throughout the years when faced with challenges:

> *I took a break and saw Spencer's Mountain . . . I adopted a motto in the movie and this is it: The world will step aside to let any man through who knows where he is going.*

—Undated letter

Only now can I thank Karina and my wife, Rita, for encouraging me to continue writing this story. I hope it will contribute to my piece of the family history for generations to follow.

PART ONE

"Once a New Yorker, always a New Yorker."

—Origin unknown

1

THE FARM

CANA, NORTH CAROLINA, 1950s

Reflecting back on all the different countries and places I've traveled, I think the most pleasurable time would be at Aunt Lola and Uncle Everett's farm, located in Cana, a farm community in the northwestern area of North Carolina. Uncle Everett was one of my dad's older brothers. The farm influenced me in many ways throughout my years and is befitting of the term "rural south." The experiences on the farm inspired me to begin a college career in the field of agriculture.

Aunt Lola and Uncle Everett (who was hardly ever seen without a pipe in his mouth) were my heroes. They led a life of hard work and toiled in such a way that only a farm family would appreciate. A typical day for my uncle was a 4:30 a.m. wake-up call to fetch the cows for milking. By 6:00 a.m., the process was in full swing, and then it was fieldwork until milking time came again around 5:00 p.m. The day would end around 7:00 p.m. and was repeated seven days a week. The only exception was on Sundays, when there was no fieldwork.

Aunt Lola was not only present for the milking but also raised three children, was a school teacher, and drove a monstrous bookmobile for the county. It was a library on wheels in which she'd bring reading material to the people in the area. I think that is where I got my appreciation for literature, excluding schoolbooks. I can still picture the country kitchen table with homemade biscuits, jams, apple pie, and chicken. The chicken was not "store-bought," but was the result of Aunt Lola running around the yard with a hatchet over her head until the right moment came for the chicken to meet its demise. After the execution, the chicken would continue running a distance without a head. Fortunately, Aunt Lola hardly ever missed.

The big home improvement came the summer we installed an indoor bathroom, and gone were the days of using the outhouse. People who have not had this experience are missing a great part of life. The outhouse was located between the barn and the house, requiring something of a journey at night. A flashlight was great when one could be found, so as not to stumble over rocks, stumps, and/or snakes. I used to occupy my time while sitting looking at the hornets' nests in the corners, hoping they wouldn't be disturbed. I had the pleasure of being there one summer when the outhouse had to be moved. The task was ranked at the same level as cleaning out the barn.

Around 10 or 12 years old, I was expected to do a man's work. Not much appreciating the milking periods or cleaning out the barn, I thoroughly enjoyed fieldwork, bailing hay while sweating, itching, and attempting to keep bees away, and mowing alfalfa. The best was plowing, when time would fly. Uncle Everett would show me a field, supervise one time around a row, and then leave me in my own world to plow. I can smell the dirt as I write.

One day at a field a few miles from the house, I got so carried away with plowing that since the tractor had headlights, I just kept working until both Aunt Lola and Uncle Everett came and told me to call it a day and stop. I would have probably continued all night if they hadn't made the visit. As much as enjoying the fieldwork, I used to wait for the days we had to go to the mill in Mocksville, driving the tractor at about 15 to 20 mph down the road, pulling a trailer full of grain sacks. It was an all-day affair and only became uncomfortable when halfway to the mill or returning, it would start to rain.

Actually, the love of the farm began years before, at four or five years old. I remember being in New York with Dahl, discussing a spur-of-the-moment trip to the farm. The more we discussed the venture, the quicker she packed a suitcase, and of course, I was off and running, avoiding my mom and dad as I went out the back door with Dahl, waving goodbye. I think she even packed a lunch for the journey. I knew exactly where the railroad station was and headed straight for it. I only had one more street to cross before arriving at the station, and the train was already there. Naturally, I assumed that was the one going to the farm. One of our neighbors happened to be coming out of a supermarket and spotted me with my suitcase in hand. She almost dropped her groceries yelling, "Jimmy, where you are going?" "To the farm," I replied very directly. I knew I was in trouble.

I can't remember who the lady called first, a policeman or my father, but they were both there in record time. The policeman picked me up so that we were eye-to-eye and gave me a lecture. This was my first encounter with the law, but not my last. I knew then that my trip had come to an abrupt halt, and I started crying. I think my dad thought the whole episode was entertaining. My mom, however, took a different stance, and of course, Dahl denied any participation in the plot. Years later, I made another unauthorized attempt to go to the farm, and that time it was successful. It proved to me that when you fail at an endeavor, try again.

My companions around Cana were two local boys, John Ray and John Lowe. Because I was from New York, a "Yankee," talking to John Lowe's sister was forbidden until I had proven myself by fighting John. We decided to raid a watermelon patch belonging to a fellow by the name of Abe, who lived up the hill from my Aunt Laurie's house. Aunt Laurie was my father's sister, a librarian in the army. She had been stationed in many locations throughout the world, which kept her away from home a good part of a year; unfortunately, she was home during this episode. Abe appeared to be blind in one eye, which may have saved our lives.

On the fateful night, John Ray, John Lowe, and I were leisurely picking and choosing watermelons when we heard "blam blam," followed by a noise directly over our heads, which sounded like a swarm of bees. It was buckshot fired from Abe's shotgun. Apparently, we were noisier than we should have been and picked the wrong night, due to the full moon. Running like hell, with melons in hand, I quickly made it to Aunt Laurie's house, leaving my bounty by the pump house. I didn't mention that night's adventure to her due to the possible reprisals, but the next day, I told Uncle Everett as we were going to spend the day at the sawmill. He felt that it would be as good a place as any to eat the watermelon, so I went and collected my prize, undetected by Aunt Laurie.

Unknowingly, while Uncle Everett and I were milling about, Abe had gone to Aunt Laurie, informing her of the previous night's activities. I guess Aunt Laurie made a connection between his story and the watermelon that she had seen before I took it to the mill. When Uncle Everett and I returned home late in the afternoon, we walked into the house greeted by Abe, Aunt Laurie, and Aunt Lola. I knew something was ready to hit the fan, with a country court trial forthcoming.

After a brief discussion, and pleading "guilty," my punishment was for Uncle Everett to put the belt to my backside. Uncle Everett hadn't even digested the melon from our lunch at the mill, and undoubtedly, he had stolen many during his youth. We proceeded to a bedroom and he closed the door so no one would witness the punishment; just by looking at each other, we had it all worked out. As his belt came down on the bedpost, I would yell, and he would ask me if I had learned my lesson loud enough for the jury in the other room to hear. This was repeated a few times, and I came out with water in my eyes, holding my butt.

We didn't fool Aunt Lola one bit, but she never said anything. Everyone else was satisfied. I felt no pain, Uncle Everett hadn't hurt me, and Aunt Laurie proved that even in the country, there was a level of law and order. Abe had cooled off, and a few days later, I thanked him for being such a poor shot. He said he knew who the villains were, and he fired over our heads on purpose. I told him if that was so, he was a sharpshooter, since the buckshot didn't go *too* far over our heads!

It was not uncommon while riding to and from Mocksville, a town next to Cana, on various trips either by car or tractor, to see the chain gang hard at work along the roadside. The prisoners wore stripes, with a guard standing by with a shotgun slung over his shoulder. It was a scene straight from Paul Newman's *Cool Hand Luke*. The only difference was these prisoners had no intention of escaping. Dad took me for a visit to the jailhouse, and none of the cell doors were closed, as the detainees sat in their cubicles watching TV or reading.

One gentleman was getting out at the time of our visit, and he cleaned his cell, folded the blankets, and neatly placed his pillow at the foot of the bed. As he was leaving, his last instruction to the jailer was, "Under no circumstances, give my cell to anyone. I will be right back." True to his word, before we left, he reappeared with the local policeman. He had gone and thrown a rock through someone's window, stayed there until arrested, and returned "home" for another 30 days. The jailer explained that it was a cycle, to be assured of housing and food.

At the end of one of my summer visits to the farm in the mid-1950s, Uncle Everett drove back to New York with my dad and me to visit New York for a few days. The driving time was extended, since Uncle Everett would get nervous when the speedometer went past 60 mph. As we approached the Delaware Memorial Bridge and he saw how it towered over the water, it took a great deal of effort to convince him that we would not fall off. I took him into the city, and we spent the day going from one landmark to another; it was great, and I enjoyed the time since he was and still is my hero.

There is an ongoing habit that I will never forget about him: his nose blowing. He would simply place his finger against the side of the nostril, more or less directing the discharge onto the ground. Why use a handkerchief when no one is around? He let one fly and hit a woman passing to his side, not realizing that he was off the farm and there were people in close proximity to one another. Understandably, the woman raised hell, and I gave her money to have her garment cleaned. My solution didn't completely satisfy her, but it was the least we could do. Returning to our home in Westbury, we took the Long Island Railroad and stood by the engineer's compartment. When the driver saw my uncle continually watching him in amazement, the engineer invited him into the cab and explained the function of all the switches as we neared home. The lesson was really appreciated, and Uncle Everett and I reminisced for years about his great adventure in New York.

Unfortunately, after Uncle Everett and Aunt Lola passed on in September 1982 and November 1994, respectively, the farm deteriorated considerably. I hope someday it will be restored, as it was a strong influence in my life. Although it's too late to tell Uncle Everett and Aunt Lola now, I appreciate and love them for the values they taught me, which prepared me for the future.

Every region has an unofficial gathering spot. Cana's was Uncle Boyce and Aunt Ina Cain's general store, which was the area's post office until 1954. Afterward, it continued to serve the local residents with goods until 1963. Uncle Boyce was the brother of my grandmother Nana Cain Etchison. The store was, and still is, a typical one-room rural country store, which was built in 1885 by his father, James Harrison Cain. My favorite selection of the store's goods included cheese crackers, Butterfinger candy bars, and Pepsi. Although I am ashamed to admit, a few times, excluding the Pepsi, my favorites would end up in my pocket without paying. Uncle Boyce had a habit of sitting outside in front of the store, while I would come through the back door to "shop." Of course, at that time, I didn't realize he knew exactly what I was doing, but being a "country gentleman," he never confronted me.

Cana, and its inhabitants, will always remain the source of some of my most treasured memories.

2

SCHOOL YEARS

WESTBURY, NEW YORK–FORT DEFIANCE, VIRGINIA, 1950s–1962

It's challenging to go back 50 years attempting to reconstruct one's life. First and foremost, I wouldn't have graduated on time were my mom not the guidance counseling department secretary at Westbury High School. I would get into trouble, she would get me out of it, and I would get in, and on and on it went. It was never serious; I just seemed to march to my own drummer. I couldn't get with the educational program, and although I passed, it wasn't by very much. I remember scoring the second lowest in New York State (not percentile) when we had to take SAT exams to determine eligibility for college.

One of my teachers wrote a letter to my mother concerning my behavior, which did not coincide with the acceptable norm of social interaction:

> *Dear Mrs. Etchison:*
>
> *Apparently, James did not listen to any of your discussions and talking that you had with him last night. He was reported today by Miss Sheridan, our gym teacher, for hurting a little boy quite badly on the playground at lunchtime. He hit him very hard in the chest and caused fights with other children. If James does not take care of himself at lunch time and does not stop the continual fights he has caused, he will have to be forbidden to eat in the lunch room and remain at school during lunch hour.*
> *Sincerely,*
> *Marilyn Silverman*

—Undated letter

In 2012, I was organizing my CDs and noticed *Avalon*, by John Tesh, which reminded me of the Westbury Methodist Church. I guess all parents have a deep desire for their offspring to follow their own religious beliefs. I was no exception, and the affiliation came at birth when I was given the middle name "Wesley," after my grandfather, derived from the founder of the Methodist church. I don't know who named me, but it was most likely my mom.

Unfortunately for them, my bond with the church never reached their expectations. I do remember attending church on Sundays with the family, sitting restlessly through the sermon, which more or less seemed the same week after week: "Be good and you will be rewarded in heaven," wherever that is. In any event, I would endure it as best as I could and would look forward to the interruption of the sermon to sing an assigned hymn.

If you ever had the privilege of listening to the Etchison family sing in harmony, you would realize that music was not a notable family trait, with the exception of Dahl; she wasn't great, but she didn't drive people out of the room and was a choir member for several years. Usually, I would just move my lips without attempting to draw attention to my vocal ability.

I guess my mom didn't comprehend the fact that carrying a melody was not one of my genetic traits. Somehow, I am sure through my mom's maneuvering, I found myself in a blue choir robe singing at church. That was how I became friends with John; at that time in his life, he appreciated being a choir member as much as I did. The procedure for Reverend Rhinesmith, our pastor, to finish his sermon was to have the choir leave the platform, walk down the aisle to the back of the church singing, and exit through a door that led to the basement directly below the congregation.

At that time in the service, the churchgoers would be on their last prayer. The choir made a lot of noise at that point, which interrupted the final prayer. The choirmaster warned in frustration: "The next person running across the basement will be suspended!" John and I looked at each other and, not having to say a word, took off running. True to the choirmaster's word, we were suspended, and I never went back. I am not sure if John did or not. He certainly did not have to, since he is a well-known musician who has given concerts in many different countries. I sing in the shower from time to time when no one is around.

Surely, much to her relief, I gave my mom a two-year break when I was sent to the Augusta Military Academy (AMA) in Fort Defiance, Virginia, for the second and third high school years. Military schools are more or less one step up from a penitentiary. Many of the cadets should have been wearing stripes instead of the school uniform. I had five fights within the first two weeks simply because I was a "Yankee" from New York.

AMA was constructed after the design of the Virginia Military Institute (VMI), the South's answer to West Point. The two-story dormitory was rectangular with an open courtyard, with all the rooms facing into the yard. There were no internal hallways, and once you left the room, you were outside.

This wasn't bad during the spring, but not too pleasant in the winter. There were two washrooms on each floor that had to accommodate at least 100 cadets living on that particular level. Showers were taken very quickly, due to the lack of hot water. There were four cadets to a room that measured approximately 8×12 feet, housing two bunk beds, four desks, and two shelf closets to hang clothes; therefore, there was very little room for stretching. The walls were so badly chipped with paint that we covered them with blankets to reduce the feeling of living in a ghetto. I would put myself to sleep by reaching behind the blanket and peeling paint layers.

Despite all this, Shenandoah Valley is an absolutely beautiful part of the country. First-year cadets had to stand in formation every morning for approximately half an hour waiting for the seniors to arrive. During that period, we had a panoramic view of the Blue Ridge Mountains.

My first year as a "new cadet" required walking around with elbows in a horizontal position and chin tucked in, "bracing," plus other silly requirements to let everyone know my status. I played midfield on the school's lacrosse team until someone struck me with a stick during one of the games, which burst my appendix. I was also on the precision drill team, "Roller's Rifles," traveling occasionally for various local parades.

The second year eased up a little, as the formalities of a new cadet ceased, and we could walk around the school in a normal manner. Things were going so well that five of us, three from our room and two from the next, decided to take an unscheduled leave that was not on the school's calendar. I guess in a way it could be compared to a prison break. It took quite a bit of planning, and I am proud to say it was very successful.

Classes were held on Saturdays, which meant that on Mondays we had all-day passes. Sunday mornings were devoted to having a parade in full dress uniform, and in the afternoon, we were free to go into the town of Stanton for a few hours. After the traditional Sunday parade, my roommates, Jim Burchette and Lee, and I went to town with our uniforms on as required, wearing our civilian clothes underneath. We went up a hill in the woods by the railroad station, undressed and hid our street clothes under rocks. Putting our uniforms back on, we returned to school.

At precisely 10:00 p.m., the guard on duty would walk the stoops and bang on the doors, and the occupants would say, "Right." This was the term that everybody in the room was tucked in bed for the night with lights out. Naturally, with no one in the room to reply, there is a good chance that the situation was not normal. Since we had all day Monday to "hit the road," we would be far away before they found us missing Monday night.

Monday arrived; we signed out on a day pass and headed directly for our clothes. When we got to the area where we had hidden our traveling attire, there was a bum sitting on our clothes, drinking wine, and refusing to get off them. He claimed that he found them, so rightfully they were his. It took a lot of convincing and a few threats, and reluctantly, he surrendered his new wardrobe.

We were now ready to go and went down the other side of the hill with our thumbs out ready to catch rides. I was heading for the farm in Cana, and Jimmy, being from Winston–Salem, North Carolina, was going back home. Lee was coming with me to the farm. The other two headed north. Recently, I tried to retrace our route on a map but could only come up with a general idea since many new roads have since replaced the older ones. I do know it took over 13 hours, and when Lee and I got to Mocksville, we couldn't walk any farther. Our feet were approximately twice their normal size from walking all night. We did get several rides; the last being a truck in which we were closed in the back with what seemed like a zillion chickens. You can imagine how refreshing it was when the driver opened the door to let us out.

In 2012, I read an excellent book, *The Wettest County in the World,* written by Matt Bondurant that focused on Franklin County, Virginia, regarding the area's bootlegging operations in the 1920s and 1930s. I studied a road map of the area since the names of the towns mentioned in the book were familiar: Rocky Mount, Martinsville, and so on. As it turns out, our hitchhiking adventure took us right through Franklin County. Actually, old habits are hard to break, and the area to this day still has its bootleggers; one article I read online called the county "the moonshine capital of the world!"

The school telephoned my parents late that night informing them their son was AWOL, "absent without leave." My mom went into a panic mode, but my dad rolled over and told her not to worry and that I was most likely headed to the farm. He was dead on. At Mocksville, I telephoned the farm and thought I would surprise my aunt and uncle. I didn't. My dad had informed them of my adventure and to expect a call. Aunt Lola answered and told me not to move and that she was on her way to pick us up. Lee and I went to sleep almost immediately after getting in the car, and when we arrived at the farm, ate a big meal, and went right to bed, not waking until the next day.

Aunt Lola was a stern lady with a heart of gold, and Uncle Everett simply had a heart of gold. He saw nothing wrong with our visit; however, Aunt Lola didn't feel it was the appropriate way to take a vacation. I am sure deep down she realized how attached I was to the farm and was proud. The next day, Aunt Lola took us to the bus depot in Mocksville, and I will never forget her words to the driver, "Under absolutely no circumstances, let these two boys off this bus until you stop at Fort Defiance." He followed her orders to the letter.

It was night when the bus stopped in front of the school and we held our breath, expecting the worse. As we stepped down, the most senior cadet, Jim Crawford, hugged us: so far, so good. He told us to get a good night's sleep, since the next day we would have the school's version of a court martial. Apparently, we had set a record being five AWOLs in one day, and if the school exists today, that record is probably still intact. The other AWOLs we had left with had already returned by the time we went to bed.

In reality, most of the teachers thought it was quite amusing, and the only person who took it seriously was the owner, Colonel Roller. He must have been 100 years old, but he still had the energy to bore the hell out of the cadets by giving lengthy speeches in the dining hall before allowing us to eat. The morning after our arrival at breakfast, his speech was longer than usual, and as he chastised us, in a phrase that was common for the time and place, he compared us to "niggers running away in the middle of the night." The penalties for wandering were not too harsh. From the time of our "crime," we had to revert back to the first-year cadet's rituals, bracing, emptying garbage cans, and working in the mess hall from mid-November until the Christmas break.

Although encouraged by my parents to return to AMA for my senior year, I absolutely refused, wanting to graduate from a normal high school as most teenagers did. I didn't date a lot that year or hang around with a specific crowd; I was simply, "everybody's friend, but nobody's best friend." I had a couple of fellows that I would run with when not attending school or working. One of them owned an old hearse that we had a lot of fun with going to the Bowery in lower Manhattan, coaxing bums by offering them a six-pack of beer to take a ride with us. We would then transport them to Westbury, and let them out in the middle of town. Very quickly, Westbury became inundated with homeless people. It became such a problem that the village council had a special meeting to solve the situation. Our group didn't realize it at that time, but our exploits were, in reality, kidnapping, and we felt that there would be serious consequences if continued, especially if caught. Therefore, we stopped.

The 1950s and 1960s were probably one of the most unique eras in decades. The Korean War finished and was almost forgotten. Placing the world and domestic events aside, the 1950s were the time when bobby socks were in, along with how much gel the guys could put in their hair to comb it back into a DA (Duck's Ass) style. It was also the time of the sock hops, where we dislocated our hips with dances such as the Twist, Monkey, Swim, and Chicken, not forgetting to step down in an area between two rows of dancers clapping for you and your partner, when it was your turn to Stroll.

On May 7, 1954, the Vietnam situation became our problem, when the French were defeated at Dien Bien Phu, and the Cold War was in full swing. All this meant little to us. Nikita Khrushchev was a familiar name in the news associated with Castro in Cuba. By 1961 the South was in turmoil with the civil rights movement, and Martin Luther King Jr.'s "Freedom Riders" were being shot and their buses burned as they drove through Alabama and Mississippi, preaching for an end to segregation.

However, my classmates and I were more interested in going to the soda shop located in the middle of town after school.

These decades encompassed a period when music was music and rhythm and blues was king, with groups such as the Drifters, the Temptations, and the Righteous Brothers. Disputes were handled by going to the back of the school building with a teacher supervising the blows; not like today where someone usually ends up shot. The movie drive-in was a must while hiding in the trunk as your buddies drove to the ticket window; you had the money to legally attend, but the thrill of trying to get in without buying a ticket was the attraction. It was amazing how many people would climb out of the trunks of vehicles once the movie began.

During this time, people sat down at dinner and conversed with each other while sharing the meal, instead of texting someone via their smartphone. In 2011, Rita and I had a young couple as houseguests, and while we were eating on the back deck, they were buried in their own individual worlds; each texting God knows who. While I appreciate technological advancements, there is also a thing called "social grace." Life today moves so quickly the young are likely to burn out before their time. Although not as efficient, I am glad to have lived during the time when you wrote a letter and had to wait a week or two for a response.

To review my high school years, I breezed through the school's yearbook reading many of the comments that classmates wrote. Naturally, they are going to write that you "are a great guy"; if they didn't, you would not have had them sign the book in the first place. They continue by writing "remember so, and so." Of course, I don't remember anything they mentioned since it was so long ago.

My energy during hours off from school was devoted to work at the Wheatley Hills Tavern, on the main street in Westbury, which was owned by the Zano brothers. There were five brothers who were very well connected to the mob. I started as a dishwasher, became a busboy, and when I turned 18 (and able to legally serve alcohol), advanced to a waiter, which was an accomplishment for the only employee who was not Italian. The brothers treated me as family, and while still a minor, each would bring me a glass of beer in the kitchen with instructions not to tell the other brothers; at 3:00 a.m. (quitting time), I would float home.

My most memorable time at the tavern was the day of the Kentucky Derby. I was asked to go to the basement for a sack of potatoes. Upon entering, there had to be at least 20 "gentlemen" sitting around a long table wearing headsets that were connected to an overhead wire leading somewhere. Off-track betting was illegal; however, I didn't think it was my place to inform the group that they were violating the law, especially if I didn't want to come out of the basement wrapped in a blanket. Odds were being shouted across a room that was so full of cigarette and cigar smoke that you could hardly see from one end to the other. The scene could have been right out of a gangster movie. I picked up my potatoes, went upstairs, and wasn't even noticed, often wondering how much the brothers had to bribe the local cops to stay away from the tavern that day. Years later, my family occasionally went to have dinner at the tavern and reminisce with the remaining brothers or their offspring. I discovered on my last visit that it was sold to a Mexican group. As the saying goes "The only permanent thing in life is change."

In addition to working at the tavern, as a teen, I also shoveled snow, had paper routes, and did landscaping. Landscaping could have evolved into a career, since I had built a client list of 13 lawns and employed Ross, my neighborhood pal, to assist. We were always "on the go" in pursuit of the dollar.

I became friends somewhere along the way with Patrick Tighe, who lived with his mom, "Aunt Ruth," in The Bronx around 188th Street and Briggs Avenue. On Friday nights I would go and stay with them through Sunday. The area at that time was predominantly Irish and has changed today to Dominican. This section of the city is now known as "Washington Heights." Pat and I would spend most of the nights hanging out with his group around Fordham Road in a park or at parties that always seemed to be in progress; it was great fun.

In 2012, I looked forward to my fiftieth high school reunion. It's absolutely amazing how fast the years have passed since my boyhood days on Long Island, living in Westbury, New York.

3

MY DAY IN THE SKY

FAYETTEVILLE, ARKANSAS, 1962

While attending the University of Arkansas, not completely into the academic environment at that point in my life, I heard about a skydiving club that was actively recruiting members. Thinking that this sport was more appealing than studying, I immediately pursued the idea. A few days later, I found myself jumping from a three-foot barbecue pit practicing landing techniques. After many bruises, my instructor felt that I knew enough not to break my legs on impact and signed me off for my first jump.

The big day came and after strapping the parachute on my back, I really had second thoughts. Actually, by regulation, I wasn't even supposed to be there. In order to participate, a person had to be 21 years old. However, if you were underage, you could get the signature of one of your parents authorizing you to participate in the activity. Being 18, I had to get around this, since after a telephone conversation with my dad, I found he was a far cry from being delighted. His line of thought was that he sent me to college to "learn" and not kill myself. Since it would be a waste of time for me to ask my mom, I simply forged my father's signature on the authorization form in order to jump. There was nothing to it: I had considerable practice in such forgeries as they related to bad school reports.

We took off from the narrow airstrip with one jumper in front next to the pilot, plus me and a third parachutist sitting on the floor in the rear passenger area of the Cessna 172. On command, the first jumper swung out of the plane, catching the wing strut with both hands and resting one foot on the door pedal and the other on the plane's wheel cover. He remained in that position for less than a minute, and then on the next command, "Off," he dropped out of sight like a bullet.

Now, completely realizing what I had gotten myself into, I expressed my feelings in many words. Next, it was my turn. I slid to the front and then out the door, into a vertical spread-eagle position as the first jumper while holding onto the airplane. I remember looking at the inside of the plane and knowing that I might as well jump since there was no way to get back in, and it sure couldn't land with me hanging on the wing.

You are supposed to kick your feet out first and then let go of the strut with your hands to establish a prone horizontal position. Right: I let go with my hands and feet at the same time and down I went, not in a horizontal position, but vertically. The next thing I remember was being yanked upward as the chute opened. Thank God I was on static line, as was required of all parachutists for their first five jumps. I have absolutely no recollection of the time from when I jumped off the wing until the chute opened.

Floating through the air was great. After the chute opens, you have to look up and make sure that none of the panels are blown out; this type of chute has 13 panels. If a certain number of them are missing, the reserve must be deployed. I was floating at a comfortable rate; therefore, I didn't see any reason to do this safety check. To this day, I have never witnessed such peace and quiet. I even remember a bird passing in front of me, probably wondering why I was in its airspace.

I was enjoying myself so much that I failed to look down at the jumpmaster on the ground to follow his signals as to whether I should adjust my flight path through the air to the left, right, forward, or backward. These signals are executed by walking in a certain direction from a fixed position on the ground. This position represents my location in the air. For example, if the jumpmaster walks to the right, I should turn to the right.

The only objects within two miles of the jump zone were an old hangar and a parking lot filled with spectators' cars, and I was headed right for both. With the jumpmaster yelling, he finally raised my attention, and I got with the program by maneuvering just enough to sail over the hangar and miss the last row of cars. A skydiver should use five parts of his body to soften the landing from the point of ground contact through the ground roll. I used two of the five, my feet and my rear end. It wasn't graceful, but it did the trick. I collapsed my chute, had the jump verified in my logbook, and never went back to try and improve my technique.

To my surprise, my cousin and his wife from North Carolina, John and Rachel, were passing through the area on their honeymoon the day I jumped. In 2012, Dahl told me that she had seen them at a family get-together. The subject of their visit to Arkansas on the day of my skydiving was mentioned. I was apprehensive about their appearance in Arkansas since I thought my dad may have sent them to see if I ignored his wishes for me not to jump.

4

LORING AIR FORCE BASE

CARIBOU, MAINE, 1963–1965

After the first semester at the University of Arkansas, it was obvious that I wasn't ready for a prolonged stay in an academic environment. All I wanted was to be a farmer like my Uncle Everett, where I enjoyed summers working and sometimes getting into a little mischief on his farm in North Carolina. However, to get a college degree in agriculture, words that a normal farmer used, such as "alfalfa" and "wheat," became what to me were elongated Greek and Latin high-society terms that were way over my head. Therefore, I simply left, went to Little Rock, Arkansas, and joined the air force. Little Rock was caught up in all the negative aspects of the civil rights movement when I arrived, and it was as though I were in a war zone before I even officially raised my hand. Enlisting was easy. However, not having my birth certificate to prove I was 18 required the recruiting officer, good old Sergeant Smith, to call my mom for verification. Well, within a few minutes, I felt very sorry for him as he turned all different colors while on the phone. It was obvious that "Mother Dear" was not keen about my career change. The next day, I was on an airplane heading for Lackland AFB, San Antonio, Texas, for boot camp training.

Since I went to Lackland directly from the university, donating my books to whoever walked by the dormitory hall trash can, I arrived there with all of my personal belongings. After our newly formed platoon was assigned to a barracks, I had to stand by the bed and empty everything I had brought with me on the mattress. As soon as I saw my skydiving logbook, I quickly tried to hide it but was not quick enough. The drill sergeant asked if I liked jumping out of airplanes, and I responded, "Absolutely not!" He said, "That's great, because tomorrow you are going to report to the paramedics and start training."

The primary mission of this unit was to go behind enemy lines and rescue airmen who had been shot down. With Vietnam escalating, this type of employment didn't appeal to me, and I was hoping for a softer classification. When I went for my medical the next morning, God was with me. Apparently, I am color-blind and, therefore, could not qualify for paramedics. On the surface, I acted as though my heart were broken, but I thanked God for weeks on end. There were only two other fields for which I could qualify: cook or air police. I chose the latter since I don't like kitchens.

For the next five or six weeks, I did nothing but sleep, fire all kinds of weapons, undergo physical training, and march. There was also plenty of classroom work. At least I could understand the words and lectures on how to control a drunk, answer a domestic dispute call, and so forth. It was more fun than learning what a preposition or a superlative was or the difference between a proper and a common noun. In any event, there were three in our platoon who were assigned to Loring AFB, Maine, after completing basic training. There may be a worse place on earth, but we did not know where that could be.

The air force was kind enough to give us tickets for a Greyhound bus ride to Loring, which was an experience within itself. From Texas to the northern tip of Maine, a bus is not exactly the way to travel. At Tulsa, Oklahoma, the three of us were not allowed to get the connecting bus, due to drinking a little more alcohol than we could handle. Eventually, as we sat in the bus station, the alcohol wore off, and we got on the next one to continue the journey. If you want to see the United States, a bus is a good way to go, providing there is nothing else to do in your life.

There is no describing Loring. I had never been so cold for so long in my life, and it actually snowed in July. Not only that but I could never understand why dog teams had to walk all night in knee-deep snow around the base perimeter guarding B-52s that belonged to the Strategic Air Command (SAC). The enemy, if there really was one, probably couldn't find the base even if they knew it existed. I did see plenty of deer, bears, and caribous on my post, but I am sure they had no intention of invading since they lived there. I would always leave a portion of my bagged meal on the trail as sort of a peace gesture. Although the animals were not armed, they were still damn big. It wouldn't be fair not to mention the mosquitoes: they didn't just bite; they ate you.

Beginning as a "ramp rat," I walked around guarding B-52s. These planes are gigantic. I became friends with the K-9 group and, approximately six months later, got a chance to join that section. When one of the handler's service commitments was completed, I became the new handler for his dog, "Jet." Jet was a brown and tan German Shepherd that was very dedicated to me. The K-9 perimeter had many advantages compared to walking in circles around an airplane. Most importantly, having an attack dog as a partner, you were left alone to find a tree in the woods and under which you could snooze.

The problem was Jet and I couldn't coordinate our sleep schedule. In many instances, we would be napping at the same time. The peace and quiet was incredible. During certain times of the year, the Northern Lights (Aurora Borealis) would appear. I used to watch their display for hours while on post as they danced across the sky in colors of white, green, yellow, and red. While there is a solid scientific explanation for them, the myths are more romantic. Eskimos have been taught that they are torches held in the hands of their departed loved one's going to a land of happiness and plenty. In Scandinavia, the lights represent the final resting place of unwed mothers who are busy above the mountains cooking fish, dancing, and waving their white-gloved hands. Also, for some reason, there seemed to be a billion stars that could be touched with outstretched hands. If it weren't for the cold, Loring could have been a good duty assignment.

I wrote to my mom, discussing the weather conditions at Loring:

> *I was talking to my "NCOIC" (non-commissioned officer in charge) and he informed me that they think nothing of it when the weather drops to 40 degrees below zero and the winds blow up to 50 mph during the winter. I saw pictures of last year's winter here, and the snowdrifts were up to 30 feet high.*
>
> —Letter, June 8, 1963

One day, a K-9 co-worker approached me with the following, "Etch, I know it hurts, but you better think about changing dogs. Jet is getting old, and sooner or later, you are going to end up in Vietnam." The advice was well taken, and about a month thereafter, I had a new dog pulling on my arm for eight hours each night.

Handlers are to walk an assigned post with their dog as an individual team. However, as it will be, the correct way is not always the method in which we follow through life. Two dog teams would walk together covering both adjacent posts. In this manner, the job got done, and the night seemed to go a little more quickly. It was very infrequent that the officer in charge would check, since we were more or less buried in the woods. Jet and I usually walked with Mac, the handler, and Rheiner, the dog. Rheiner was an absolutely beautiful 110-pound full pedigree German Shepherd with a coat mixture of silver, black, and gray. His pedigree name was Rheiner's Holiday. Everyone gave him a lot of room due to his aggressiveness. A police dog is trained to increase its bite, measured in pounds per square inch, "psi," from a normal 250 psi for a civilian dog to 1,500 psi. Studies have shown that while only 20% of civilian dog bites require hospitalization, over 50% of people bitten by police dogs have to be hospitalized. The average person's bite only represents approximately 150 psi. Through many hours of walking posts with Mac, Rheiner got used to Jet and me; however, without a doubt, I gave him his desired space. He was one of the most feared dogs in the K-9 section.

Mac's service time was coming to an end, and night after night, he would tell me to give him my word that I would take over Rheiner. A request like this could be equated to asking an individual to take and raise your child. I promised I would try; however, it depended upon Rheiner accepting me. Mac was discharged, and Rheiner was penned. I walked by his kennel daily and got braver as time went on. One day, the sergeant saw me and said, "Etchison, you can get in on him, can't you?"

I replied, "I don't know, but he's been penned up for about two weeks, and I am sure he wants to get out and run in the training area." The handlers who were present went into the assembly building and took bets on what would happen as they scrambled to get the best view from the window. I opened Rheiner's kennel gate, went inside, closed the gate behind me, and prayed. I extended my arm, turning my palm up, indicating I had nothing in my hand to harm him. Mac had taught him to shake hands by the command "Paw." As Rheiner approached, I momentarily asked myself, "Why the hell did I ever volunteer to be a handler?" We looked at each other thinking, *"What do we do now?"* I said "Paw" and Rheiner placed his paw in my hand. From that moment onward, a bond formed that only a handler could understand. Rheiner and I became one, with a trust in each other that was unparalleled in times of peace or war, not to be found between two humans. I began calling him "Spanky" which stuck until my tour was over.

I think the best song I have heard that would describe a K-9 team's night on post is entitled "Have You Ever Seen a Night So Long." As the truck discharged a handler and his dog, the team evaporated into the woods, disappearing from everyone. Most of the handlers trusted their dogs off leash for the first few minutes they arrived on post, but if caught, it was a court-martial offense. By letting the dog loose, it gave him the freedom to relieve himself, run through the snow, and generally cut up, burning off stored energy from spending all day in the kennel. Each dog had its own personality, and Spanky was no different. During the first minutes on post, I would let him go off-leash, and our ritual would start. I would head down a path, acting as though I wasn't watching. He would run ahead and suddenly dart into the woods out of sight. I usually knew his general vicinity, and as I passed, slowly moving at a shuffle with head down, he would wait and wait. At his proper moment, he would sneak up behind, burrowing through the snow, and launch his attack at my back, knocking me down. I'd grab him, and for the next five minutes, we'd roll over and over in the snow like two little kids. *There was no one else in the world but us.*

One of the most memorable nights that had the entire K-9 section laughing the next day involved two handlers, Jack and Tim. Jack was a big Polack, and on this particular night, he had a post adjacent to mine. At about 3:00 a.m., he came flying onto my post, swearing that there was a bear on his post, and he wasn't going back. I asked if he saw the animal, and when he said, "No," I asked him how he knew it was a bear. He said his dog alerted and led him to a big pile of crap that only a bear could have made. He walked with me the rest of the night. When we got on the truck in the morning, Jack told his story to the other teams. Tim, the handler on the other side of Jack's post, started laughing like hell. Apparently, Tim had been constipated for a week, and it was time for relief. He was on Jack's post when the call came. It turned out that Jack's bear was Tim. Tim further rubbed it in when he asked Jack, "When did bears start using toilet paper?" Jack had overlooked that detail in his excitement.

Sadly, K-9 was called to guard the wreckage of a KC-135 aircraft that blew up as it was flying over the base perimeter at approximately 20,000 feet, throwing debris for miles. K-9 had this duty for a week, and the stench of fuel mixed with body parts was terrible. I stumbled across an object and, when I turned my flashlight on it, saw that it was the helmet of a crewmember with his brains still attached. Needless to say, those were long and terrible nights; it was worse for Spanky, since a dog's scent is many times more acute than that of a human.

The K-9 section enjoyed the respect of almost everyone on base. As any former or present GI knows, obtaining items through proper channels is almost impossible; the barter system is widely utilized. The sole requirement for the K-9 handler to successfully engage in this system was to inform the person with the desired items that he was from the dog section. For extra assurance during these requests, we always wore our dog gear, used for work on post, attached to our belt. The supplier, or one of his friends, usually had a dog, and we made sure that his pet was well fed from the time of our transaction forward.

Because of this bartering system, our room furnishings were superior to other air police sections. Once, one of the barracks that housed the B-52 and KC-135 aircraft alert crews was closed. Three days after it closed, and many midnight truck rides between the billets and our barracks, we had plush furnishings, and of course, we got carried away. Consequently, our rooms were inspected, and most of the newly acquired home comforts were confiscated by air police officers for their own use. We did keep enough to maintain the rooms in a very comfortable state.

The animosity between town civilian police and air police, or any GI unit for that matter, was incredible. I guess they felt we would steal the hearts of the local girls and carry them off into the sunset.

Many of these women exhibited the results of the "potato diet" for which Maine is famous, and that, combined with heavy beer drinking, made very few of these ladies eligible for such a trip. I had the pleasure of being an overnight guest in the Caribou jail and a week later in the "police hotel" located in Presque Isle, near the town of Caribou. I had to call Sergeant Perdue, who was my immediate supervisor, to inform him that once again, I had a small problem. It was about 3:00 a.m. and his wife answered the phone. She was very polite, and I heard her waking him by saying, "George, it's Etchison, he is in jail again." The sergeant was great, but a little excitable. He asked me how much the bail was this time, and after inquiring, I responded $10,000. He hit the ceiling and asked whether I had raped a nun. The police started laughing and told me there would be no bail if someone from the base came and got me. The good sarge showed up the next morning, very disturbed to say the least, and I was free.

Comparing the comfort and hospitality of each "hotel," they both would have received one star at best. Although roughed up by my hosts in Presque Isle, I was treated decently in Caribou. I finished my day in court visits with a 50% success rate, found guilty in Caribou for disorderly conduct and innocent in Presque Isle. Leaving the courthouse after winning my case, I passed the officer who had incarcerated me at Presque Isle. He politely told me never to come back; I responded by telling him to never come to the air base. We both adhered to each other's advice. Actually, I acted as my own lawyer in Caribou and did get the policeman to admit that the only person that I was disturbing was him. When I asked him how, he said, "by pointing at him in a dance hall." I guess my legal skills must have been impressive, because the judge called me back into his chambers to make a deal; I had to pay a small fine. It could have been worse.

As the old saying goes, "every dog has his day" and Officer Joe got his. Approximately one month after the other verdict in Caribou, Jim Manwaring and Tom Kelly, both air policemen, along with myself, were sitting in a diner about 11:00 p.m., approximately three blocks from the police station, and in walked our friend who politely said, "You are going to jail." It was an absolute "cat and mouse" game. We didn't even inquire as to what the charge was, since it really didn't matter. As we walked out with Caribou's "hero," Joe the Cop, he radioed his station that he was bringing in three individuals for lockup. Outside, as we were getting in the car, Jim was the first to break and run. Now, Officer Joe was down to two. Kelly and I were in the backseat, and at that time, there were no internal locks on police car doors. At the first stoplight, Tom went out one side, and I escaped from the other. The cop was so startled that he didn't even give chase. We often wondered what Officer Joe told his co-workers when he arrived at the station empty-handed.

The squadron commander, Colonel Dohnke, had to observe the trial of any airman who ended up in the hot seat with the civilian populace. He told me that while he was thoroughly entertained during my trials, one more incident and I'd be out of K-9. He was a great guy, and I had a lot of respect for him.

Within a few weeks after arriving at Loring, I asked our squadron education officer if I could enroll in a night accounting course offered on base by Ricker College. My request was rejected with the explanation that prior to participating in the college, I had to complete the air police upgrade training that was to take four months.

Being a very obedient airman, I went to the education office to obtain admission forms for the class and then borrowed a bulletin off the board containing my squadron commander's signature. The next night, after transferring the commander's signature to the application, I began classes. This was kept secret until the course was complete and grades were sent to the squadron education office. I caught hell but was allowed to continue. On my first attempt, I failed the police upgrade test. The second time around I managed to gather enough answers prior to the exam to pass with flying colors.

Classes were held on the other side of the base from our barracks. The distance was approximately five miles, which seemed much farther during the winter. For a good part of the time I didn't have a car but managed to hitchhike and faithfully attended classes. After joining the K-9 section, I was relieved from post when school hours conflicted with duty. As a result, the classes were uninterrupted, but I became very unpopular with my classmates during the winter months.

Relieved directly from post, I would place my dog back in its kennel and proceed to school. Being around the kennel area, I would arrive in class with dog crap frozen to my boots. No matter how hard I tried to scrape it off prior to entering class, some remained intact. Since the temperature was anywhere from 0 to -10 degrees outside, anything frozen thawed quickly once inside. After 30 minutes, with the windows shut and heat on full blast, it smelled as though I brought the K-9 section to class. By break time, it became apparent to my classmates where I worked. When the second half of class had begun, I would find the windows opened, with the class members moving to various parts of the room maintaining the greatest possible distance from my seat. Meeting one of these classmates two years later in California, we had quite a laugh over this topic. Taking the good with the bad, I left Loring with over a year of college credits.

Most airmen looked for part-time employment, since enlisted pay barely kept you above the poverty line and frequent trips to the local pawnshops were the norm. I was no exception and found a job with another K-9 handler, Tom. A civilian company had been contracted to redo the aircraft ramp area, and somehow Tom and I met the foreman one morning. Due to our nightly K-9 schedule, we could work during the day. There wasn't much sleep those days between the two commitments, but at that age, you could survive.

The contract was coming to a close, and the company had crews assigned to different projects up and down the East Coast. At that time, Interstate 95 was being worked on in Connecticut, and the leftover supplies from our operation were needed for that area. The foreman asked Tom and me to drive the material in a big truck to the waiting crew. I had no idea how to drive it, and although Tom said he did know, he really didn't. I looked in the cab and saw so many gear shifts that I didn't have a clue where to start. After changing our K-9 schedule with a couple of other handlers, we were off and running.

I don't know how the hell the truck stayed in one piece during our initiation period, but it survived. I jumped a curb in Houlton, Maine, and knocked over a mailbox on a corner. Nobody was around, so naturally, we moved on. I am sure the mail was delivered on schedule. By the time we roared through Bangor, in southern Maine, we were "King of the Road" and could turn the truck on a dime. The supervisor had instructed Tom and me to avoid all weigh stations if possible along the route.

Approaching Massachusetts, we were coming upon a weigh station, and after a brief discussion, Tom and I drove past it looking the other way, hoping it would disappear. I glanced in the rearview mirror for a police chase, but no one was there. Halfway through the state, another weigh station appeared, and since two police cars were at the entrance, it was time to obey the law. It was not my lucky day, since I was driving. I rolled onto the scales, and the first violation was that we were overweight. The conversation between the station officer and me was more or less:

"Where is your manifest?"
"My boss didn't give me one."
"Let me see your driver's license."
"Yes, sir."
"This is your automobile license. I need to see your commercial driving license."
"I don't have one."
"Son, pull that god damn truck over to the side and park it."
"Yes, sir."

I parked where he had directed. The officer continued:

"Let me see your log books."
"I don't have any."
"How long have you been driving today?"
"About ten hours." (The maximum allowed was eight.)
"Where are your flares?"
"Where do they usually keep them?"
"Behind the driver's seat."

None were there. By this time, the officer couldn't keep a straight face. We told him we were GIs from Loring AFB and just trying to make some extra money. I wasn't aware at that time that Tom actually had a commercial driver's license. The officer let us go with Tom driving. Our employer was given a substantial fine and never offered us another job, and we didn't get paid for the trip.

The relationship between a handler and his K-9 partner and companion can never be underestimated. For that reason, I include the following eulogy for a dog, which was presented as testimony by future U.S. Senator George Graham Vest during his time as a lawyer, in 1870. The trial concerned the killing of a dog by a sheep farmer. The dog's owner sued for damages totaling $50, which was the maximum allowed by law at that time. This eulogy has been widely published over the years and even appeared in two movies: *The Voice of Bull Run* (1936) and *The Trial of Old Drum* (2000). My inclusion here is dedicated to the K-9 serving in our armed forces in different capacities throughout the world.

Senator Vest's Tribute to a Dog

> The best friend a man has in this world may turn against him and become his enemy. His son or daughter that he has or was reared with loving care may prove ungrateful. Those who are nearest and dearest to us, those whom we thrust with our happiness and our good name, may become traitors to their faith.
>
> The money a man has, he may lose. It flies away from him when he needs it the most. A man's reputation may be sacrificed in a moment of ill-considered action. The people who are prone to fall on their knees to do us honor when success is with us, may be the first to throw stones of malice when failure settles its clouds upon our heads.
>
> The one absolutely unselfish friend that a man can have in this selfish world is the one that never deserts him, the one that never proves ungrateful or treacherous, is his dog.
>
> A man's dog stands by him in prosperity and in poverty, in health and sickness. He will sleep on the cold ground

where the wintery winds blow and the snow drives fiercely if only he may be near his master's side.

He will kiss the hand that has no food to offer, he will lick the sores and wounds that come encounter with the roughness of the world. He guards the sleep of his pauper master as if he was a prince. When all other friends desert, he remains. When riches take wings, and reputation falls to pieces, he is as constant in his love as the sun in its journey through the heavens.

If misfortune drives the master forth an outcast in the world, friendless and homeless, the faithful dog asks no higher privilege than that of accompanying him to guard against danger, to fight against his enemies.

And when the last scene of all comes, and death takes the master in its embrace, and his body is laid away in the cold ground, no matter if all other friends pursue their way, there by the graveside will the noble dog be found, his head between his paws, his eyes sad, but open in alert watchfulness, faithful and true, even in death.

—George G. Vest
United States Senator (1879–1903)
Excerpt from a trial summation
delivered in Warrensburg, MO
September 23, 1870

I will never forget and will always appreciate Jet and Spanky protecting me in war and Little Fellow protecting my family during peace.

5

VIETNAM

While writing this book, I corresponded with retired Lieutenant Colonel Martin F. Heuer, who was gracious enough to provide his thoughts, which are excerpted below.

> The story of Airman First Class James W. "Jim" Etchison, U.S Air Force, and his flying as a crewmember/gunner on both 174th and 161st AHC "Slicks" is really quite rare, yet it is something that actually happened during the Vietnam War. Jim was a sentry dog (K-9) handler assigned to the 366th Air Police Squadron at Phan Rang AFB in February 1966 and served there until he finished his tour in February 1967. It was March 1966 when he started flying missions with Army Aviation.
>
> When Jim first approached me with his story in early 2011, I found it hard to believe. At that time, I was the president of the 174th Assault Helicopter Company Association and had already had some rather unsettling experiences with people who we categorize as "Wannabes." Jim said he'd flown many times as a gunner on U.S. Army helicopters of the 174th and 161st during the conduct of regular missions flown by both companies while they operated out of the Air Force Base at Phan Rang, RVN. He said he'd kept a written record of each flight mission, including the crewmembers names of those he flew with and a statement of the mission. I could hardly comprehend such a story because it was so repetitively against all the regulations I was familiar with. He was a member of the U.S. Air Force, had no orders authorizing him to fly as a crewmember on

U.S. Army aircraft, nor did he have permission from his own Air Force unit. Yes, there were many personnel of all services who had flown as a gunner on Army helicopters from time to time, but it was usually an emergency requirement, or it was often done when the missions were of the "Ash and Trash" variety with little danger involved. Up to this point, I'd never heard of an individual from another service flying regularly with Army aircrews. One of the most basic considerations for the crew was that the person riding as gunner was qualified to fire the M-60 machinegun; that he knew the rules for engagement and could be counted on in the event of an emergency. Jim, it turns out, was qualified and had obviously convinced the flight crews he would perform his duties, if needed.

Jim and I corresponded for the better part of a year during which he sent me the meticulously prepared reports of the missions he flew with pilots and crewmembers of the 174th and 161st. I still had reservations, so Jim sent me photos, orders, biographies, and other written material to prove what he was saying. I then began to believe he was exactly who he said he was and what he had done in Vietnam were real life experiences. The final confirmation came from a former 174th pilot, then First Lieutenant Curtis P. "Curt" Laird, who I knew very well and had transferred to the 161st shortly after the arrival of the 174th at Lane AHP. Curt remembered the missions he flew with Jim in the gunner's position on his aircraft. With that, I was convinced and encouraged Jim to provide all of the information he had to complete the story.

Some of you who read Jim's record may remember him as "The U.S. Air Force guy who flew gunner on our aircraft in Vietnam."

Martin F. Heuer, LTC, USA (Retired)
174th AHC 1965–1966
14th CAB 1966–1967

Phan Rang, 1966

Those that I fight, I do not hate.
Those that I guard, I do not love.

—W.B. Yeats

First, I must be honest and tell you why I went to Vietnam. Was it for democracy and patriotic duty? Absolutely not: It was to get out of the cold, although a letter home dated November 27, 1965, seemed to imply that it was my contribution to our country's freedom that led me there. The reward to leave Loring came when Colonel Dohnke called me into his office one morning and asked if I would be willing to volunteer for Vietnam. If you didn't have 12 months left on your tour, you did not have to go, and I had 11 months remaining. This conversation took place in November with another winter already upon us. My exact words were, "Does it snow in Vietnam?" With his answer, "No," my reply was "On behalf of 'Spanky' and I, we are ready to serve our country and go to war." After a 30-day leave, I returned to Loring AFB, packed my belongings, and prepared Spanky for the trip, and we flew to Vietnam.

The trip took us from Maine to New York by commercial airline. At Kennedy Airport (JFK), my dad met me for a brief layover, and Spanky and I continued to Texas for tropical warfare training. After a week of throwing grenades and firing several types of weapons, we headed for Saigon in a C-141 airplane. There were 52 dogs and handlers, with what seemed a million pounds of dog food. Our route went through Wake Island, Guam, Manila, and finally into Saigon. After a night's rest, the K-9 teams heading to northern bases from Saigon continued on a C-123. The C-123 shook, rattled, and rolled, with most of its windows missing, toward Phan Rang, located along the coast of the South China Sea. Spanky and I arrived there completely exhausted, approximately three days after leaving Texas.

I left Tan Son Nhut on the 10th and got up here in the morning on the same day . . . We came up on a C-123, and on the way, one of the dog handlers cracked-up, and five of us had to hold him

> *down until the plane landed . . . I had the honor of being the first dog man on the base; Spanky and I were the first ones to leave the plane.*
>
> —Letter, February 11, 1966

When the two of us left Loring, it was the middle of winter, and Spanky had his thick coat of hair. When we landed in Vietnam, the temperature was approximately 100 degrees F. With the tropical humidity, along with the temperature change, Spanky really fought the elements for approximately the first three months. Due to his heat exhaustion, I almost had to carry him around the perimeter while we were on duty. He finally shed his winter coat and was back in action.

For the next year, we endured the tropical heat and monsoon downpours. We walked, ate, played, and put our lives in each other's hands. As a result of daytime activities, and not being able to sleep when we got off post in the morning due to the heat, I would doze off on post many nights. Spanky picked up my habit and snored louder than I did. I'm sure every Viet Cong (VC) in the area knew exactly where we were. Actually, I was more concerned with the guards in the security towers on the inner perimeter. The dog team was caught in the middle between the tower guards and the VC, resulting in a possible cross-fire position during an attempted penetration.

Nights can get very boring, and there is just so much you can discuss with your four-legged partner. After elaborating on plans for when you get out, daily newspaper articles, bar girls you had tea with, and so on, there were still hours of walking or finding a nice quiet place to relax. The handler's philosophy was that if a penetration were going to happen, it would be well known within a few minutes. The base didn't need K-9 teams to tell them that we had visitors. AK-47s, the Viet Cong's favorite weapon, in addition to their other calling cards being fired, were enough in essence to say, "Hi, we're here."

To illustrate how the dog team's night can go from one extreme to the other, there are two situations. The first was a firefight that erupted on the post adjacent to mine. We were being shot at from the other side of the perimeter and in turn, naturally, returned fire. It was only for a few minutes, and the handler next to me, collecting his composure after the excitement ceased, went looking for his helmet. When it was found, there was a bullet hole right through the middle. We never strapped our helmet on since if it were hit and went flying, most likely your head would follow.

The helmet ended up in our captain's office, who claimed it was his. Everyone knew the real story, but we allowed him to preserve his ego. It was also well known that the captain wouldn't leave his quarters after dark, so I would have loved to read the letter he probably sent home, along with a picture of the helmet, describing his heroic stand defending the base that night in the name of "freedom."

Another extreme illustrates how dangerous "boredom" can be. When we arrived at the base, it was small, with construction activity 24 hours a day in preparation for fighters, F-100s and F-4s, plus other support aircraft to arrive and call Phan Rang their home. The air for the entire year was filled with red clay dust that attached to everything you owned. As a result of the expansion in its early stage, for the first few months, the outer perimeter was not a great distance from the middle of the compound, showers, mess hall, etc.

We had a handler who was very much a loner, never mingling with the other K-9 members. Around 2:00 a.m., the handler had nothing to do, so he took aim with his rifle at someone wrapped in a towel who was going to the showers. He was clearly visible, due to a light on the shower walkway. The handler put a little too much pressure on his trigger finger and fired. The M-16 bullet missed the guy by inches. A witness said the fellow went one way and his towel the other. The handler was court-martialed. It is not known whether the guy with the towel ever took another shower until he left the country.

One of our posts contained the base waste dump where all items thrown in the trash wound up. It was nothing but gigantic piles of garbage. Two dog teams worked "The Dump" every night, and if there was one Vietnamese going through the garbage, there were between 50 and 100 each night. Although you see pictures of people picking through refuse, you don't realize the reality of life for many in the world until witnessed firsthand. Many of the young girls would come up within 8 feet of you, with the dog leash being 6 feet, and ask if you wanted to make love, naturally for a certain amount of compensation. Their other request, holding a baby in their arms, was for you to take it to America. It was simply one of the scars of war.

There was a sergeant from Alabama who was short, fat, and a complete idiot, and it showed in all his actions. The first episode was when he came in a jeep to my post about 11:00 p.m. As we were talking, he swore he heard a noise on the next post. Without the least bit of hesitation, he started firing his M-16 in that direction. All of a sudden, we heard, "Don't shoot, don't shoot!" The noise he heard was from the dog team assigned to that area. The handler's name was Andy, and to say the least, Andy was pissed. Somehow, the ordeal did not get reported, although it should have been reported as a "friendly fire" incident.

The second incident involving "Sergeant Alabama" occurred when we were driving on a dirt road around the perimeter in a jeep. He was driving, and I was in the front seat with another handler in the back. He stopped so quickly that I almost went through the windshield. A Russell's viper snake, very poisonous, crossed the road and caused that panic. Instead of simply running over it, he jumped out, fixed his bayonet to the rifle, and threw it at the snake. The rifle stuck in the ground in a vertical angle, and the snake coiled around it.

I started laughing like hell and asked, "Well, Sergeant York, what are you going to do now?" We had to wait until the snake took its time to uncoil and continue across the road. It disappeared into the brush unharmed, probably laughing like hell, and the sergeant's ego was crushed. Since the main area of the base was under construction, the snakes migrated toward the perimeter seeking safety from the construction equipment.

Vietnam had more than its share of poisonous snakes, including the "spitting cobra," and they were an ongoing threat to us. Many of our posts were in elephant grass, where the snake would be unnoticed until you or the dog stepped on it. None of the handlers were bitten; however, the dogs were continually taking snake bites, Spanky being one. A bite that would kill a person would not kill a dog. The dog would become very sick and remain off duty for a few days while recovering. One moonlit night, while I was walking post in grass up to my hip, I noticed a cobra watching me that was coiled with its head taller than the grass, approximately 20 yards away. Obviously, I avoided that part of the post for the rest of the night, with the feeling that if any VC came through that area, it would be the snake's responsibility to capture him. The largest one we killed measured 9 ½ feet long!

After the Korean War, handlers were not allowed to take their dog home. The government was getting sued for the dogs back in civilian life biting the mailman and others that got too close. The line of thinking was that since the government trained them to be aggressive and attack people, they were responsible for the dog's actions. Therefore, I knew the day would come when I would have to leave, and Spanky would remain to be put to sleep or retrained. I am not aware of what eventually happened and do not want to know. All I know is that when the departure day from Vietnam came, it was like giving away my child, knowing we would not be reunited in the future. To this day, there have been very few people I have met and would put my trust and faith in over him. A dog handler fully understands the saying "A dog is a man's best friend."

Years later, in Brazil for a family wedding of one of Rita's cousins, I met two Brazilian military dog handlers during the reception. We got along great after they were told that I was a handler in Vietnam. The next day, they took me to the kennels to see their dogs, of which they were rightly proud. During the reception, as the drinks were refilled several times, one of them asked, "Who would you trust more, your wife or your dog?" We just looked at each other without having to give an answer.

Since our duty was at night, several days a week, I took an illegal side job as a door gunner on helicopters, "Huey Slicks," with the army's 48th, 161st, and 174th Assault Helicopter Companies based at Phan Rang. To a point, the "powers that be" turned their backs, since the army was short of door gunners. One of our primary duties was to take the 101st Airborne in and out of firefights they always seemed to find. We also conducted resupply missions for the Korean troops (ROKs) in the area, plus medevac flights, transporting the wounded from areas of conflict, in addition to those who suffered from everyday accidents. I still don't feel comfortable around gas-operated objects, such as generators, due to medevacing a Korean troop out of the field that had a generator blow up in his face. Everybody has a story returning from war. Although I had the "blood and guts" moments, which most listeners prefer, there was a psychological incident that will remain with me forever, which began years before during my time at the University of Arkansas.

My first college semester was at the University of Arkansas, and I lived, as most students did, in the dormitory, three to a room. Across the hall lived my close friend, Roy. Where you saw one, the other would be. After the first semester, realizing that for the moment, college was not my "cup of tea," I enlisted in the military; three and a half years later, I was in Vietnam.

During one of my helicopter missions, we brought back a 101st infantry squad to their base camp, shut down, and returned to the ship approximately an hour later. As I was walking back to the chopper, but not yet in, I turned, and approximately 10 yards from me, Roy was sitting by a hut with a few other troops dressed in field gear, indicating they had just come from or were going out on a mission. I noticed he had black officer's bars sewn into his fatigues.

We stared "eye to eye" for what seemed like an eternity ("thousand-yard stare"), yet we never spoke or advanced in recognition. I wanted to hug and embrace him, with memories of our past in college, but could not move forward; my legs just would not take me to him. Only a vet can truly understand, and it's beyond my ability to explain why I couldn't. As I returned to the gunner's position on the chopper and we lifted off, I noticed his eyes, void of life, following our ship's path. I never went back to find him, and now over 40 years later, I see his blank stare cutting through me as though it was yesterday.

The K-9 section arrived at Phan Rang approximately three months prior to the fighter aircraft: first, F-100s, followed by a variety of other attack and support airplanes. The closest town was Thap Cham, approximately 5 kilometers from base where we would spend most of our off-duty time. Because the K-9 section was the first line of perimeter defense, we would not wear identifying dog patches on our fatigues, as apparently, there was a price on our heads offered by the VC.

In any event, it didn't take us long to feel at home and know where all the bars were. We found small rooms to rent by the month furnished with a chair, bed, dresser, and an all-purpose maid; the total price for this package was $40 per month. What else could you ask for being so far from home? "Chad" was the landlord and a hell of a nice guy. The only problem was the local military carried him away one morning, accused of being a Viet Cong. As soon as the planes arrived from the United States, the price tripled for our comforts, and being on an enlisted pay grade, most of us surrendered the luxury of these hideaways.

Our living quarters on base were nothing to write home about. There were eight handlers in a tent, plus we had a monkey as a pet. It was absolutely impossible to keep clean, since Phan Rang was in a construction mode 24 hours a day and the dust from expanding made it an absolute dust bowl. The bathroom was a "two-hole" outhouse that was in continual use. During the first few days after arriving, everybody had dysentery due to the change in diet and climate. If you want to laugh, imagine 52 handlers lined up waiting their turn. By the time you finished, you had to get back at the end of the line, knowing that one trip was not going to be enough. You didn't even buckle your pants, and you always carried a roll of toilet paper as a treasured commodity, knowing that the next time around, there may be none at your disposal.

> *It reached 115 degrees today, and I am getting splinters from using the good old outhouse. When I get back to the States, I am going to go to the bathroom the very first thing just so I can use one of those automatic flushers!*
>
> —Letter, February 26, 1966

Taking a shower was also a difficult task, since the facility was on the other side of base. Anyone wanting to shower had to meet at a particular time and take the section's truck. It was a pain with all the coordinating, and we probably smelled worse than our dogs. God bless the monsoon season. It simplified matters greatly. We knew the approximate time of the afternoon rains and positioned ourselves with soap in hand; many stark naked outside the tent, waiting for the downpour. Once in a while, you would get your timing off and be completely lathered with soap from head to toe, and suddenly, the rain would stop. During these cleansing periods, the area resembled a nudist colony more than a war zone.

Tell a handler *absolutely not* to do something and, guaranteed, he *absolutely will* do it! Stan, another handler, and I became good friends. After nights of hearing activity from a hamlet not far from the northeast corner of the base, we decided to make a daytime public relations visit. It was posted as an "off limits" area due to suspected VC activity. Therefore, one morning after putting up our dogs, off we went. We knew how to get there, and it was just a matter of not telling anyone.

With extreme caution, we walked into the hamlet with big smiles on our face, no weapons, and pockets full of candy for the children who swarmed around us within the first few minutes of our visit. I am sure they had not been that close to an American and probably heard tales of their fathers and uncles shooting at us. During the day, the VC usually hid their weapons, carrying on with their regular lives. In any event, as the elders rendered cold stares, we began to think there was a good reason why the area was off limits.

While strolling, I noticed out of the corner of my eye, down by a river that ran through the hamlet, a guy in uniform about 20 or 30 meters from us raising his weapon over his head signaling *someone, somewhere* and telling them *something*. Although the local militia walked around in uniform with a weapon, you were not certain which side they were fighting for. I did not inform Stan until later as he would have to turn to see, and I didn't want the guy to know he was being watched. The VC attempted to remain anonymous, so I wasn't really worried, due to the number of children surrounding us.

Stan was, and I am sure still is, one of those fellows that can make friends at the drop of a hat, and the kids completely enjoyed him. Villagers other than children started coming over to us, and a man approached with instructions, by pointing, to follow him. I could only look at Stan and think, "Oh, shit, we're dead." They didn't speak English, and we certainly didn't want to practice our local barroom vocabulary. We were led to the "mayor's hutch," and through moaning and groaning, supplemented by hand signals, we found him extremely friendly. He offered fruit that contained bugs, resulting in dysentery for the next few days, and ended the visit by sharing his fully loaded opium pipe. Any fear we had literally went "up in smoke." In due course, excusing ourselves, we were escorted back to the main road. From there, we bid goodbye, never mentioning our K-9 occupation or telling our co-workers about the adventure. We never returned. I used to send film home for my mom to develop, and when done, she would send the pictures to me.

> *Received the pictures; even though they are in black and white, they are good. Your son took quite a chance going there for the village was off limits for it is located at the north perimeter of the base, and as several of our planes have been on final approach they have drawn a lot of ground fire from there . . .*
>
> —Letter, September 16, 1966

Stan and I had a previous episode that almost got us thrown in jail if it hadn't been for a "not too bright" air policeman at the main gate. As mentioned previously, the K-9 section and the army's 101st Airborne arrived at Phan Rang prior to the fighter pilots. The air force would not issue grenades to dog handlers, and the army did not issue good mattresses to their troops. You know where this is going, and you are correct, "barter system" once more. Stan and I were in one of the local "boom-boom" houses, the polite term is "tea house," at the end of the base when we began a conversation with a couple of airborne troops, and within minutes, negotiations began.

The air force pilots' living quarters were ready for their arrival with the thickest mattresses that would compare to those in a five-star hotel; we were guarding this area, so we were familiar with the furnishings. It would be quite easy to acquire a "six-by" truck (six wheels), load it up, and deliver the cargo to our clientele. In turn, they would give us a case of grenades, and everyone would be happy, as any business transaction should end. The midnight "commando raid" was going great. Stan and I had the truck loaded with five or six mattresses, and just as we were getting into the truck, an officer stuck his head into the hutch and noticed the mattresses missing from the beds, and with a quick glance, he saw them on our truck. There wasn't much of an excuse to come up with, so Stan saluted as he got into the truck, never wavering on his protocol. I told him to forget the formalities, because if we didn't get out of there, his saluting would not prevent jail time; I drove like hell directly to the main gate.

Because the officer immediately called the air police explaining the theft (a better term is "relocation of government property"), the radios became alive, relaying messages to the regular air police patrols to be on the lookout for a truck filled with mattresses. Since we were air police and had our radio on, we heard all transmissions. Stan broadcasted over the air that he saw the truck going to the southern part of the base, only because we were in the northern sector. Slowing down to a roll at the gate, not giving the guard a chance to look in the back, we flashed our badges, and off in the night we rode. I knew then what "mules" (drug smugglers) must feel like when they approached customs while carrying contraband.

We unloaded at the 101st, being treated as "heroes," received our grenades, drove back to the K-9 section, and the next morning, in the chow hall, heard all about the missing items. I am sure the air force pilots' mattresses were replaced, the original ones now being enjoyed by the 101st, and Stan and I with better protection on the perimeter. Everybody was happy, except for the officer who blew the whistle.

Toward the end of my tour, I received a telegram that my dad was operating a Pan Am flight through Saigon as a flight engineer. A leave was granted, and I flew to Saigon on a military transport. I met his plane on the tarmac, and it was a great feeling. Somehow, he had arranged for another engineer to continue his trip from Saigon, giving us some time together. I had only been in the city once when transferring to Phan Rang, so both of us were tourists. At Phan Rang, GIs were not allowed to have civilian clothes, but in Saigon, they were encouraged to be worn, as circumstances would allow. I took him to the K-9 section at Tan Son Nhut Air Base and met a handler who I was previously stationed with in Maine. He was more or less my size, so I borrowed his shoes, shirt, and pants for our adventure.

Big Etch and Little Etch hit Saigon, and hard. There wasn't a bar on Tu Do Street that we missed, and all the tea ladies thought it was great for a father and son to be together. They made our visit as pleasant as possible until funds began to get close to the poverty line. It was a great evening, and I saw him off the next day on his flight to

Hong Kong to rendezvous with my mom, who was waiting for him there on vacation.

A few years later, my parents had some neighbors to dinner at our home in Westbury, on Long Island. The subject came up about people not paying attention to exchanging money when traveling through foreign countries. To emphasize her point, my mom told the story of when my dad came from Saigon to Hong Kong. She explained how Etch paid the taxi driver a Hong Kong fare in U.S. dollars, which cost him about 50 times what it should have. Naturally, this left them short on funds for their vacation. It took me about a second to connect the dots, and when I looked up at him, he was already staring at me indicating to keep quiet. I did, and the subject was never mentioned again.

The sad part of the story is that the handler I borrowed the clothes from was killed in a VC penetration at Tan Son Nhut before I could give them back. I had taken the clothes to Phan Rang and was going to mail them to him, but after hearing the report of the attack on his air base and that he was one of the fatalities, I threw the clothes away.

Phan Rang is located south of Cam Ranh Bay, and because we worked at night, approximately once a week, our unit members would provide security for convoys between the two bases. A unit member manned an M-60 machine gun in the lead jeep and another GI in the rear jeep with an M-60 protecting the convoy from the back.

There was a rubber plantation approximately halfway along the route, and it was a perfect place for engagement.

> *I got back from the convoy all right, but not without a little trouble as I had anticipated and exactly where I had anticipated, the plantation. Your son was credited with discovering eight cases of stolen ammo, 7,750 rounds, which the VC obtained by way of black market. With the gunner giving me fire coverage with the machine gun, this other guy and I threw the cases of ammo in the jeep and got the hell out of there for it was as much VC territory as you could get. Two VCs were cut in half by the machine gun, and all I can say is God was with us . . .*
>
> —Letter, March 6, 1966

I volunteered as a door gunner on the Hueys with the 48th (Jokers), 161st (Flying Pelicans), and 174th (Dolphins) Assault Helicopter Companies when time permitted. My total hours were approximately 175 while in-country, with God knows how many missions throughout our area of operation; some were boring, while others were quite memorable. The most challenging part of this undertaking was trying to convince my mom and dad that I still had all my faculties, so I wrote to them and explained:

> *Mom and Dad, I know you feel that I am crazy for doing things like this and they make you worry, but it's not that I am crazy. Some people feel that God has led them into their occupation, such as the ministry. Well, see, I feel that he has led me into my occupation, and I feel that he is always right beside me and guiding me. I am not pushing my luck for I feel that life is something, which God gives you, leads you through, and then takes away from you at his choosing for a reason.*
>
> —Letter, March 11, 1966

I always looked forward to flying with Aircraft Commander Captain Carl Kernwein and his copilot Captain Donald Higgins, with Lionel Grover in the crew chief position. They could always incorporate humor into our flights. Most of the time, we flew with the side doors open, leaving the gunner on the one side and the crew chief on the other completely exposed. Glover told a story of when he was flying as a gunner and that while hovering approximately 20 feet off the ground, the crew chief accidentally leaned over the edge of the chopper too far and fell out. The captain's first words were, "I wonder how much paperwork this is going to take?" The comment was made before seeing if the crew chief was injured. Apparently, the crew chief was lucky, only breaking an arm.

When Kernwein and Higgins flew together, they would compete to see who could fly closest to the ground, "contour flying," and come up *over* the trees; many times, branches scraped my gun mount. On one mission, Kernwein was following a road as if in a road vehicle. He came up behind a wagon being driven by an old man and ox carrying a high load of hay piled higher than the chopper, since we were flying so low. As the ox was slowly plodding along, Kernwein got "bumper to bumper" with him and came up over the wagon's rear, missing it by inches. The ox, driver, and wagon went in different directions, and there was one more Vietnamese that wanted the "ugly Americans" to go home. Another time, the good captain noticed a Red Cross worker and a Vietnamese girl riding in a "Lambretta," similar to a taxi, and flew down alongside so the occupants could talk to one another. The girls loved it, so one day you make a foe, and the next, you make a friend.

Kernwein was a pro as a pilot, always on the lookout for a trap. One such flight took us over a "free fire zone" meaning if anything moved, you could engage without any questions asked; this area was the bad part of town. The captain had the ship at approximately 4,000 feet, which kept us out of the small arms ground fire range yet close enough to see activity. Someone was walking in the middle of an open field with his back to us. This was considered suicidal on his part. Kernwein's instinct targeted the person as a decoy to lure us down to a lower altitude, where we would be in a cross-fire situation from the woods adjacent on both sides of the field. Kernwein didn't take the suspected trap, and we lived for another day. Another mission illustrates how a number of South Vietnamese soldiers were not keen on being exposed to "harm's way." They felt that the Americans were present to fight their war for them. We flew a search-and-destroy team composed of five or six Vietnamese to a drop-off point where they were to spend two days in the "bush" seeking out their brothers fighting for the opposite side. The patrol was to return to the landing zone (LZ) for pick-up two days later. The procedure for off-loading was to come in fast, hover above the ground for literally seconds, while the troops jumped out, and then get the hell out of there as fast and high as you could.

When off-loading, you are a sitting duck. As we started our climb out, approximately 10 feet above ground, I noticed one of the Vietnamese with his arms wrapped around the skid dangling from the chopper on my side. I guess he wasn't too patriotic and felt he had better things to do than go into the bush. I stomped his arms with my feet, and whether wanting to go or not, he dropped to his comrades.

We came back in two days for the pickup, and nature can be very informative. The LZ was composed of high elephant grass, which had obviously not been walked through for the two-day period. Their search-and-destroy mission turned out to be a fireside cookout right where we let them off.

One of the first missions was to pick up three or four VC suspects being flown to an area for interrogation. They were sitting in the middle of the ship off to my left, with their hands and feet tied, guarded by a Vietnamese officer. Since we seldom flew with the side doors closed, there was nothing stopping a VC suspect from falling out, which reportedly occurred on several occasions. Before realizing what was happening, the officer took a prisoner and threatened to throw him out into the wild blue yonder a few thousand feet above the ground. After I stopped the officer, assuring him that it wouldn't happen in this chopper, he reluctantly sat back down, staring at me, not in a loving manner, throughout the remainder of the flight. In hindsight, it probably would have been better to let the suspect *fall* than go through the interrogation techniques that were being used.

While flying, I used to write a brief summary at the end of each mission. By the time I left Vietnam, my diary was composed of two books. Through the years, only one has survived, and I hope that someday the other will be found. It contained a write-up on a mission that has remained in my thoughts, and without the book for reference, I can only describe what is remembered concerning one of the flights. The mission was to fly a colonel on a resupply/inspection mission, where he could fly over his troops who were dug in somewhere in the jungle. We flew from Phan Rang with the ammunition and picked up the colonel at Nha Trang. After taking off and reaching God knows where over the jungle, the aircraft commander signaled me to start lowering the ammo boxes. The colonel took my position, and he was momentarily probably Vietnam's highest-ranking helicopter gunner. Hovering at treetop level, lying flat on my stomach and halfway outside the chopper, I let down the ammo through the triple canopy trees. Once the box went through the treetops, it disappeared, and due to the multiple layers of palm leaves obscuring the ground, I had absolutely no idea who was receiving it on the other end of the rope. Even if it were the enemy, they wouldn't have shot us down since, if they crippled the helicopter, the chopper would most likely explode, which would have ruined the ammunition and food. There's a saying "Don't bite the hand that feeds you." Whoever was on the ground would pull hard on the rope, signaling me to pull it up and start again with another load. While all this was going on, the colonel was shouting, "Those are my boys, those are my boys," smoking a big cigar while waving his hands. Actually, he wasn't smoking the cigar; he was chewing it. The colonel was right out of one John Gotti's social clubs. He was as Italian as they come and quite a character. We did receive ground fire from the crew chief's side for a few seconds that was opposite to the helicopter's side I was resupplying from. The crew chief wasn't in a position to return fire, since he was in the middle of the ship, holding my feet so I wouldn't fall out. We weren't hit, and the aircraft commander quickly climbed to gain altitude. Heading back to the base, the colonel settled down, and I wanted to ask him if he knew any of the mob back home but felt it wasn't an appropriate time.

That was a good mission, since it broke the monotony of many routine resupply flights termed "ash and trash." Most of them were around Phan Rang, going back and forth to the Korean outposts that surrounded the air base. It was a matter of carrying ammunition, food, and water; the water was transported in five-gallon jerry cans. On the outbound, the cans were lined up in two neat rows in the middle of the chopper for easy extraction. Filled with water, they were heavy and stable. The trouble was bringing back the empties that were light. I would line them up, and when we reached altitude, because of my nightly K-9 duties, I would fall asleep. Due to the chopper having its side doors opened during most of these flights, two or three cans would fall overboard by the time we got back to the flight pad. God knows who or what was hit down below. Can you imagine being killed or wounded by a jerry can falling from a helicopter? Inventory was never taken of the cans, so nothing was ever said.

The Korean troops were hardcore fighters, respected by both sides of the conflict. The following excerpt was found on a captured Viet Cong:

> *Orders now stipulate that contact with the Koreans is avoided at all costs unless a Viet Cong victory is 100% certain. Never defy*

Korean soldiers without discrimination, even when they are not armed, for they all are well trained in Taekwondo.

A mission flown on August 23, 1966, got me in a situation where I had to come up with a quick story to explain why I hadn't shown up on time to go on post with the K-9 section. K-9 patrols started at 6:30 p.m. around the Phan Rang perimeter, and at that time, I was in Nha Trang on a helicopter mission that got extended past its scheduled time. The day started by departing the pad on routine supply missions for the Korean outposts surrounding Phan Rang. About midday, we were called out for a medevac run due to a soldier having his hand blown off by a grenade. By the time we got back to Phan Rang, we quickly refueled and took Captain Kernwein north to Nha Trang, where he was being reassigned. The trip was an approximately 30-minute one-way flight, and although I knew it would be tight, I could make the trip and return just in time to go on my post. I was wrong; we didn't depart Nha Trang until 7:00 p.m. and realized that I would have to do some creative talking to explain my late arrival when I got back to the K-9 section, especially since the air force had not approved my flying with the army and my seniors at the K-9 section were not aware of my extracurricular activities with the Hueys. That time of year, night fell around 6:00 p.m., and the flight back was my first time I had flown during darkness. Vietnam looked completely different. The only thing you could see were flashes from artillery fire from ground units or air strikes. The air force was conducting several strikes along the route we were flying, and our pilots had to stay alert to avoid a midair collision with these fighter aircraft as they dropped their ordnance and strafed the area.

Actually, it was quite entertaining. After time spent "in-country," you became immune to the fact that these displays ended in people being killed. Captain Higgins had been upgraded to aircraft commander and asked if I wanted to be let off at the kennel. I immediately responded that it would be a disaster. All I could picture was a chopper landing in the middle of the kennel with me jumping out. We arrived at the Huey pad at Phan Rang located on the other side of the base from the K-9 section at 7:35 p.m., and I began the half hour walk to the kennel; this gave me time to compose a story.

My explanation to the supervisor was I had gone down to the tea house area by the base in the afternoon and after a few beers, fell asleep in one of the back rooms of a local bar. Looking like hell from flying since 8:00 a.m., he mistook the reason for my rough appearance and told me to go sleep it off. I never heard any more about the incident and ensured all future flights got me back to the kennel on time to go to work.

Another flight with Captain Kernwein and Captain Higgins is recorded in my diary. Both pilots had to be on their good behavior for this one:

> *Departed pad 11:30 for VIP run with three-star General Heinges and three of his aides. We departed here with a one gunship escort. Both our ships were supposed to make a quick stop at Dalat, but as we made our final approach, the airfield was completely abandoned, and a C-47 had been pulled off into the woods, whereas there was no possible way it could take off from the field. We bypassed Dalat due to the above information and continued on to Bro Loc. I felt I would freeze to death because we had to fly at a high altitude to avoid ground fire. After landing at Bro Loc and getting mission coordinated with the pilot of the gunship, we took off and landed at a field close by to refuel and pick up the general and his aides. After accomplishing this task, we took off and landed at Tra Tan Ra, a Special Forces outpost. As we landed, the ARVNs had a color guard for the general. It was funny as hell, because they didn't know what they were doing. I was very much interested with an outpost of this type, for I had read about them in the book The Green Beret. This was the first time I had actually been to a Special Forces camp. It was fortified to a maximum and very impressive. As we were waiting for the general to finish his business at the outpost, we were sitting in the ship at the end of the small airstrip when, without warning, a caribou-type aircraft landed and could not have missed hitting our rotary blade by three inches. It was so close that the crew chief jumped from the ship and ran like hell. After leaving Tra Tan Ra, we headed for a town called Diling and landed after ground troops marked the "LZ" with a yellow signal smoke grenade as the troops had done*

at Tra Tan Ra. "Green"—come on in, "Yellow"—if you want, but be careful, "Red"— stay away unless you're a fool! The general left on business, and we waited around the ship for his return. The "LZ" was right in the middle of town, so we passed the time away watching the local girls walk by. Upon leaving Diling, we took the general back to Bro Lac, dropped him off, and headed for Phan Thiet at approximately 18:00. Following another meeting, we departed Phan Thiet with our passengers and arrived at Tral Loung San, another Special Forces outpost. After this stop, we departed back for Phan Thiet. On the way back, the general wanted to circle a forward position camp. It was shaped in a triangle with each side approximately 100 yards in length. A couple rows of barbwire were strung the length of these sides on the outside with a deeply dug trench along the inside. All I could say is that these troops must be brave bastards, for the ground surrounding their fortification showed hundreds upon hundreds of mortar craters from the fence line to approximately 600 yards out. Upon completion of this circle, we flew over one of the major operations that was taking place at this time. Tanks were seen maneuvering off to the left of our ship, but I did not observe any firing. We arrived back at Phan Thiet, and the passengers departed for their own ship. The gunship that acted as our escort departed for its home base.

On the way back to Phan Thiet, I studied the general and observed how he had two personalities. On the ground, he is always smiling and shaking hands, but in the air, he sits in his seat and stares out into dead space showing deep concentration. Upon leaving Phan Thiet, we headed for Phan Rang and landed at pad at 19:45. On the way, we spotted tracer fire in an area where we had flown a previous mission. The ground fire was not directed at us.

—End of Mission, August 19, 1966/19:45

This flight was conducted around the southeast area of the country, Phan Thiet, throughout the central highlands, Dalat and Bảo Lộc. I had the latter town's name spelled incorrectly in my diary. How's that for a part-time job? This was a good example of why the Huey was so important during the war. I was watching the Military Channel the other day, over 40 years later, and the Huey still ranks number one in performance. Any crewmember who had the privilege to be assigned to this helicopter will never forget the *pop, pop, pop* sound the blades created while making its way through the sky. Approximately 10 years after returning from Vietnam, I was refueling one of Academics of Flight's training airplanes at Islip Airport on Long Island. While completing paperwork, three or four Hueys landed that belonged to the Air National Guard. Naturally, when the crew came in the office, we started talking. The aircraft commander invited me to the ramp to view one of the ships. Accepting his offer, I walked to within approximately 20 feet of one of the choppers but then stopped. I couldn't make myself go closer. Time, which as they say cures all ills, has erased my disassociation with items I was familiar with during Vietnam. I also had "survivor's guilt" for many years, which rushed to the surface at that moment. Finally, one morning I woke up to reality. I had given my opponents the opportunity to cut my life short, exposing myself on the base perimeter at night and as a door gunner during the day. If he couldn't shoot straight and hit my ass, that was his problem, not mine.

Rummaging through some personal effects, I once came across a few moth-eaten ribbons that had been awarded during my military years. I wanted to display them on a plaque in my den. I hoped to include the Army Air Medal, since I met all requirements, due to the helicopter operations. However, there was a catch: since I was in the air force and the flights were with the army, it was never listed in my military separation papers. I am still working on trying to receive the award and feel, with more effort, I can achieve this goal. By keeping a record of all my missions, I began this project. The high point has been establishing contact with the aircraft commander of my last mission on November 7, 1966, Captain Curtis Laird, who is now retired and living in Texas. It was one of my most unforgettable telephone conversations. We had much to talk about, and my eyes filled with tears after I hung up. It's true when they say that you never leave it behind. I sent Captain Laird some photos taken while we were flying and joked that while he thought I was protecting him at the gunner's position from possible ground fire, I was really just taking pictures. Two missions of several flown with Captain Laird when he was a first lieutenant were recorded as follows:

> *Departed pad 07:45 to resupply ROK outposts around Phan Rang perimeter. Felt good flying again after so long of an absence. The ROK Tiger Division has been replaced by the White Horse Division. AC and pilot are real good flyers. High gusty winds made flying rough.*
>
> —End of Mission, November 1, 1966/11:00

> *Departed pad at 08:00 to resupply ROK outposts around Phan Rang perimeter; good flying weather. Arrived back at pad to refuel at 14:00. Went back to resupplying. Crew chief thought he heard a shot and thought we were shot at. Crew chief jerked ROK Troop off chopper and fight broke out between them for a few seconds. A 2/Lt. from the ROK's started to chew the crew chief's ass, but crew chief told him to go to hell in a nice way. Very interesting afternoon.*
>
> —End of Mission, November 7, 1966/17:00

The other pilot on both missions was Chief Warrant Officer Dale Beggs. I never knew his unique story until speaking with Captain Laird not too long ago. Beggs had been in the Army Reserve and Army National Guard for six years, with his last rank, a sergeant. He wanted to go to the regular army but was refused, since this required previous active duty and not more than one dependent. Beggs had no such previous active duty; at that time, he had two dependents, his wife and son.

Dale had a solution. He divorced his wife, got around the requirement of previous active duty, and joined the regular army. From there, he went to Warrant Officer Candidate School, a helicopter school, and was assigned to the 174th Assault Helicopter Company in Vietnam. He remarried the same girl three months after he was accepted into the regular army. As they say, "Where there is a will, there is a way!"

Laird said that in the beginning, he had no idea, as the others, of Beggs' story. Dale was a quiet person, and I assumed he wanted to keep his background to himself. However, it was leaked by someone in Dale's hometown. Laird was returning off a mission with Beggs as his copilot, and as they approached the helicopter pad to land, Laird saw a multitude of press, with cameras waiting for the helicopter to land. Laird's first thought was, "Oh God, what did I do wrong this time!" As it turned out, the press was there to interview Beggs concerning his journey to get to Vietnam.

Another conversation was with Carl Kernwein, who now resides in Washington State. Apparently, he was transferred to the 1st Cavalry Division after Phan Rang. The 1st Cav was continuously engaged, and I am sure Carl was in the middle of it all. He told me he wanted to forget that part of his life, and I certainly respected his feelings.

The last contact in 2011 was with Lieutenant Colonel Martin "Marty" Heuer, the president of the 174th Assault Helicopter Company. He was an officer with the 174th in 1966, and because he was stationed at another base than Phan Rang, he was unaware of my flying with his unit. Captain Laird and Marty have remained good friends, and after speaking to Laird for confirmation, Marty called me, and again, we had a few laughs. Marty claimed that if he had been aware of my flying, he would have never authorized such activity, but he was grateful and sent the following e-mail:

> *It was great talking to you today. You sure had an unusual experience during your tour in VN, and the 174th was the beneficiary of your volunteer service.*

Marty asked if I had been officially checked out and certified with the M-60 machine gun prior to my flights, since it was the main armament on the "Slicks." I explained that it was the primary weapon we used on our convoys and I was completely familiar with its operation. I can't remember if I was ever formally checked out or not; I just started using it.

He subsequently published a book, *Sharks, Dolphins, Arabs, and the High Priced Help*, about the 174th. He told me if he ever got to a second edition, he would update the book with my activity. He sent me a copy, and reading the book has been very refreshing, since the majority of the crewmembers I had flown with were mentioned throughout.

On one page, Marty expressed his thoughts about the people assigned to guard duty:

> *Guard duty was never a pleasant task, especially during the monsoon seasons when the bunkers were cold and wet. It certainly wasn't as dangerous as those who pulled perimeter duty in the field; the thought of snakes, rats and the threat of enemy attacks were enough to unnerve the strongest.*

A friend sent me an e-mail last year regarding a Medal of Honor recipient, Ed Freeman, who was assigned to the 229th Assault Helicopter Battalion, 1st Cavalry Division (Air Mobile) involved at the Ia Drang Valley battle in November 1965. The following took place at LZ X-ray:

> *Your infantry unit is outnumbered 8–1 and the enemy fire is so intense, from 100 or 200 yards away, that your own infantry commander has ordered the medevac helicopters to stop coming in. You're lying there, listening to the enemy machine guns and you know you're not getting out. Your family is halfway around the world, 12,000 miles away, and you'll never see them again. As the world starts to fade in and out, you know this is the day. Then—over the machine gun noise—you faintly hear that sound of a helicopter. You look up to see an unarmed Huey. But. . . it doesn't seem real because no medevac markings are on it. Ed Freeman is coming for you. He's not medevac, so it's not his job, but he's flying his Huey down into the machine gun fire anyway. Even after the medics were ordered not to come. He's coming anyway. And he drops it in and sits there in the machine gun fire, as they load 2 or 3 of you on board. Then he flies you up and out through the gunfire to the doctors and nurses. And, he kept coming back! 13 more times! He took about 30 of you and your buddies out who would have never have gotten out.*

The author was not mentioned; however, you can be assured that for the rest of his life, he will look skyward and regress to that time in his life whenever a chopper passes overhead. Ed Freeman was wounded four times and passed away on August 20, 2008, at the age of 80. This is an amazing piece of writing, illustrating what a person will go through under intense fire to extract his fellow combatant out of harm's way. Every now and then, a person hears a song that is remembered for life. I had a cassette tape from 30 years ago that was stolen from my car. One of the songs recorded was "More Than a Name on a Wall" by the Statler Brothers rendering tribute to the mothers, the *real heroes*, who lost a loved one serving in Vietnam. This is for all the moms who had their lives changed forever:

I saw her from a distance
As she walked up to the wall
In her hand she held some flowers
As her tears began to fall
And she took out pen and paper
As to trace her memories
And she looked up to heaven
And the words she said were these . . .
She said lord my boy was special
And he meant so much to me
And Oh I'd love to see him
Just one more time you see
All I have are his memories
And the moments to recall
So Lord could you tell him,
He's more than a name on a wall

Excerpts from Letters Concerning K-9 Perimeter Duty, Phan Rang, 1966

February 26, 1966

Had a little action last night. The dog man on the post next to mine heard something outside the perimeter fence. He light his flare to light the area, and it reveled three individuals coming toward the fence about 75 yards out. He opened fire on them, and they disappeared back into the mountains. We figured it was VC trying to plant booby traps around the perimeter where we walk or snipers trying to get into position to harass us.

April 3, 1966

Three dogs have been bitten by snakes—two by Russell's vipers, one by spitting cobra. The dogs got sick, but did not die."

Two nights ago the dogman on K-1 was shot at with an automatic weapon five times. They captured the two individuals, and I don't know what happened from there.

Last night, a dog team was just being posted when a water buffalo started charging them. He raised his weapon to fire but didn't have a round in his chamber. The posting truck had not yet left, and one of the dog teams that was sitting in the back of the posting truck quickly fired on the bull with automatic fire and dropped the bull about ten feet in front of the dog team it had been charging. Apparently, the security troops were trying to run it off the runway, and the bull got mad.

April 10, 1966

Last night, I wandered a little too far from the perimeter and landed about a mile off base. Spanky alerted and pulled me to about 50 yards from a house where I observed a group of Vietnamese men. I kept hearing sniper fire, but I am so used to it by now that it didn't bother me. I found cover behind a bush and radioed in to control if they knew anything about a house being on my post with Vietnamese around it along with sniper fire. After checking my position out, they told me I better get the hell back on base for my own good. These people are so security-lazed (U.S. military) that they (Vietnamese) took down the barbwire around the outer perimeter. As it turned out, I didn't get shot, for I got back on the perimeter with much speed. Here is a diagram of where I had wandered. We had another dog bit by a snake; this makes five so far.

April 13, 1966

Two nights ago, we had a very active night. Remember I said they would try and attack the base; they did on our south perimeter, but were pushed back. They also blew up a fuel line of ours, and K-9 as harassed by sniper fire. I had a tracer round go by my helmet not more than five feet and was the closest one yet, but I don't think he really knew where I was. he snipers know where we have our posts, but they don't know where the handlers and dogs are a good part of the time. By shooting rounds on our posts, they hope we will fire back. By doing this, the explosion from our weapon will create a muzzle flash, and we would give away our position. Also, we had another dog bite by snake, which makes six.

June 6, 1966

Two nights ago, a water buffalo hit one of our dog teams, two posts down from mine, and in the confusion, the dog got away, and we haven't found him as yet. The buffalo was killed, and the handler is OK.

July 11, 1966

We finally got back into the war. Five VCs tried to penetr7ate our north perimeter two posts down from mine. The firefight lasted for about one and a half hours because they kept sending up reinforcements.

Spanky and I hit a bank for cover and watched for them to come through our post that was being illuminated by flare ships, but none tried to come through. One VC was found dead, and we had no casualties. One or our boys had a bullet hole right through his helmet, but was not hurt.

The other night, Spanky took a snake bite out on post, and needless to say, it would have been me if not him. He got sicker than hell, but we rushed him to the hospital, and he recovered.

August 18, 1966

Well Spanky is out of work for a while, so I have some extra time. He has some kind of skin disease which means he cannot work and must be isolated for a while.

October 23, 1966

The other night, a troop turned his dog loose on alert, and the dog came back a few minutes later after making contact with a wild boar. The dog's whole side was ripped open. He is alive, but it will be a long time before he works again. I would be happy if the VC were the only thing we had to worry about. We are all about underwater and the snake situation is worse than ever. About two weeks ago, they killed a cobra, which measured nine and a half feet. Now, what in the hell can you do about something like that? You know why I say that the VC is the least of my worries.

I found the following newspaper article from *Stars and Stripes*, written in 1966, which referred to the unsuccessful enemy penetrations at our K-9 unit at Phan Rang.

Four-Footed "Detectives" Defend Phan Rang AB

The main lines of defense at Phan Rang AB, Vietnam, against perimeter penetrations are the four-footed "detectives" which patrol the base perimeter. The sentry dogs can "sniff out" an intruder at 600 yards under ideal wind conditions.

TSgt. Rodney G. Arnold, 35th Security police Squadron canine section supervisor, says that the presence of the sentry dog on the perimeter has been "a deciding factor" that the base has never had an enemy penetration.

The dogs react in many different ways to let its handler know that it has "sniffed out" an intruder while on patrol. Some dogs bark, some moan, cry, or jump into the air. Without their "four-footed radar," the handlers could pass within a matter of feet of the enemy during the dark of the night, without detecting him.

A2C Donald V. Houck summed up the reliability of sentry dogs: I rely more on my dog "Dutch," than I do my weapon.

6

WEST COAST

MERCED, CALIFORNIA, 1967–1968

Leaving Phan Rang, the next assignment was Castle AFB in Merced, California, south of San Francisco. Thank God I was not reassigned to Loring AFB. It was amazing that after a year in a war zone, I was more or less "dumped" into a civilian environment after disembarking at Travis AFB, California, with absolutely no time given to adjust to my new environment. I was wired through training and exposure to a battle-torn country for a year to be extremely aggressive, yet now, I was expected to behave like a gentleman. It took a long time not to feel like a fish out of water. I felt empty, bitter, completely disoriented, and scared. Many of us came home with invisible wounds that we will carry for the rest of our lives. I wanted to go right back to Vietnam, where I felt I belonged. Not only did I go through the normal readjustment period, but I didn't realize the amount of hostility toward returning vets as baby killers, and so on. I just had to live with the mood that swept the country. There were certainly inexcusable actions committed by both sides during the conflict, as in any war.

I came across a song that was written by U.S. Army Major J Billington. "The Eagle Cried," excerpted below, really nails it in expressing the emotions experienced by the majority of returning vets after a short time back home:

A 12 month tour behind him
and all his hopes ahead
A pride that beat with his young heart
for all the things he did
As he stepped off the airplane
He stooped and kissed the ground

And he traded a war on foreign soil
For one in his hometown

I saw them spit upon him
And I heard them call him names
Something changed within his eyes
He didn't look the same
He hid his wounds from battle
so others didn't know
But he couldn't hide the damage from
Their scars upon his soul

Welcome or not, I was home for 30 days prior to having to report to Castle AFB. Much to my surprise, my parents bought me a brand new 1967 Corvette Stingray, which I still have today. I had and still maintain a friendship with Ross Salt, who lived up the street from our house in Westbury and with whom I attended my last year of high school. If there was a way of finding trouble, we found it, in and out of school. Ross also spent a couple of years in military school. I asked him if he would drive to California with me in the Corvette, and I couldn't have picked a better traveling partner. Since it was winter, we decided to take the southern route, so as not to get snowbound in the middle of the country.

Off we went with the first stop at my uncle and aunt's farm in Cana, North Carolina. Ross hadn't been on a farm before, so I felt that he should get a "little country" and become familiar with an electric fence. When we were at the barn, I asked him to hold down an electric wire strand on a fence so I could get over. Ross then learned why they called it an "electric fence," and he didn't hold it very long. The next day, we went to stay the night at Dahl's house in Tabor City, North Carolina. Up to this point, the trip was great, and we were within our budget.

If I did the trip again, two items would be changed: the license plates and the car. To drive a brand-new sports car with New York license plates through the Deep South is asking for a whole lot of trouble from the police and others still sore that they lost the Civil War. Remembering when we left Dahl's, her last words were "Be careful driving through South Carolina due to the police." We weren't across the border for more than 10 minutes when we got our first ticket. The next scheduled overnight stop was Alabama, to see a buddy, Mike Cooper, who had been a dog handler at Phan Rang. We were very close friends, even though one night while on the perimeter I almost shot him. Mike wandered onto my post, and when challenged with Spanky alerting, no response was given. My finger was already on the trigger, and at the last minute, I recognized his dog's outline against the moonlight. I had a lot of choice words for him, but I don't think the seriousness of the situation registered, since he was laughing. The friendly fire incident that almost happened would have scarred me for life, especially involving a close friend.

Ross and I arrived in Alabama after driving through South Carolina and Georgia. We met Mike at a predetermined location. I got out and hugged him, and immediately, there was a cop on the scene. Remember, we had a Corvette with New York plates. He thought we were "transporting." However, the cop backed off after hearing Mike and I were together in Vietnam. At least there was one person that didn't hate us. Mike took us home to meet his wife and brother.

Mike's brother was also in Vietnam for two tours with the 1st Cav and certainly saw more than his fair share. In a unit such as his, your sixth sense was to react in a deadly manner without thinking; if not, you were dead. Day after day in that environment, after a period of time, the gentlest person is converted into a seasoned killer who reacts in a split second. Not only was this trait required to stay alive, but the soldier was rewarded with ribbons and medals. Mike's brother had been shot two or three times and had not adjusted to civilian life at the time of our meeting each other. To this day, many returning vets have not been able to leave the battles behind, and never will. A significant number volunteered for a second and third tour simply because they felt they couldn't adjust back to the demands of civilian life. They would rather take the risks of war.

Mike and I both requested to extend our tour in Vietnam; however, we filed our paperwork too late to remain there. A good number of GIs simply didn't have anything or anybody to come back to and didn't want to leave their unit members. The bond GIs form among themselves in a combat environment is sacred and unbreakable. The greater the intensity of hardships they endured together, the stronger the bond.

We went to the Playboy Club that night, and Mike's brother had a flashback in the men's room. While relieving himself, without warning, he coldcocked the hell out of some unlucky guy who was using the next urinal. The fellow went across the room with a mouthful of broken teeth. We left by the time the police arrived, and needless to say, Ross and I didn't get much sleep that night. I sincerely hope that his brother adjusted to civilian life as time went by. The next morning, or what was left of it, Ross and I hit the road. It was still a long journey to California.

The Mississippi Delta was next, and we decided to get off the main road for a while to see the state from the secondary roads. We gained two things from this decision. It was an education seeing the sharecropper shacks that still existed, as though it were the 1930s. Then we got our second ticket for driving through a rural "municipality." We were well aware that the speed limit was 45 mph as clearly posted. I reduced to 35 mph to have a buffer, but it wasn't quite good enough. Since it was raining, the officer, upon stopping me, explained that I should have known the speed limit was automatically reduced to 25 mph. After a long discussion with the trooper, we were given the choice of paying the ticket on the spot or waiting in jail for the judge to return from a two-week vacation to hear the case: not much of a choice. After paying, we took heed and continued out of town below 25 mph and returned to the main highway to continue the trip over the mighty Mississippi River.

Louisiana was next, followed by El Paso, Texas, in the late afternoon. Juarez, Mexico, was right across the border, and we had heard so much about it, so we opted for a stop. The night was spent dining, drinking, and dancing with the "señoritas." What transpired remains unclear, but Ross and I each had a hell of a headache the next morning.

On our way through Arizona, we got our third ticket. It was time to put the pedal to the metal with the roads so straight and the engine broken in. It was a perfect place to see how fast the car would go, or so I thought. At 120 mph, I was ripping up the road and happened to glance in the rearview mirror. There was the cop, bumper to bumper with us without his siren on or lights flashing. It appeared that I wasn't the only one ripping up the road. Had I stopped, he would have sailed right over the car, and I am sure he was getting a big kick out of the chase. I told the officer that we were late reporting to our base and had to go to Vietnam.

Lying will get you nowhere, but he was very polite; he even called me by my first name. Officer Such and Such instructed us to continue to the next town and make a left to the courthouse and wait for a judge named Walker. We were on the honor system and contemplated skipping town and moving on down the road. We noticed that passing police were giving us special attention, and since the cop proved I could not outrun the highway patrols, we decided to do as told and go see Judge Walker.

It wasn't hard to find the courthouse, since there were only about four buildings in the whole town. Ross and I waited approximately 30 minutes, and in came the judge, wearing dungarees and appearing to have been plowing fields. As he was lecturing us, Ross and I glanced at each other and, for some reason, started laughing. I guess the trip was finally getting to us. Judge Walker didn't see anything funny, and it was reflected in the $180 fine.

With the tickets and the stop in Juarez, the trip came to a temporary halt, as we had to wait for money from my dad or Ross's father. We only had Nevada to cross before California and then north to Castle AFB. Ross got stopped in Nevada but, somehow, talked his way out of a ticket. I should have taken lessons from him. In any event, we finally arrived at the air base. I reported in, and Ross left for New York the next day by plane.

Ross passed due to ill health in November 2022.

Castle AFB's duty was mundane compared to Vietnam. Although at one time I was seriously thinking of reenlisting and going to officer's training school, I finally decided to turn my government uniform in and meet the challenges of civilian life. I have absolutely no regrets for being part of the military, and I think, all in all, it came at the right time in my life.

After my discharge from the air force, I remained in Merced, California, to complete my two-year college degree that was provided by a great tuition policy at the local community college. Being stationed in California, an ex-military person was considered a resident and, therefore, could take as many credit hours for $50 per semester. My most memorable teacher was Mr. Jones, who taught economics. Despite being close to 300 pounds, he never stopped moving. Becoming a teacher later in my life, I admired the energy he expended during each lecture, and he was truly one of my mentors. He had his lectures perfected, wherein he would start writing on the blackboard at one end of the classroom, working his way across from left to right, and by the time class was over, he was drawing his last graph at the far end; his timing was perfect. I also became good friends with my philosophy teacher, and we spent many barroom hours discussing Plato, Socrates, and their Greek associates.

Regressing back to Vietnam, I saw an advertisement for a correspondence course to become a claims adjuster. The ad had a very pretty girl stretched out on the road with a short skirt, apparently hit by a car. I never met her, but completing the course while in Vietnam paid off when I got to California. While attending classes at Merced College, I went to the first claims adjuster's address that I found in the yellow pages and was hired part-time. The owner of the company, a fellow named Dave, would grade my reports as though he was my college professor. Being a claims adjuster is very challenging: you have to be very flexible and think fast.

I remember one of my first cases, which involved a young man in jail who stole merchandise from a local gas station. I had to go to his father's house in an attempt to recover some of the property. Realizing it wouldn't be pleasant and that the man could turn on me, I backed into the driveway and left the driver's side door unlocked with the window down, in case I had to leave in a hurry. When he answered the door and realized who I was, I saw in his eyes that the shit was about to hit the fan. After verbally abusing me, God, and the chicken that ran across the front porch, I more or less told him that all this crap wasn't going to change the situation and that the quicker he cooperated with me, the sooner I would be gone.

Actually, I had no legal right to be on his property, and he could have run me off at any time. His attitude changed and he became cooperative, inviting me in and telling me his life story, in which I was really not interested. At least I was getting closer to achieving the purpose of the trip. He led me to a room where some of the stolen merchandise was stored. The outcome of this was that I became a counselor to his son, who I met in jail. I would go once a week and visit him in his cell to discuss anything that came to his mind. This certainly was not required of the office, but if I had a chance to turn someone around in a positive way, it was my pleasure; besides, jails were not foreign to me. In the end, Dave gave me a good grade.

On another assignment, I had to drive to take pictures of an auto accident scene in Yosemite National Park that was about a two-hour drive from Merced. I took the pictures and stopped by a bar at the park. Returning to the office where Dave was waiting, I discovered that after a few drinks, I had left the camera on the bar and had to drive all the way back to retrieve it. Dave wasn't too happy with my performance.

The most challenging assignment was to prove that a man claiming total disability was working, which was classified as insurance fraud. This type of case has to be executed very carefully; if not, you could find yourself being physically harmed. The accused man lived in a house at the end of a U-shaped street with only one exit. He had several children aged about eight to early teens, and I felt that they were probably unsupervised, which would be in my favor: they were probably the neighborhood terrors. I composed an economic status survey checklist with my story being that I was a college student at Merced College, which was true, and I had to conduct an income survey for a class project. That part was false. I planned to go to the man's house last, so he would get used to seeing me around the neighborhood over a two- or three-day period.

The neighbors were unbelievably cooperative: it was at a time when people still trusted others. In a few instances, I was invited into their homes for coffee. At the house directly across from his, I mentioned his name, and the lady went "bananas." I had been correct about the children's reputation and decided it was time to tell why I was really in the neighborhood. She thought it was great and became my assistant. She told me the man's work schedule and allowed me to watch his house from one of her windows.

Sure enough, he was coming home dressed in a uniform, and I took pictures. It was already easy to prove him guilty of fraud, with the information I'd collected, along with the pictures. I could have called it quits, but the next day, knowing his work schedule, I went to his house and he invited me in. I hadn't noticed the weapon he was wearing with the uniform from the neighbor's house and thought maybe I had pushed the envelope too far. I went through my survey items and just wanted to get the hell out of there. Actually, he was nice, and I felt kind of guilty but had to do my job. Dave was ecstatic and forgave me for all my previous blunders.

There were other cases, and each one had its own twist. I learned a tremendous amount about human nature as a claims adjuster since the field is so people-oriented. I once had to investigate a home fire on the wrong side of the tracks in which arson was suspected. I am sure that I looked like a pimp, driving my Corvette. When I entered the neighborhood, all eyes were on me, and naturally, no one knew anything when questioned about the fire. After explaining that I had a check from the insurance company for the owner of the house, which was not true, suddenly everyone became very informative. They felt part of the funds should be for them since one claimed he called the fire department and another said he aided in some other way. It was all quite comical. The man who set the fire was found, turned over to the police, and later convicted.

Other jobs I held included selling shoes and working as a bouncer at a local bar. These jobs didn't compare to being a claims adjuster, but I had to make a living. One night in the bar, someone felt he could get past me while checking IDs, which started a brawl. It was as if we were making a Western movie, diving and being thrown over tables with glasses breaking all around. I avoided a great deal of pain due to a barmaid who knocked a beer bottle out of the hand of an opposing brawler just as it was coming down on my head. I had the brawler in a headlock and saw blood all over the floor. I was proud of myself for teaching him a lesson. After the police separated us and things settled down, I saw that the blood was from a cut on my hand. My Mexican girlfriend, Delores, was there, and I was her hero. California was a great ride, and if I hadn't chosen to return to Vietnam, I am fairly sure it would have become my home.

7

HERE WE GO AGAIN

SAIGON, VIETNAM, 1968–1970

"Jim, would you like to go back to Vietnam and work in Saigon with Pan Am?" The call came from my dad unbeknownst to my mom. It was like asking a child if he wanted candy. I thoroughly enjoyed being a claims adjuster while dating my Mexican girlfriend, Delores, who lived in San Francisco. However, I was trying to find an excuse to end the relationship. It had nothing to do with her or her family, because they were great.

One of our best, but longest, dates was the night we drove from San Francisco to some place in Mexico, danced all night, and drove back the next morning. The trio was Delores; her brother, Art; and me, all in a Corvette, which is a two-seater. A change was needed, and Vietnam was the perfect exit.

I had been to Rio de Janeiro, in Brazil, approximately a month prior to the call, and became friends with a philosophy student, Ingram, who was studying at a university in Rio. I was taking philosophy at Merced College, so she and I had a lot in common. Ingram would quote some philosopher, and I would come back with another. I invited her to California; she accepted and planned to arrive on a United Airlines flight the same day I left for Vietnam on a Pan Am cargo plane. I sent her a telegram at the last minute, on the day of her arrival, explaining my urgent departure, but never received an answer. I am sure that time proved it was to her benefit.

Military friends who had returned from Vietnam after I left strongly advised me not to return because the Viet Cong were becoming very sophisticated with their updated Russian weapons as the Tet Offensive was underway. The Viet Cong were determined to overrun the major South Vietnam cities, bringing the war to an end. This goal created the Offensive. The typical 24-year-old doesn't listen to such advice (and I didn't).

After a long flight arriving in Saigon, Pan Am booked me in the Caravelle Hotel directly across from a cathedral in the middle of the city. I arranged a wake-up call for 5:00 a.m. the next morning, since the company van was to come at 6:00 a.m. to take me to the airport for my first day of work. Before going to bed, a few of my new Pan Am co-workers took me around Saigon to their watering holes, which, of course, were filled with tea girls. I was in heaven and on top of the world. It sure was a step up from my previous Vietnam tour.

All this changed a few hours later when the shit hit the fan at 2:00 a.m. One-hundred twenty-two Russian-made rockets sailed over the hotel and slammed into the cathedral blowing off the top (very sacrilegious) and turning the hotel lobby into rubble. As the rockets came inbound, I started running around the hotel room trying to find a place to hide. Now, how the hell do you hide from rockets? I ran into the bathroom and thought, "No, I am not going to stay here, because people would laugh like hell if I got killed by a flying toilet." The only place left was to make a speedy exit to the hallway. Once there, the other hotel guests were already sitting, and I felt as though I were late for the party. One looked up and said, "This must be your first night in Saigon, Welcome."

I wasn't doing very well as a vet, and my friends back in California were absolutely correct when they warned me of more advanced weapons. If whoever was trying to kill me had aimed about an inch lower, the rockets would have come through my window. When I was at Phan Rang and had incoming fire, there was always room to maneuver, but in a hotel room, your dancing area is very limited. I preferred the good old days on the perimeter during these attacks, compared to being helpless in a hotel, as I was at that moment.

After everything settled down, I went to the lobby by the stairwell, since the elevator was severely damaged: the last five steps were scattered around the lobby. I managed to get to the floor level and went outside to take a look. My first thought was "Thank you Dad, here I go again getting involved with the Vietnam conflict." I picked up a small piece of shrapnel from a rocket and mailed it home with a note "From Russia with love."

The 5:00 a.m. wake-up call came on the dot, only two hours after the disruption ended. Somehow, the phone survived, and my caller said, "Good morning, Mr. Etchison, would you like a continental breakfast?" as though nothing had happened.

Being on a line station away from Pan Am headquarters was an excellent way to learn all of what makes an airline function. One day you are in operations completing paperwork for the flight crew, and the next you are assisting maintenance personnel changing an airplane tire on the ramp. For many days, fighter airplanes were strafing areas in Saigon that were on our way to work; it was like watching a war movie without having to pay for tickets.

By contrast, I remember one incident when I went back to work for Pan Am in the company's operations at Kennedy Airport (JFK) after leaving Vietnam. I was on the ramp that required coordinating all ground personnel movements around the aircraft to achieve an on-time departure. One day, I was supervising a unionized fleet service crew and picked up a piece of luggage that was near the conveyor belt and placed it on the belt, sending it to the airplane's cargo compartment. The fleet service crew stopped working and accused me of doing their job. Their team leader understood that I had come from a line station in Vietnam and calmed them down, so they went back to work.

All Pan Am employees at Tan Son Nhut, Saigon's major airfield, knew one another, and it was quite a group. We worked side by side with the locals, and they proved to be very efficient and reliable team players. I learned that two or three were VC, but they never tried to disrupt our operations.

> *I now have 20 Vietnamese, 12 Malaysians and 5 Americans, How's that for a melting pot? They gave me a surprise dinner the other night, and all I can say is that they're the greatest people going.*
>
> —Letter, July 26, 1966

Several of the American co-workers married Vietnamese partners, and their marriages are intact. The rest of us left as we came (solo) and were nicknamed using the Vietnamese word "butterfly." This term was for men who appreciated the variety of available young women as opposed to courting only one. An American security co-worker, John, upheld this term by using the location of his apartment as a nightly boarding house for the tea girls. Saigon was divided into rings around the city starting at 5 miles from the center, then 10, and the last 15. Depending on where the Vietnamese lived, a curfew was in place. The farther the ring, the earlier they had to be home. For example, if you lived in the 15-mile ring, the curfew was 5:00 p.m. As you got closer to the middle of town, the required time was later; the latest a Vietnamese could stay out was 10:00 p.m.

Many of the tea girls lived in the most distant ring, so they had to leave work by the afternoon, missing all the opportunities offered by GIs patronizing the bars at night. John had a simple remedy for all concerned, especially himself. Instead of the tea girls having to go home early, they crashed at John's apartment for the night. At any one time, there would be as many as five or more girls staying over. By this arrangement, they could work in the bars until the last minute to make it to John's apartment in the middle of Saigon. His phrase, which became famous among the Pan Am workers, was "Just leave the apartment key in the mailbox." Nothing was ever stolen, even though many times he was at the airport and his "guests" were there by themselves. It was a great arrangement. Needless to say, his mother's begging for him to come home where it was "safe" was ignored.

John did have a problem with one tea girl who misunderstood his hospitality. He came home tired from working a flight and went to the closet to put away his clothes. There was no room for his clothes since it was lined from one end to the other with women's clothing. The problem was even worse. The owner of the clothes had invited her mother from the country to live in the apartment. Naturally, this particular tea girl was removed from the guest list, which killed her dream of going to America.

Like John's off-duty life, ramp duty at Tan Son Nhut was never routine. One day I saw a crowd around an Air Vietnam DC-4, and I ventured over to where it was parked. An American GI was in the process of hijacking the plane and wanted to go to Hanoi, North Vietnam; I could have thought of a lot better places to visit, but it was his show.

While he was in the cockpit with the flight crew, the ground crew quietly deflated the tires. When the captain found out what they had done, he was really upset, cursing from the cockpit window. A few minutes later, a man fell out the cockpit window and dropped to the tarmac below. It was a good 15-foot fall, and the victim broke his back. The onlookers thought the hijacker had stabbed him, but in reality, it was the flight engineer, who had seized the opportunity to escape. I didn't think the side cockpit window was big enough, but he proved me wrong. The crewmember should have stayed put, because the hijacker gave up about five minutes later.

On another day, I was working Pan Am's Flight One, which goes around the world. The standard procedure is to put the meals in the aircraft's cargo compartment and bring them up to the passenger cabin prior to the aircraft taking off for its next destination. The meals at that time were packed in dry ice, which is compressed carbon dioxide that consumes oxygen. When the flight landed, I had the misfortune of being assigned ramp duty.

A woman dressed to the hilt, complete with jewelry, walked down the steps from first class to the ramp and asked if I could get her dog out of the cargo and hold it for her to walk for a few minutes during the layover. "Sure, it would be a pleasure." I had the worker bring the cage out of the airplane's rear lower cargo compartment, and the woman opened the door. Nothing came out. I realized in a minute that at one of the previous stations, the ground crew placed the dog in the same cargo compartment with the dry ice. The little dog simply went to sleep and didn't wake up. When the woman realized the dog had died, it was as though the airport was under a full-blown attack. I ran to the airport manager's office so he could earn his keep confronting the passenger. He did, and I can guarantee it cost Pan Am, "The world's most experienced airline," a bundle. Between flights, I would go to the far end of the ramp to Air America's operations office, which was no more than a concealed shack. It is well known that the company was a CIA airline, and they were all over Vietnam and surrounding countries; many of their flights were covert with the government claiming ignorance. The pilots were among the most colorful a war zone could produce. One of their missions was transporting munitions to General Vang Pao's Meo in Laos, who the

United States convinced to fight Communist China. I would sit for hours and listen to the transmissions between operations and the pilots in the field. On several occasions, even though an operations person would radio the pilots that their landing strip had just been hit with mortars and they didn't have to continue the approach and land, in most cases, the pilots would not abort. It was great listening entertainment. Laos, on the western border of Vietnam, was part of the Golden Triangle, famous for opium production. Many pilots became very wealthy by transporting more than arms, but what the hell, they deserved any possible arrangement they could negotiate.

Ron MacCloran was an Irishman who wore thick, dark-rimmed glasses and was always on edge. He was transiting through Saigon to work in operations at Cam Ranh Bay with Pan Am. I had him spend the night with me in an attempt to calm him down and render a few pointers to assist while he was "in-country." Thank God the VC didn't pick this particular night to be active, as I am sure Ron would never have recovered emotionally. The next morning, I was able to get him on a hop up to Cam Ranh Bay on a military transport C-130 loaded with marines in full gear. I explained that this is how we got around, and reluctantly, he climbed aboard, suitcases in hand. Thanking the aircraft commander, I went back to work and didn't think anymore of Ron. Approximately two hours later, still on the ramp, I noticed the C-130 taxiing, returning from Cam Ranh Bay. The aircraft commander flashed his wing lights after seeing me, and I went to the plane. There was Ron, in total shock, sitting alone in the back of the airplane. Apparently, when they landed at Cam Ranh, the field went under attack, and as the aircraft was taxiing slowly, the marines rolled out the back onto the tarmac. Ron, absolutely shaken, said if he couldn't disembark by walking off an airplane, he wasn't getting off. He left on the next Pan Am flight to the United States. I'm quite sure that Ron must hold the record for the shortest Vietnam tour of a Pan Am employee.

After approximately a month of living in Saigon, I joined night school at the University of Maryland. The university had a program for military personnel, and Pan Am employees were eligible. Many classes were interrupted by red alerts, since the city was continuously under artillery fire at night. Because of this, we would have to leave class to sit in a bunker. I made very good friends with a marine colonel, thinking that he would be the best one to tag along with when the fireworks started. I glued myself to him. It was a hell of a way to get a college education, and I left Vietnam with my four-year degree.

Mike Gullino was an employee of Pacific Architects and Engineers. The company was contracted for various construction projects throughout the country. Mike taught management classes as a part-time endeavor, and we became good friends, spending a lot of time riding our motorcycles around Saigon and the surrounding areas. His position required continuous "in-country" trips to all of the major cities. I was fortunate enough to accept a flight that is described below.

> *Two days ago, I took a plane ride to Cam Rhan Bay, Quin Nhon, DaNang, Pleiku, and back again to Saigon. My teacher last semester works for PA & E in Saigon. We became close friends and started to build relations between his firm and Pan Am.*
>
> —Letter, February 19, 1969

I had a 350 CC Honda and I believe Mike had a 750 CC. Both were considered big since the normal Viet motorcycle was a 75 CC. Although small, they could carry the whole family, plus a couple of chickens. It was quite a balancing act. The motorcycle police were the only ones with larger bikes, and they bothered us continuously. I remember one cop following me home in order to collect a bottle of scotch as my fine for some imagined infraction. They were bold and always had the upper hand, but after a while, they got used to us, and we learned who the good, bad, and ugly were. I kept in touch with Mike after we left Vietnam and visited him in Washington, DC.

Another close friend was Vic Roxas. On one of our many adventures, we had to go to Bien Hoa, northeast of Saigon, to cover Christmas and New Year's contract flights that Pan Am had with other U.S. carriers. We lived in a trailer with another employee, Jan, who had come from Pan Am operations in Los Angeles. He was born in the Netherlands and was a very neat, proper, and great guy. His routine phrase to Vic was "Are you shitting again?" Vic was one that used the bathroom as a library, making it difficult for us to use the bathroom ourselves. We came across a supplier of "funny cigarettes" and would light up when the occasion arose. Pan Am employees had a government GS-13 rating that afforded us the privileges of an officer, including the use of their club. Vic and I would take a few hits before going to the club. One night, we were asked to leave due to our boisterous laughter when there was nothing to warrant such a relaxed composure.

One evening we were sitting on top of the bunker by our trailer watching what we thought was a holiday fireworks celebration. As we toked away and watched the red tracers going outbound, green tracers began coming inbound; red was our side, and green was used by the foe. Everyone was heading for their respective bunkers, and Vic and I just sat there, engrossed in the display. I remember Vic saying, "Smoky, isn't this beautiful?" Jan broke our mood by grabbing us while trying to explain that the base was under attack.

Somehow, we started calling each other "Smoky," and to this day, it has stuck. Karina met Vic years later when we went to have lunch with him at Teterboro Airport in New Jersey, where he worked for the FAA. For a while, she couldn't understand why we called each other "Smoky" and finally pieced the puzzle together herself. During the Christmas season, probably in 1969, Bob Hope and his troupe came to Bien Hoa Air Force Base for their famous Christmas show. They arrived on a military transport, and Vic believed that if we posed as maintenance personnel, we could get up close and wouldn't have to watch the show from the sidelines. The military maintenance crews were used to seeing us on the ramp, so Vic borrowed a set of maintenance headsets and told me to follow his actions. I did, and we went up to the transport in our Pan Am attire as though we were part of the ground crew. When the doors opened, we were one of the first to meet Bob and his group and were given front-row seats.

A week in Bien Hoa could compare to an assignment in the countryside with the bright lights of the city in view. It became very boring, especially with Saigon within an hour's drive. Vic telexed his boss, Bud Shone, requesting permission for us to drive to Saigon for the New Year Eve's festivities. It was already 9:00 p.m., and we went into a panic mode fearing the New Year would come in with us in the bush. The reply was a definite "No," due to VC activity along the highway. However, we got in the van and headed for the city anyway. Our excuse would be that communications were broken and we never got the response. After all, there was a war going on.

Vic was driving, and about half an hour down the road, a small tank with three or four Vietnamese troops stopped us. After a very unfriendly greeting, one of them shoved his rifle barrel down my throat, and I began to wonder if I would ever see the New Year. I reached ever so slowly to retrieve a cartoon of Kool cigarettes on the seat next to me and offered them to my captor. He accepted, removed his weapon, and we were signaled to be on our way; we didn't have to be told twice. After lighting a joint a few minutes later, we laughed all the way to Saigon and got there at the tail end of the celebrations. I can't remember where we spent the night, but I am sure we didn't drive back to Bien Hoa until the next day. Bud didn't believe we never received his message.

Due to the labor and tax laws, employees who worked in Vietnam for about 60 days or more had to leave the country for a week. This afforded us a change in scenery, and I visited several countries as a result. The first trip was to Cambodia with Carl Hanson from Hawaii and Norman, a New Yorker. It was most interesting, since we toured Angkor Wat, which is now a Buddhist temple complex and the largest religious monument in the world. It was representative of a civilization that had completely disappeared and become buried in jungle growth, and at the time of our visit, the buildings were being excavated.

I was able to save the film I took of the area, and watching it was absolutely amazing. Approximately two weeks after our visit, the North Vietnamese took it over for the next few years, halting any further productive work. Returning to the capital, Phnom Penh, for the last day, we could hear B-52s pounding parts of Vietnam, so the war continued close by. Norman was one of the very few in our group who didn't smoke or drink. However, while vacationing at his parents' home in the United States, he suffered a fatal heart attack. He had played basketball in the evening and returned home to watch TV. His parents found him the next morning in his chair with the TV still on. We were all shocked and missed him.

Other trips were made to Bangkok, Thailand, with Bill Kristoka, Jan to Singapore, and John Fraiser to Jakarta. John told a story about himself and another employee of Pan Am on a previous trip to Jakarta; a maintenance and security rep would usually fly with the scheduled trip from Saigon to Jakarta and return the next day. Apparently, John and his co-worker got in a taxi to hit the town during the evening and couldn't resist asking two ladies standing on a corner, the usual spot for these working girls, to join them when the taxi stopped at a red light.

The taxi was styled after the Lambretta, where you sit sideways on a bench in the back. It resembles a pickup truck with a roof. As the taxi proceeded with the four passengers in the rear, as luck would have it, one of the tires went flat. John noticed the spare tire under his seat, and before he could get to it, his new companion reached down and threw it to the road with the intention of assisting the driver. John was startled at the strength of the girl and felt that although beautiful on the outside, possibly the young lady may not be a "young lady" after all. A quick check between "her" legs proved his suspicion was correct: they had picked up two "he–she's," and needless to say, their new acquaintances had bid farewell.

I had also made a couple of solo trips to Hong Kong and Taiwan, China. There were always tour guides available to show the sites of each country, and it was an educational experience. I spent a night in the Hong Kong Harbor on a small sampan with a Chinese family and was very happy to return to the hotel the next morning, not being the seafaring type.

Erskine Rice, a Pan Am senior vice president, came to Saigon for a station inspection and recognized me as he lived in the same area as my parents. I met him several times in Westbury, though he was originally from Georgia. I brought him to my apartment in Saigon and forgot to explain that I was raising quail in the kitchen. I had found a *Farm Journal* magazine and ordered an incubator with eggs.

There is a saying, "You can't take the country out of someone," and I suppose it fits. He got quite a kick out of my hobby, especially since the quail decided to start hatching during his visit. Erskine couldn't wait to get home to tell my dad that his son was farming in Saigon during the war.

> *My poultry business kind of collapsed, so I think I better stick to the airline business! Don't tell Uncle Everett and Aunt Lola that I am a failure at farming.*
>
> —Letter, January 21, 1969

One of the letters I sent home while working for Pan Am illustrates that it's a small world:

> *About two days ago, I was eating in the officers' club with one of the fellows in the office. I noticed this man sitting next to us and was sure that I knew him from somewhere. To make a long story short, it was one of the helicopter pilots I flew as gunner with four years ago at Phan Rang. We had a real nice reunion.*
>
> —Letter, February 21, 1970

Leaving Vietnam was bittersweet. I acquired a tremendous amount of knowledge to prepare me for future challenges in life, made many lifelong friends, and, in general, enjoyed two years working as a civilian in a war zone. However, there is an innate feeling that tells you when it is time to leave, and my time had come. I completed a four-year college degree and saw about all there was to see, so it was time to move on. Vic threw a going-away party at his villa in Saigon, with food shipped in from Bangkok and other countries. There were about 100 people, but we only knew a few. Word of a get-together travels fast in that type of environment, and the party was a great success. The next day, the Vietnamese workers gave me a farewell lunch, and I was very touched. I still have the gifts they presented. In my experience, Asians can be extremely humble people, and once you earn their respect and trust, you have often gained a true friend for life.

As the B-707 taxied out to the runway at Tan Son Nhut International Airport, Saigon, and lined up for takeoff on the departure day in August 1970, I was riding in the cockpit. The call from the tower was simply "Clipper, cleared for takeoff. Have a good day." Although I knew it was time to leave, I had to hold back my emotions. Nevertheless, my eyes filled with tears. Once more, I was leaving the country that in so many ways shaped my character from that point on. I told myself I would return, but as of yet, I have not. Hopefully I will.

At the beginning of 2000, Rita, Karina, and I attended a Pan Am reunion in Washington, DC, for workers who had been employed in Vietnam by the company. In 1975, the final year of the war, many of the local Pan Am Vietnamese workers escaped to the United States. Most were assisted by Pan Am, since had they remained, they would have been executed for working for an American firm. The more fortunate would have spent years in rehabilitation camps.

There have been several documentaries on Pan Am's final employee evacuation mission from Saigon on April 24, 1975. Among those on board were a number of embassy personnel, plus CIA agents carrying several million dollars in cash. The FAA issued a waiver so that passengers could be seated on the floor, and double-up in seats, since there were far more passengers than the legal number the plane was permitted to carry. The *Washington Times* quoted one of the passengers recalling the event:

> *The memories are still vivid: A steaming bus ride through the humid morning, the acrid odor of jet fuel, the clouds of smoke from distant gunfire, getting closer. Then, about 450 people boarded the last commercial flight out of Saigon.*

Six days after the flight departed, the North Vietnamese tanks rolled into Saigon, and the war came to an end.

8

GERMANY

ERBENHEIM, 1970

After being in Vietnam for three years, I wasn't ready to go back to the United States, and a transition period was needed. The University of Utah was offering college courses for military personnel stationed in several areas of Germany, and I was accepted into the MBA program at Wiesbaden. The plan was to spend eight months there and then proceed to Salt Lake City to complete the degree on campus.

I had never been to Germany and was a little apprehensive as to how the people felt toward Americans. Arriving from Vietnam, through Tokyo, map in hand, I took a train from Frankfurt to Wiesbaden. My first personal contact was with a woman on the train in her fifties who saw me struggling with two big Samsonite suitcases. She placed them on a rack over my train seat, and from that moment on, I felt a lot more comfortable with the Germans.

Arriving in Wiesbaden absolutely not knowing where I was going to stay, I went to a real estate office at the train station. The realtor spoke a little English and told me about a farmer who was offering accommodations in Erbenheim, a town next to Wiesbaden. I walked about a mile to his farm to meet him. He was more than happy to have me since his entire household consisted of females: his wife, mother, mother-in-law, two daughters, and a female dog. I wrote about my stay while I was there:

> *"Silent night, holy night.*
> *All is calm, all is bright."*

"Who's singing that Ralph?"
"It's one of Germany's top male singers, Karl Gott."

I could hardly hear his reply to my own question but managed to reply, "It's beautiful, but the best I think I have ever heard is the version by Mario Lanza."

A song, an artist, what does it really mean to a person? On this particular night, the song was a catalyst, spinning my head with thoughts of the past. I wanted obscurity from the human race long enough to ponder over memories that I had voluntarily and involuntarily forced upon myself in my 26 years of life. How many different circumstances, countries, and versions of "Silent Night" had I heard? Why now in Germany?

At this time, I was living in Erbenheim, a small farm town approximately 30 minutes by car from Frankfurt. I rented a room on one of the town's most prosperous farms, which belonged to the Stein family. The large stone house and barn were connected at a 90-degree angle. Flowers lined the long driveway leading to the house and had beautiful red, white, and yellow blossoms. My room occupied the space between the house and barn, and for $35 per month, it fit my student budget quite nicely. It was exceptionally clean, with a desk, bed, two chairs, and a utility table, plus a sink that faithfully produced hot water. The shower was located in the main house and was at my disposal from six in the morning until approximately 10 at night.

I had the option of using either the toilet in the house or the one in the barn. By day, I chose the house and was forced at night to use the barn. With this choice, a few drawbacks were encountered. During the night, I would leave my room, cross the driveway, go to the first room in the barn that housed the tractors, and with my hand, fumble along the wall for the light switch. During this task, I usually managed to knock over a few of the master's hand tools, which set his watchdog barking.

Once the light was on, I then proceeded to another room where five bulls were being fattened for their future slaughter. I am sure these filthy creatures of God didn't appreciate my nightly intrusions, since they would begin protesting that fell in tune with the dog's howling. By the time I passed the bulls, I was almost there with just one more room to cross, and this was where three pigs were housed. Thank the Lord they were totally unconcerned, for all the noise already had everyone in the main house cursing my nightly business calls.

Once I was finished, it was a matter of retracing my steps, but my return included turning out the light and replacing the tools. Back in the room, I would hug the radiator, and after the noise subsided, there was peace in the valley once more. After a few weeks of these frequent ventures, the noise from the animals was replaced by me opening and closing the window located on the back wall of my room. I am positive the family is still puzzled over the ensuing quiet nights after the second week of my stay. A little uncertainty in everyone's life is good for the soul.

The human kindness shown by the Stein family made up for what I lacked in physical comfort. Helmut, my landlord, could have played a lumberjack, construction worker, or any other occupation requiring a macho-looking guy. He was 50, with tanned lines in his face, a hooked nose, thinning hair, and a stare that would melt ice. He had a heart as big as the world, and I doubt very seriously he would raise his hand to swat a pestering fly with fear of doing it harm.

One night, as many others we spent in discussion, Helmut revealed his role in World War II. I have probably encountered as many personal stories concerning this era as the next person my age but never from a member of the opposite side. The worst part listening to him that evening was due to the language barrier and Helmut's extremely comical method of telling a story. I never knew whether to laugh or cry. I must have done what was expected, for his stories lasted until the wee hours of the morning. During that time, we killed our mutual foe and a bottle of apricot brandy.

Helmut Stein, corporal, SS trooper of one of Germany's artillery units, was assigned to advance into Russia. He marched with the German south army through Poland, crossing into Russia around Brest. He continued through Smolensk to Bryansk and halted at Ora, not far from the Oka River. The length of this advance was approximately 2,000 kilometers by train, horse, and wagon, including much on foot. It was the Germans' intent for the south army to join the north army at Stalinogorsk (now Novomoskovsk). This would surround Moscow. The *Russkies* started their drive against the German occupying forces, and Helmut's unit dwindled from its initial strength of 204 on June 22, 1941, to 16 by March 8, 1945.

Being aware of the cold and its hardships, I still had to chuckle as my hero tried to explain how he had to continuously rub his face and hands in the snow to keep warm. Two of his friends, along with Helmut, who was driven by hunger, approached a farmhouse occupied by a Russian woman and her three children. A cow was in the yard, and one of his friends started at it with a knife. A sparkle of Helmut's inner self appeared regardless of his own suffering. He refused to let his comrade put an end to the cow's life, being aware that it was the only means the family had for obtaining milk.

He conveyed this adventure by grabbing a kitchen knife off my table, one minute portraying his friend and the next moment himself. He continuously pranced around the room with his chest expanded after the part of taking the knife away from his fellow soldier, who had his heart set on the cow. Helmut was the family's savior and stayed fairly comfortable for the duration of his time spent in that area. The Russian woman and her children now live about 100 kilometers from Erbenheim.

After making motions of loading artillery pieces, shooting machine guns and every other type of weapon the Germans and Russians possessed, and showing me his scars from grenade wounds, which covered a large area of his legs and back, Helmut's performance finally came to an end. As the door closed behind him, I could only ask God why it was necessary for men such as Helmut to be driven to war. I never received an answer.

I had spent the last hours in the house of Ralph and Doris Dauer. The Dauers spent five years in the United States and spoke English well. This, along with their charming company, drew me toward them for conversation. They lived next to the Stein family. Ralph was a record wholesaler, and practically every night, I wandered over to their house to talk and listen to the latest hits. Since the spirit of "Old Yule Tide" was in the air, Ralph selected a Christmas album.

The version of "Silent Night" was penetrating me to the point where I had to leave, excusing myself as being tired and in need of a good night's sleep.

"Gutten nacht, Ralph, Doris. Bis morgen."
"Gutten nacht, Jim. Schlafen Gut."

Once outside, I slowly started walking home. The first snow of the season was lazily and silently floating to earth. It tried in vain to cover the surroundings in a blanket of pure white. The snow reminded me of a resolution I made five years prior while stationed in northern Maine. Fed up with the harsh winters, I promised myself that once I had left that part of the country, I would never put myself in a position where I would face such winters.

For the next five years, it held, but like other promises a man makes, from the person fighting to stay off drugs, to the politician swearing false intentions, usually a promise, sooner or later, becomes broken. Why bother to make one in the first place? It might produce short-term gains, but in reality, promising and lying are usually synonymous terms leading to the same end results.

As I continued walking toward the farm, the night was crisp, and I turned up my coat collar. Having gone a few meters, I stopped and sat down on a log with my back against one of the many trees scattered along the road. There, my thoughts continued as trying to find and establish myself to be worthwhile and self-accepted, not necessarily by society. Would I rise above the average man, achieve the same level, or fall beneath him?

In retrospect, at one time or another, I fit into all three categories.

Since writing this, I have to add a situation that actually began when I was working with Pan Am in Vietnam, with the adventure ending in Austria. One side of the mountain in Austria was where the rich and famous went to ski, and the other side was for "commoners"; I was on the commoners' side.

Pan Am had daily military and commercial flights in and out of Saigon. The crews that flew these flights were mostly from San Francisco, Hawaii, and Los Angeles, and the chatting time we had with flight attendants was held to about 45 minutes per flight. Since the VC were showing their muscle during this time, the crews wanted to land and take off as soon as possible, with minimum ground time. This cut our socializing short, but with the same crews reappearing, I made many friends over the two-year period.

During that time, I had met a Chinese flight attendant, Carol. In one of these conversations, she mentioned that she was an avid skier, and I filed this information in my brain for possible future use.

After arriving in Germany where skiing is second nature, the old brain started ticking. Remembering Carol, I wrote a letter encouraging her to come for the weekend and go skiing with my group, since we did this every weekend. It sounded harmless, but in reality, I didn't have a ski group, nor even had put a pair of skis on in my life.

Thinking no more of my invitation, approximately three weeks later, I received a telegram from her saying she would arrive in Frankfurt on a Pan Am flight in two days. I told Helmut of my predicament, and we rushed to a Volkswagen dealer and bought a ski rack for my car. Once installed, we beat the hell out of it with a hammer to have it appear highly used. His family watched from the kitchen window thinking we had both gone absolutely mad.

On the day of her arrival, I kept hoping Carol would be bumped from the flight, since she was flying standby as a company employee. I waited where passengers came through immigration and customs, and it seemed as though my prayer was answered. People had stopped coming from the area, and I turned to leave, praising the Lord.

Then it happened. I heard, "Jim, help me with these skis." My friend had arrived in all her glory, well equipped for the slopes. After the greeting formalities, we attached the skis to the car rack. I had read the manufacturer's instructions over and over again as to how to use the rack and didn't miss a beat securing the skis.

Arriving at the farm, meeting the Stein family, not being able to look at Helmut, I suggested she go to sleep and rest while I went to night class. After school, I would come back with the group that was going with us, and we would all drive to Austria. Returning from class, I told her the bad news that the group had to cancel, but we would go anyway. Also, my friend didn't return my skis, so I would have to rent a pair when we got to our destination. I began to believe my own lies.

The drive took all night and when we arrived at the German–Austrian border, the Austrian guard asked for our passports. I didn't have mine, so I thought, "Finally a legitimate reason not to continue." Well, wrong again, he let us go across after looking at my driver's license. It was obvious that there was no way out of the hole I had dug. As the sun came up, we arrived at Kitzbuhel, and the scenic view was beautiful as the sun reflected off the snow-covered surrounding mountains. We drove by a church on the way to the hotel, and being Sunday, people were singing hymns led by guitars, which added to the town's tone.

After a few hours' rest, we headed to the ski shop. Up to this time, Carol was convinced that I was a seasoned skier, due to the ski jargon I would often incorporate into our conversations. I had actually learned these terms by listening to weather reports on the radio. However, the truth finally surfaced when I tried on a pair of skis. I couldn't even walk, and said, "Look Carol, the fact is, I have never had a pair of skis on in my life. There's the mountain, go have a ball." With very few words, only understanding a few, since they were directed at me in Chinese, my little "China Doll" disappeared up the slopes.

All alone now, since I got myself into this mess, I thought, "What the hell, I might as well try it," and headed for the beginners' area. I spent the entire day falling, getting up just to fall again. On one try, I was even going backward. This little brat, about 10 years old, was attempting to assist speaking in German; I think she was showing off more than being concerned with my welfare.

I saw Carol approximately twice the whole day as she was having a great time way up at the top of the slope. When we rendezvoused at day's end, her mood toward my false pretense was somewhat calmer, and we headed back to Germany as friends. Helmut was waiting for us and said he couldn't sleep until receiving my report.

After Carol left for California, I was surprised to find that the Stein family had elevated my status to "family member," and I was given my own room in the "Big House." It was getting close to the time to leave for Salt Lake City to finish the last months of the MBA program at the University of Utah. One of Helmut's daughters was becoming very friendly, with Helmut's approval, and if it hadn't been for my required departure, I probably would have become a farmer in Germany. I remained in touch with Helmut, and he visited twice in New York.

Rita, Karina, and I also went to Frankfurt to visit Helmut and his family. Unfortunately, his wife passed away, and we were introduced to his new friend, Erica. Rita still corresponds with her, and every year, we promise to get together, but it never seems to happen. Helmut took us to a Wiesbaden sauna that is world-famous due to underground springs. Rita elected not to go in the water and remained at the health bar, while I was led to the locker room to change into my swimming suit.

No one told me that we arrived on the day everything was co-ed, and when I entered the locker room, men and women, some very beautiful ladies, were walking around in their birthday suits. Off came my clothes, and I joined the activities. I am sure my discomfort was certainly observed by many. Men will shrink in several body areas during cold temperatures, and I ended my naked health routine in a sauna with two beautiful German girls without clothes. While sweating like hell, all I could say was how *cold* it was in the sauna in an attempt to give a reasonable explanation for my present condition. I don't think my sauna buddies were convinced.

In Vietnam with Pan Am, I became friends with Bill Roberts, an army captain. We remained in touch after his Vietnam tour ended when he was reassigned to a base in Frankfurt, Germany, approximately 30 minutes from the farm where I was staying. Realizing we were both going to spend Christmas away from home, the decision was made to visit Sweden for the holidays. It was a great plan, and we left Germany heading north just in time to catch the last ferry from northern Germany, across the North Sea to Copenhagen, Denmark. The boat ride took all night, and it was an incredible sight to view the sun rising above the water in the wee hours of the morning.

Due to the extremely high number of Vietnam deserters settling in that part of the world, the attitude toward Americans was not the best, and the farther north we went, the worse it became. As a result, we scrubbed our plans for Sweden and headed back south to Amsterdam, Holland, continuing through Belgium and Luxembourg, returning to Germany. While in Amsterdam, we went to the famous red-light district, where the young (*and old*) ladies sat by the windows displaying a portion of what they had to offer.

Bill and I followed our better judgment by looking but not touching. After touring the area, we went to dinner at one of the many restaurants and met a well-known couple in the performing arts, she a ballerina. They planned to be married in the next few months, and we were invited to their wedding. We returned for the event, and it was simple with a few people attending, but classy, and we had a great time. I felt that Belgium and Luxembourg were very impressive and very clean.

Whatever apprehension I had about Germany when I arrived diminished by the time I left. I can only say that it is a beautiful country with very humble people. They take time to hear your story and are very respectful. I was told that Helmut had passed away, and the news hurt me deeply. I will always regret not going back for a visit, while he was living his last days in a retirement home. He suffered from chronic circulation problems, resulting in both legs having to be amputated. His family felt that he would have better care in a nursing home than they could provide. Helmut, maybe in our next life, we can get together and finish those stories.

During a Christmas season, I was listening to music from tapes that I had acquired over the years of traveling. "Silent Night" in German began, and I cried like a baby thinking of Helmut. It was a release of emotional guilt, since I never went back to see him while in the nursing home as I had promised. I can't bring back what I didn't do since "time" is not always a friend; however, I am going to make every possible effort to visit his grave.

9

UP, UP, AND AWAY

SALT LAKE CITY, 1971

The people who know me will agree that I am not a religious person. Whether there is or isn't a "super being," I feel that incidents are out of my control.

I was in the process of completing my master's in Business Administration at the University of Utah at Salt Lake City. Although being raised in an aviation environment, due to my father being a flight engineer with Pan Am, I really did not have any desire for flying. I was content to keep my feet on the ground.

Awakening one morning in my apartment, I got up and went to the yellow pages, as though being led by an unexplainable force, to make an appointment for flight training the following day. The next morning, as I was leaving for my first lesson, I remember hesitating at the front door, telling myself that this was going to change my life. I went to the airport, and, as they say, "the rest is history."

I could not leave the subject of learning to fly without mentioning a few episodes. The first has to do with Sunday flights with a fellow named Leonard who also had his pilot's license. Since I was flying with the government paying for my flying via the GI Bill, I flew as much as possible in the shortest amount of time. A student had to accumulate 250 hours of flight time in order to get a commercial pilot's certificate, and I wanted to get it done quickly. I flew so much, and the controllers at Salt Lake International knew me by my voice transmissions when I called for takeoff and landing clearances.

One of the aircraft's navigation systems was the automatic direction finder (ADF). If you tuned in to a radio station, you would hear the program playing as though you were listening to any radio. The instrument also incorporated a needle that continuously pointed to the station you were tuned in to. All you had to do was fly the airplane in the direction that the needle was pointing to arrive at the station.

Nevada is approximately an hour and a half flying from Salt Lake City, it allowed "companionship," and there were various fly-in ranches providing this service. Leonard was a local fellow, living in the middle of Mormon country, who owned a TV repair shop. He had very little money and loved to fly. Part of Leonard's constant lack of funds was due to supporting a wife and seven children. Somehow, he did save enough to be in the company of women other than his family.

Leonard had his favorite, called "Ida's Fly-in Ranch," which had a radio station compatible with the ADF at the ranch's landing strip. On Sundays, Ida would keep to the spirit of the day and play church music. As a result, Leonard and I would fly to Ida's listening to hymns. I never went in and stayed by the plane. I must have missed a good time, since when Leonard returned to the airplane, he was always in a better mood than prior to his visit. To this day, every time I teach the ADF to students, I always think of these Sunday flights.

During the private pilot certification process, there are two required tasks that must be performed. The first is the solo flight and then to fly a solo cross-country. For the first solo flight, you must go to an airport at least 50 miles away and return to your airport of origin.

The first event went smoothly. After about three takeoffs and landings with Bill Frandsen, my instructor, he radioed the tower that I would handle the next circuit. Bill left the plane and off I went. The landing was very good, and I was on my way to becoming a pilot.

The solo cross-country flight did not go as well as the first solo. I planned a flight from Salt Lake City to Tooele, Utah, a small airport to the north. I had no problem finding the airport, but I was distracted during my final approach for landing. There was a rodeo in full progress close to the runway, and being from the city, I had never seen a cowboy riding a bull other than on television. Finally realizing that my priority was to land the plane, I was halfway down the runway before landing. As the plane came to a halt, the propeller was cutting the grass at the end of the runway. I gave power to turn around toward the hangar, but the plane wouldn't go anywhere with normal power applied to the engine, due to both main tires going flat. I did manage to taxi to the airport's hangar by applying full power on the flat tires and was greeted by a mechanic who commented, while scratching his head, "Never seen a landing like that before!" I believe I stole the show from the cowboy on his bull.

After calling Bill, I briefly told him what happened and explained that two tires were needed to get back home. He was so calm that I called him back to make it clear I needed *two*. Bill flew to the airport with another pilot and gave me the tires without getting out of the plane. He was using the philosophy that if you get thrown from a horse, you must get back on and ride. The mechanic changed the tires, and I flew back to Salt Lake City with a new lesson learned in flying, which was to pay attention to what you are doing and don't allow yourself to be diverted from the task at hand.

My flight examiner for the private pilot certificate, Abe, had one eye and was quite a character. He instructed me to take him to an airport where I had to demonstrate three different types of landing. I expected him to remain in the airplane through my demonstration, as is the normal practice. Instead, he told me he would be on the side of the runway. If he wanted me to abort a landing, he would wave me off. I asked, "Abe, why are you not going to stay in the plane?" His answer was, "You may kill me!" This was a great confidence-builder while taking a flight check. I didn't kill either of us, and when I returned to Salt Lake, I was a private pilot, with my life changed forever.

To obtain a commercial pilot's certificate, a pilot has to fly solo to two airports that are at least 250 miles apart. I chose Boise, Idaho, and at that time, it seemed like a trip to the end of the world; I stayed up all night going over navigation charts. Actually, the trip wasn't quite solo. I taxied away from the office after everyone wished me good luck, made a quick turn around the hangar, and picked up Leonard, who wanted to come along. Naturally, on the return, I let Leonard out behind the hangar before taxiing to the office to get the other pilot's congratulations.

At the time I was going through flight training in Utah, my dad was doing the same in North Carolina. Apparently, the Pan Am flight engineers, through union contracts, were given the opportunity to choose a flight school and obtain their commercial certificate. I didn't let him know I was also flying and would call periodically to find out how he was progressing. We were neck and neck.

I received my private certificate on July 13, 1971, and he became a certificated private pilot on July 31, 1971. When I went to visit my parents the next month and told my dad of my achievement, we did several flights together, buzzing the farm in Cana and touring the northwestern area of the state. I remained in North Carolina for a few weeks to complete my qualifications for the commercial certificate. When I returned from the flight check, someone asked the examiner about my performance on the check ride. He said he didn't know how I did what was required, but I got the job done. This was August 28, 1971.

10

ONCE A NEW YORKER, ALWAYS A NEW YORKER

1971–PRESENT

With an MBA, plus a commercial pilot's certificate, I went back home to New York to resume my employment with Pan Am at the end of 1971. The company assigned me to a small team of men whose task was to reduce the amount of lost, or more like stolen, cargo that came through JFK. It was well known at that time that the mob controlled airport freight movements. To date, the biggest heist involving cargo was at JFK with Lufthansa Airlines as the victim. That heist was backed by the Lucchese crime family and planned by Jimmy Burke and netted $5.875 million ($27.6 million in 2023), with $5 million in cash and $875,000 in jewels. It was in the news again in January 2014, when a series of arrests connected to the heist were made in New York. The crime was the basis for the 1990 Martin Scorsese film *Goodfellas*. Our group did our best under the circumstances. It was reported that we decreased the cargo losses; however, a deep recession engulfed the country, and the group was terminated.

Prior to the layoff, I had an apartment in Long Beach that was adjacent to the boardwalk. The neighborhood was predominantly Jewish, and once while checking mail in the lobby, a neighbor inquired if I was Jewish. When I replied, "No," the lady said it was a shame because she had a granddaughter she would like me to meet. The grandmother did finish by saying, "We will talk to you anyway."

Long Beach throughout the summer months was a great place to live. The boardwalk was built against the apartment building, and I would spend hours watching the women on the beach promenade back and forth in their swimsuits. Winter terminated all my socializing with its cold weather and early darkness.

After the layoff, I returned to live with my parents until they retired to North Carolina in 1972. My dad rented a truck that we were to drive to their new home. My mom didn't want to go and the move was quite an experience. My dad would put an item on the truck and my mom would remove it. I think we loaded everything at least three times. After they moved, I roomed with Bill Kristoka, who returned from Vietnam approximately a year before I did, in his apartment located in Astoria, New York (Queens). During this unemployed period, I continued flying with the Aero Academics school, at Republic Airport on Long Island, to get additional certificates. The owner, Don Estes, and I got along well, and he hired me to increase his charter business. The most nonsensical trip was for a company that was in the process of moving from Long Island to Nashua, New Hampshire. During the transition, one of the secretaries forgot her typewriter, and I had to fly it to Nashua. She could have bought 20 for the cost of the trip, but it was great for me to build flight hours. On one trip, we flew Paul Newman to Pennsylvania for the movie *Slap Shot*.

During my time with Aero Academics, Doug Johnson was an Eyewitness News correspondent. During his segments, he would visit different companies as one of its employees for a day. I suggested that he become a pilot for a day, thinking that it would be great exposure for Aero Academics' charter division.

I contacted ABC-TV and asked Doug if he would be interested in flying an airplane around Manhattan. He said it would be great for the show but questioned his safety. I had recently heard statistics indicating that more people died in a bathtub each year than when flying an airplane. After relating this comforting information to him, his reply was, "That's nice to know Mr. Etchison; however, you are asking me to fly an airplane, *not a bathtub*!" After his initial apprehension subsided, he came to the airport and flew with one of the school's pilots.

While working with Don, I met a gentleman named Dan, who rented aircraft from the school and was a vice president at European American Bank in lower Manhattan. After learning I had my MBA, Dan asked me to join the bank in the financial analysis department. I was never the Wall Street type, but due to finances, I accepted and actually enjoyed the work. The main focus was to analyze the balance sheets and profit–loss statements of European and American companies to provide loans. During this period, I met Rita Mourao from Brazil, who was also working at the bank, and on May 4, 1974, we were married.

After working at the bank for a couple of years, I went to the Pan Am building and asked Ray Jewett, the personnel director for Pan Am, if the company's hiring freeze was over. I was delighted to hear that a position was open in corporate finance, and I would be able to start immediately. Since I enjoyed the position at the bank, I asked my supervisor how long it would take to increase my salary to Pan Am's offer. After hearing four years, I turned in my resignation and once again was working for "The world's most experienced airline," as Pan Am's slogan goes.

I couldn't have asked for a better boss than Jim Murphy, and my co-workers were also great. The only problem was the work provided no challenge, and after approximately a year, I went back to Ray and begged to be placed closer to the airplanes, where I could at least smell aviation. Again, Ray pulled through with an operations position at JFK. Once a pilot, it's difficult to maintain any distance from an airplane. After another layoff hit while I was still the new kid on the block, I was back on the street.

I joined a flying club at Republic Airport that was owned by two brothers, George and Pete Garambone. They were in the construction business and very well connected with the "boys." Peter was more reserved, and George was the "charmer." Unfortunately, George died early in life. I began flying charters for the brothers, along with another pilot, Andy. Most of our flights were round-trip to Atlantic City, which was George's and Pete's playground. We also made a couple of trips to Miami, and now that I look back, God knows what we were carrying.

One charter request came at 3:00 a.m. with a telephone call from George. The flight was to take a guy who missed a loan payment or two over the Long Island Sound and dump him out 3,000 feet above the water. I heard the guy screaming in the background, as he didn't want to go, and I told George it would be better to get the other company pilot for the flight. Apparently, the fellow worked out an immediate solution to his debt, and the flight was canceled.

Our flying club purchased a new 402 Cessna, and after the salesman had Andy and I complete one landing each, we flew him back to Boston. I brought Rita along, and after Andy and I dropped the fellow off in Boston, engines still running, he waved "goodbye" and more or less told us we were on our own. Andy and I looked at each other, both thinking, "How the hell are we going to get this thing off the ground?"

Rita was sitting in the back not realizing that we were completely unfamiliar with the airplane. We took off for Republic Airport, and with our confidence building, we began pushing buttons and flipping switches. The plane would go in a steep climb, then a rapid descent, and so on. Throughout our test flight, Rita was screaming in the background. She later relaxed, believing that since the flight was over water, the crash wouldn't hurt as bad as if we had land below. In any event, by the time we got back to Republic Airport, we had everything under control, and the plane was a pleasure to fly on future flights. Somehow, the club acquired former President John F. Kennedy's Convair and planned to start a commuter service between Long Island and Atlantic City, New Jersey; however, after George's death, many plans faded away.

George and Peter were very good to me. They arranged to have the plane available to fly Rita and me to a resort in Pennsylvania for our honeymoon and then have Dave DeAngles, a Pan Am co-worker and my instructor for the multi-engine rating, pick us up for the return trip.

After Pan Am's layoff, I flew cargo at night for approximately a year. The company went bankrupt. Due to the bankruptcy and Pan Am's layoff, I was tired of placing my destiny in the hands of other people and corporations and thus founded Academics of Flight in 1976.

Home, Sweet Home

Rita, Karina, and I pushed on through whatever was placed in our path. Rita quit her job at European American Bank and joined VARIG, Brazil's international airline. With Rita's fixed salary from the airline, Academics of Flight beginning to stand on its own, plus the GI Bill available for those who served in Vietnam, we got brave and went house hunting. I also sold a lot next to my parents' house in North Carolina that I purchased a few years before, which covered the down payment for a home we saw in Queens Village during the summer of 1978. I don't know how many we looked at; however, when you enter a house, you know whether it's for you without a real estate broker. I didn't have a clue how we were going to cover the ongoing costs of a monthly mortgage, maintenance, or my construction fetish, but after 30 years we are still here and happy to say that the mortgage was paid in full in 2010.

I swore I would not move again, due to so many resettlements in my life. After a few months, Karina really blossomed with the growth and color of the environment. Her playground now was a backyard, instead of an apartment hallway. We were ecstatic to leave the sounds of the city with its constant traffic, ambulances, fire truck sirens, and drunks behind, but being raised in Westbury, a typical Long Island town, I should have remembered the birds. During summer months, they start "chirping" around 4:00 a.m. and continue until their mothers feed them, which seems to take forever.

The neighborhood hasn't changed much throughout the years. Naturally, many of the homes have been renovated in one fashion or another; however, for the most part, the occupants have remained. Rita and I have maintained close relations with a few neighbors, Claudia and Ed Graham, along with Florence and Edward Omotoso who live on the other side of the street. Claudia is from Brazil, and Ed's roots are from Jamaica. Florence and Ed are Nigerians.

It seems as though every time you mention someone on the block, another country's name surfaces; I think it's great and keeps the neighborhood in balance. Bob and Shirley live directly across the street from our house. Shirley, being a nurse, many times, would come to the house rendering medical advice when one of our family members was sick. Ed Omotoso is retired from the UN and wrote a book, *A Life Around the World*, based on his life with the UN and career in OPEC. On more than one occasion while sitting around the dining room table, he would captivate us with his tales, and the sun would startle us as it rose to begin a new day.

A couple dearly missed is Judith and Logan Campbell; they were the fourth couple that formed our social group. Judith was from

Liberia, and Logan was from Grenada. When they moved into the neighborhood, they were not a typical family for the area. For weeks on end, limos with diplomatic plates lined the street day and night. There had been an overthrow of the government in Liberia around this time, and I believe that Judith's family was somehow involved. After about a month, the limos disappeared, and the tranquility of the neighborhood was restored.

Campbell and I would chat at every opportunity, usually during front yard work, since the two houses faced each other. On one occasion, we watched the boyfriend of a Caribbean neighbor, a few houses from ours, fixing his car with the front end raised by homemade jacks. It looked like a ghetto operation, and I mentioned to Logan that since he and this guy were both black, he should go and tell the guy that this was not the place to set up shop for car surgery. Logan thought about it for a few minutes as he looked at the guy working on the car. He was bigger than both of us put together. Logan then replied, "You know, Jim, I appreciate what you are saying; however, since it is on your side of the street, it would be better for you to reprimand him." Neither one of us approached the mechanic. One of our closest friends from the neighborhood is Nestora Hiraldo Altamira, who lived on the block with her daughter, Mercedes, and son-in-law, John. The couple has two children, Ingrid and Chris, playmates with Karina through their childhood. Although Nestora was born in the Dominican Republic, she was a true New Yorker. Both Chris and Ingrid, now successful in business and living in other states, have on several occasions asked Nestora to leave New York and live with them. Although I am sure her life would be more comfortable, there is no way that she will be uprooted from New York.

Nestora babysat for most of the children in the area and takes great pleasure being around them, now adults who have remained close to the neighborhood. At 85 years old, she maintains a schedule that a younger person would have a hard time keeping up with; Nestora is constantly moving around. Most of the city bus drivers forbid her to pay when she takes mass transit, and there isn't a local store you can walk into that doesn't know and respect her. On most Sundays to this day, she comes through the back door using her own key, makes coffee, and chats with Rita. Next, she heads for church and then returns for the two of them to go shopping. Nestora is certainly an important member of our extended family. The neighborhood has proven to be safe, and for over 30 years, I have heard of only a few home break-ins. Our car was stolen from in front of the house years ago, but I recovered it from East New York after receiving an anonymous call as to its location. After repairs, I drove it well past 200,000 miles; the theft did no harm. Recently, a neighbor was having the trees trimmed along the side of his house toward the backyard, and the worker pruning one of the trees discovered someone dangling with a rope around his neck. Apparently, he had been there a few weeks, since the body was well decomposed. Climbing to the top of a tree with a rope to put around your neck for the purpose of hanging illustrates a lot of determination. Even with the above events, the area is far from being termed a *hood,* and I have no future plans to move.

Within the first year of living in Queens, the last member to join our family came from a lumberyard. I had gone for wood, and the yard's dog had puppies; being a good customer, I was offered one. I could not refuse, despite knowing I would pay dearly when we got home, since Rita is not too fond of dogs. Rita was working on the front lawn as I turned into the driveway with lumber in the back of the car, and the dog between me at the steering wheel. I thought I could ease up the driveway unnoticed with my new little friend. Not a chance.

Rita's reaction was what I expected. She was not keen on the idea of a new family member. Upon swearing that I wouldn't let it in the house, and it wouldn't grow too big (both obviously not true), Rita didn't exactly say OK. However, he became an "Etchison" until his death approximately 13 years later. I named him "Little Fella," hoping Rita wouldn't know how large he would become. Within a year, he weighed approximately 80 pounds and, more or less, would be described as a short, brown-haired, lovable, and protective mutt.

Karina and Little Fella wrapped their love around each other from day one. He was the guardian of the family and provided Karina with an unparalleled security blanket. Kids have a tendency to play rough with their peers, and Karina was no exception. The accepted level of roughhousing when her group played in the backyard was determined by Little Fella. He would growl if he felt things were getting out of hand. In one episode of group play, I saw him nudge a playmate of Karina's away from her with his head, and I just watched in amazement.

He wasn't as gentle all the time. A UPS man carrying a package and a woman with a box in her hand came too close to Karina and were bitten. The UPS guy ran across the street to our neighbors, who calmed him down with Scotch and sewed up the crotch in his pants. Needless to say, it was a long time before we received any packages from "Mr. Brown." The woman sped her departure down the driveway with her skirt pulled up around her waist showing the wound on her behind to the neighborhood while screaming something in Spanish. I thought it was funny as hell and couldn't keep from laughing. One moment I will never forget was Karina and Little Fella lying side by side on the dining room rug with Little Fella's front leg draped over Karina's back. It took me back to the days with Spanky in Vietnam! Both dogs would have both given their lives for us without a second thought. Little Fella and I had a ritual whereby when I got home in the evening after dark, we would go to our tree in the backyard and I would pee on one side, while Little Fella did likewise on the other side. As time takes all of us, he passed and still to this day is missed tremendously.

If I Had a Hammer

I think that my construction activities began the moment I walked through the front door of our new home. The house had a lot of empty space that wasn't utilized, and all rooms needed remodeling. We bought it from an Italian family, and the décor gave away their roots with green and silver wallpaper throughout, plus other colors that were fashionable in the "old country." It had to come off, and it did in every room of the house, layer by layer.

Most projects were small renovations that I managed to do between school and family duties. One weekend, I had my eye on redoing the kitchen ceiling, but Rita wasn't quite up to this undertaking, due to the mess that I am well known to create during my home improvements. My title around the house was, and still is, "Mr. Construction/Destruction." She accused me of having attention deficit disorder since I could never sit still without having some kind of project in progress.

Her accusation is probably not far from the truth. I had a plan involving the open porch that is attached to the back of the house. I felt it would be a good idea to build a half bath–laundry room there, so we wouldn't have to go up or downstairs to the bathroom or down to the basement to do the laundry as the existing layout required. Actually, at one point, the porch was covered and served as Little Fella's living quarters. After Little Fella's passing, for the second time in my life, I started to raise quail. The porch was my make-believe farm. One day, I let the birds all go, after they outgrew their living space and continually woke the neighbors around 5:00 a.m. during the summer months.

I knew that at my pace, erecting a laundry room would take a couple of years to complete, but at least as the mess would be outside, I was safe. I am not one to draw plans and estimate material costs. I simply start to think of what should be done, and when I run out of material, I go buy more. I found the closest Home Depot and was off and running. I began carrying all the supplies with my trusty station wagon, "Old Betsy," which was well known in the neighborhood for its "aged" appearance, and a few operating modifications, such as touching two wires to make the horn "beep."

Actually, my little invention saved me a ticket one day when a cop pulled me over for a crack in Betsy's windshield. When I showed him how the horn worked, he shook his head and said he never saw a system as such, laughed, and said goodbye. Although none of the neighbors would ride in her, I was very proud of Betsy and bragged endlessly about her material-carrying capacity during construction projects.

I did want someone with experience to periodically supervise my work and felt I had met the right guy during one of the nightly runs to Home Depot. I was wrong. After giving him some money, he disappeared, but not before giving me the name of an architect. Actually, that contact was in itself worth the money, so I wasn't too upset and wrote the loss off as another lesson in life. After God only knows how many trips to Home Depot, I found the secret to obtaining assistance from the employees. You have to wear clothes that are ripped and covered in paint, with untied construction boots, and have a measuring tape clipped to your belt. If you are in regular street attire, the employees will run from you when you attempt to flag them down to ask a question.

Now I was on my own. Armed with a number of books bought at Home Depot on framing, electrical, plumbing, roofing, and building a deck, I had the confidence to begin. I was pushing along rather nicely with the framing and had only one accident when I missed a step coming down off the ladder and ended up in some kind of flowering bush next to the house. If I had landed another inch or two to the left, it would have been rather embarrassing to find someone to extract the branch from my butt. Other than the ladder incident and, of course, a few cut fingers and mashed fingernails, I was accident-free.

I met what would become my construction partner in crime from that day until the present, which has been more than 12 years, Mr. Thomas, from Jamaica. I was walking to a hardware store that at one time was close to my house when I noticed a guy doing some brickwork for a neighbor. Knowing that sooner or later I would need to brick the enclosure of my house, I briefly told him what I was doing, and if interested in assisting, he should stop by. He did later that afternoon, and after seeing my creation, I caught him laughing to himself. We worked out an arrangement where he would help between his other commitments. A typical day, regardless of what we were doing, would be a book in my hand, reading the way I felt it should be done, while he had another method. We would compromise, and the task would be completed. Tom kept asking when we would be getting to the brickwork, his specialty, and I always answered "Soon."

Throughout any construction period, there were reports of neighbors calling the building department, informing them of "next-door activities." I wasn't worried about the Indians on one side of us, since they didn't have a good command of the English language, but wasn't sure about the man living on the other side. He was not well thought of by the majority of the local residents, so I kept telling him about phantom meetings I was having with the architect. This seemed to satisfy him, since I never got a visit from the building department, which would have resulted in substantial penalties for starting a project without a permit. If caught, I would have to pay an initial fine with 30 days to dismantle all the completed work. If the dismantling was not completed within this period, a fine of $250 per day until it was done would be imposed.

I had many sleepless nights, especially when Mr. Thomas constructed a scaffold that looked like it was attached to a shack down in the islands, made up of a combination of rope and two by fours. Even though it was on the side of the house, it could be seen from the street. My greatest fear of exposure came one day when Rita had invited a longtime friend, Mary Fawzi, over for an afternoon at the backyard. Rita was in the kitchen, and I was sitting talking to Mary in the backyard when her head went down and slumped over. Naturally, a heart attack was on everyone's mind, and 911 was called.

Knowing that this would bring the fire department, EMS, and the police, I started to have a panic attack, especially due to Tom's scaffold, which could be seen by all. I contemplated moving Mary to the front yard but knew nobody would understand my concern, so I sat and waited. Here they came, sirens roaring with all the associated lights. They focused on Mary, and nothing was said, although I caught a couple of the response personnel looking at the work. Rita and I had never known how many Indians were living next door, but swear, as Mary was being wheeled down the driveway, there must have been 20 heads popping in and out of their windows! Mary was fine and diagnosed with an improper diet.

Tom and I pushed on, learning as we went, with electrical, framing, and plumbing, and finally after a year or so, we got to his specialty, bricklaying. Tom was familiar with an old church that was being torn down in his neighborhood, and we made cash arrangements with the demolition team to reclaim the bricks, since the style of bricks being removed matched those of the house perfectly. I had planned to make the extension only one story; however, since a roof had to be put over it, I went up one more level and built an extra bedroom.

Usually, when children move away, the parents start reducing living space; however, not here. If we had to sell, the extra bedroom would be a plus. The big advantage was it kept me occupied for another year or so. The only access to the second-level bedroom area was a ladder from the first floor, the future laundry room, through a cutout in the ceiling to the new bedroom above. Rita has an access problem with the ladder, so with the exception of a few unannounced visits, I was left alone in my own little world.

When the new bedroom was completed, with pictures hanging, Tom and I opened our new masterpiece to the rest of the house by replacing the second-floor hallway window with a door to the room. It has been regularly occupied by out-of-town visitors, and Tom advised me not to build any more rooms, as the number of visitors increases with the number of available rooms. He is a very practical person.

We once had to end the workday halfway through, due to a call from his wife notifying us that she'd left home in an ambulance and just delivered a baby in a local hospital. Of course, the hospital's name or location was not mentioned, and Tom didn't have a clue. Thank God Karina was visiting, and after driving Tom to where she guessed his wife was, we were right on the money. The baby was a girl named Faith.

I felt it would be to everyone's advantage if the addition to the house were made legal, due to insurance requirements and in the event that the house was ever sold. The building plans would then coincide with the actual layout of the house. This required paperwork and money, which were the hard part. I had a meeting with the architect and literally had my butt chewed by him. "Mr. Etchison, you are well aware that a project such as yours first requires an architect to draw plans, then file for a work permit, and finally get approval from the county to start building. You have completed construction on a building and asked an architect to draw plans and obtain a work permit, so you can start work on your already *completed* project!" He continued:

> "How in the hell I am I supposed to do this?"
> "*Cash.*"
> "OK, however, the next time you get restless, follow the rules!"
> "Sure."

The permit was filed, and the only complaint I had was that workman's compensation insurance had to be purchased in case one of the workers received an injury on the job. Naturally, this wasn't an issue, since it was already completed, but I had no choice. In any event, I now had the permit and scheduled the three required inspections: general, electrical, and plumbing. The workmanship passed all three on the initial inspections, and the architect said it was the first time he had witnessed such an outcome when dealing with the city.

I can't brag about the electrical, since the inspector never went near the panel box or looked in the new rooms. I wasn't there, but apparently, as Rita was taking him to the electrical panel in the basement, he got distracted by a model I had built of a Vietnam-era helicopter. Rita told him I had been in Vietnam, and apparently he had also done a tour there. That was enough to successfully pass the electrical inspection. It's been eight years since his visit, and nothing detrimental has happened with the electricity, so I guess all wires were connected in the proper manner.

Tom and I still keep Rita on her toes with our projects including the current one, extending the garage. Again, I "forgot" to obtain a work permit, and when I get brave enough, I will call the architect. I have the deepest respect for Tom, and although not highly educated, he is very practical and a man of his word. I only have two ongoing problems. Even with my experience in training people in Trinidad, I still can't understand him when he speaks, and about half the time I have to ask him to repeat what he's said. I'm getting better because it used to be almost all of the time. The second is that Tom attends church all day on Saturdays. Whatever was discussed on Saturday in church becomes his topic of discussion on Sundays, our primary workday.

I consider him part of the family, and without his dedication and labor, the house would never be in its present condition for us and future generations to enjoy. Unfortunately, tragedy struck Tom's family with the passing of his wife, Joyce, while she was home in Jamaica through an act of violence involving the notorious drug trade. She had stopped at a red light and was caught in cross-fire between two rival drug factions. Since then, he has been a single parent, and I can't put in words the respect I have for him. I look forward to the days Mr. Thomas and I work together; stories and philosophies are continually discussed. One of my favorites concerns the topic of "greed." Tom told me about how a baboon's greed gets him in trouble. The African natives often have a hard time finding water and know a baboon is very inquisitive and can find water without trouble. Knowing that the baboon was watching in the bush, the native would dig a deep hole with a small diameter, filling it with grain. He will leave only to return a short time later to find the animal with its paw stuck in the hole. The baboon can get away, but greed will get the best of him, with the paw remaining stuck in the hole, not wanting to let go of the grain. Once caught, the native will feed his captive salt, creating thirst. The baboon will then be cut loose and will locate an obscured watering hole to get a drink. Naturally, the natives will follow.

One of my various "yard projects," which required roughly 50 bags of sand, resulted in a meeting of the minds between me and a highway patrol officer. The city was in the midst of repairing roads after the winter's damage. Approximately every 100 yards along the side of any road, there were numerous piles of sand the highway department used to fill the potholes created in the cold weather. Being "frugal," I took "Old Betsy" to the Clearview Expressway by our house and began filling the bags with sand.

After filling approximately 30 bags, my "happy as a lark" mood and labor were interrupted by red lights flashing and an officer with his microphone instructing me to come to his car. His suggestion for me to avoid a summons for stealing state property was to place the sand back on the roadside. Without my objecting, he continued, "I am leaving now and shouldn't be back in this area for a few hours."

I guess the officer felt sorry for me, seeing both the condition of "Old Betsy" and the sweat running down my face from filling the bags. I also remember telling him that this reminded me of making sandbags in Vietnam to use for protection against mortar attacks. In any event, off he went in one direction, and after a few minutes, I left the crime scene. The sand did get back on the ground, however in our backyard.

Everyone has their own building style, and no matter what room I designed and built, there had to be wall or ceiling speakers, due to my love of music. The neighbors know when I am home alone, especially during the summer months; the house rocks on its foundation, keeping tempo to the music as it blares out into the street.

Toys "R" Us

They say dedicated modelers have plastic in their veins. It is probably true, since there has to be a reason why year after year, we continue to build.

Like many men of my generation, instead of today's video games, as a boy, I built model kits, proudly displaying them on shelves or hanging airplanes from the ceiling in the bedroom. They would look great until my mom decided to dust them. With all good intentions, she never could explain how pieces began to disappear. She simply hoped that I wouldn't notice the missing propellers or antennas. Then there were my friends who never failed to look with their hands. In the long run, it didn't matter, because when my parents decided to move, the models never followed me to our new home.

As the years went by, I began to rekindle my interest in this childhood hobby. I believed all the previous problems had been solved, since now I'd be building in my own home: an incorrect assumption. My new work area slowly took over the entire house, and the smell of glue and paint bothered everyone but me. I was finally forced, and rightly so, back to a restricted area. The house started to need repairs, but this took away from my golden moments. When major structural problems did not go away, I had to sacrifice those creative periods and repair our domain.

Another hazard is when the model is built in the summer, placed on a shelf, and winter comes with its fury. Naturally, you didn't notice the heater close by during the summer, but when the heat is turned on, there's meltdown. Another area of concern was when Rita would accidentally break a piece and decide to get glue and repair the damage herself: "He will never notice." The only problem is that several times the required amount of glue was applied and/or the part was attached backward.

In all fairness, Rita is always ready to assist in finding a piece that has landed on the floor. It is absolutely amazing what you find under your worktable. I have read several articles with illustrations on how to build an organized work area. They look great, and I am convinced that it's the way to go. However, it's not in my character, and I will be the first to admit that seldom can I find what I am searching for on the first attempt.

With all of the above problems under control, and to a point, I now realized that after inventory, I was the proud owner of over 100 unfinished kits. The temptation was always too great to pass a hobby shop or model contest without adding to my collection. After the unfinished models sat in the closet a few years, I realize they really weren't all that necessary. I visited a fellow modeler in Panama, and he had an entire room dedicated to boxed kits. At last count there were 1,500; at least I felt a little more normal. Becoming so damn good, I decided it was time to participate in a few contests. No one told me to carry a repair kit for "transportation damage." Usually, the model on the display table at the contest looked nothing like it did in the backseat of the car when I left home. I learned from experience. My most distant contest in terms of travel was held in Buenos Aires, Argentina. Have you ever sat between a hippie and a punk (with orange spiked hair) for a 12-hour flight from New York to Argentina?

The two models never left my lap, meaning that I had to forego all food service (remember those days when you actually got a meal on an airplane?). The most challenging moment was explaining to Customs at the airport in Buenos Aires that the models were fragile and I'd like the agent to handle them with care. With all the inconveniences, I did get a medal at the ceremonies, and the model club members sponsoring the contest were very hospitable. I was introduced in Spanish for my award, so God knows what the explanation was for my presence. Over time, several of my models have been illustrated in trade publications.

Since serving in Vietnam, I wanted to have the world's best and most complete model collection of all things that moved in Vietnam: planes, armored vehicles, artillery, troops, farm animals, and insects. It took almost 20 years to realize that I would have to live to be approximately 300 years old to accomplish this goal. My dad flew everything from flying boats to the B-747. Because of this, not only was I going to finish the Vietnam project, but I planned to build all the planes that Pan Am had flown over the years. This would take another 200 hundred years.

Regardless of whether the category is an aircraft, ship, armor, or figurine, a model represents an event that remains part of history. Often the people involved push the envelope and give their lives, whether in peace or war.

Although the models are not perfect, it has been more than an honor building on behalf of these people.

Be Like Water

> *Be like water making its way through cracks. Do not be assertive, but adjust to the object, and you shall find a way around or through it. If nothing within you stays rigid, outward things will disclose themselves.*
>
> —Bruce Lee, Action-film actor and martial arts instructor

In my mid-forties, being told that I had a "big belly," and having a shirt button pop and fly across the room when I exhaled, I headed for the gym, and time permitting, I was able to keep a fairly decent schedule. The best part of the program was a step aerobics class that I participated in as much as possible. Karina came for a session, and as we went up, she would go down; we would go to the left, Karina to the right. I could hear her swearing as she tried in vain to "get with the flow."

Many maintain that going to the gym is essential for good health, but for me it can get boring. I wanted to expand my physical program by joining a Taekwondo martial arts school that was located a few blocks from Academics of Flight. It was probably one of the best periods in my life, and I thoroughly enjoyed the discipline and workout. I should have been involved at a much younger age. I began at 46 and continued for six years until Academics of Flight expanded to Miami.

That I stopped participating in the sport, due to obligations with the new Florida office, is one of my biggest regrets. I had only one more test for my black belt, but after a certain age, it was time to stop. I probably could have squeezed in a few more years, but with the time I did practice, I am suffering today with torn ligaments in both legs. Taekwondo is a showcase form of martial arts, with a wide variety of kicks. However, in close quarters with restricted room to maneuver, it's not practical for self-defense. Throughout my time of doing martial arts, I had formed a father–son relationship with Komal Kungeesing, a pre-med student from Trinidad. We hit and kicked each other for years, and since he was at least a head taller than me and had a black belt, I would get the short end of the stick. We both took the program very seriously, with additional workouts in one of Academics of Flight's classrooms when it was available. Academics of Flight took on the appearance of a gym, instead of an aviation school. My office was our locker room, with sweatpants and sparring gear spread from corner to corner. At times, a ground school instructor in an adjacent classroom would ask that we hold the noise down, since it was difficult to teach when our workouts were in progress.

Komal and I wanted to expand our knowledge to other forms of martial arts and branched out to seido, which is a much more disciplined Japanese form of the arts. The "dojo" (literally, "place of the way"; the formal training place) was in midtown Manhattan, and after attending twice a week, long enough to receive our first upgrade, we left. It was too formal compared to what we were accustomed to, and there was no touching allowed during sparring sessions. This was completely contrary to what we were used to with taekwondo. With the greatest respect for our sparring mates, we tried to beat the hell out of each other.

During one seido session, I barely touched my opponent (probably "brushed" is a better term), and the guy went ballistic shouting, "He hit me, he hit me." Komal and I couldn't stop laughing on the way back to Queens. After seido, we ventured up to Jackson Heights to a school that taught sipalki (literally, "18 techniques"). We were the only non-Latinos in the school and had to prove a certain level of machismo. We did, since by now I had approximately five years of training, and Komal, much more.

Sipalki involves fighting with sticks, and we practiced disarming foes who had weapons; the lessons were more useful for real-life situations compared to taekwondo. Since the area is notorious for drug dealing, the members were very attentive during class. Komal will never admit it, but we even went to dance lessons after learning that a famous martial arts movie actor did. The dancing didn't last long; I couldn't get used to doing the merengue with a male instructor.

I believe that there are few sporting events that compare to a martial arts tournament. Komal and I made the rounds: Queens College, another school on Long Island, Brooklyn, and my favorite, Jersey City. We left for New Jersey at the crack of dawn and found it about 9:00 a.m. If you ever watched the TV series *The Wire*, the area looked as though they filmed it there. I heard that the police don't even respond to calls in that section because they feel you shouldn't have been there in the first place. I asked Komal why he couldn't find a tournament in a safe location, and his response was "Sorry, James, I didn't know."

For some reason, he always called me "James." We made it inside without being mugged or shot and then were informed by the tournament organizer that it was only for "black belts." Again, I had choice words, and again his response: "Sorry, James, I didn't know." At that time, I was a third-degree red belt, just one level below black, but I signed up to fight after the tournament organizer offered me the chance. Usually, the winners receive trophies, but in this case, cash prizes were being given instead.

I was losing it and said to Komal, "Do you realize, half of these guys look like they are on drugs, and probably here only to get money for a fix? All the rules of discipline will be thrown out the window during the match!"

"Sorry, James, I didn't know."

"Komal, I hope you get the shit kicked out of you!"

We both did. Actually, I had so much adrenalin pumping that I came off the line and got the first point. Two more and I would've walked away the champ. It never happened. My opponent was a big black guy who was not going to let a red belt beat him. I will never forget him saying after he won, "Sir, I have a lot of respect for you." Not many people have told me that, and it was compensation for my defeat. He was a nice guy, and I hope the money was spent wisely. Komal and I left, and I never let him choose another tournament location.

After losing contact with Komal for a dozen or so years, he appeared at the office one day in early 2010. He had gone to England for medical school and returned to Trinidad to practice. On a teaching assignment to Trinidad a few months later, I spent the day with him and his family. After being on the wrong end of his kicks for six years, he is now my physician, with all the "island" remedies. Life has its way of going backward at times.

I have to laugh when comparing the gym in New York to that in Miami Springs, Florida, I attended. I went to the gym in Florida when I had to be at Academics of Flight's Miami location for teaching. I think a more appropriate term for the Miami Springs gym would be "penitentiary." I have yet to see anyone without a tattoo, ranging from small to those that would take hours to explain; this also included the female patrons! Along with this body art, while I am straining to lift at most 75 pounds, they followed with double to triple the weight. Of course, most were Latinos with bandanas wrapped around their foreheads, signifying connection with a gang. There was a bulletin board containing information on those who had just died. The notices simply gave the time and directions to the funerals.

Trains, Trains, Trains

For me, having a train set as a young boy was nothing but the ultimate dream. My dad made it come true. I began with a circular track around the Christmas tree in our apartment at an age when I could barely walk. In my teen years, the train layout expanded in the basement of our Westbury home to approximately 8 × 12 feet. My dad would work on the tracks and other equipment involving wiring, while I created the scenery. The largest layout I saw was during my high school years and owned by a friend, Skippy. His basement was completely dedicated to Lionel trains, and there was barely room to walk. When I met him years later, the first thing I asked was whether he still had his layout, and unfortunately, he lost it to a family member due to a feud. I am sure it tore him apart, because of the endless hours it took to construct his pride and joy.

The Lionel brand was the most popular at that time, and still a favorite of many old-timers because of its large-scale size, "O" gauge. Today, many railroad enthusiasts use "N" scale, one-quarter the size of Lionel. Bruce Burleigh, a neighborhood pal who lived a few houses from us in Westbury, had a beautiful HO scale, one-half the size of

Lionel. I tried to convince my dad to convert to that scale as it appeared more realistic, and compared to Lionel, one could double the contents on any given layout. Being overruled, we stuck with Lionel, which provided hours of entertainment. When my parents would have a group of Pan Am flight crewmembers and their wives to the house for an evening of socializing, approximately 10 minutes after they arrived all the men would be in the basement running the trains while the women sat in the living room feeling neglected. Obviously, the men were eventually called upstairs, which would end their short-lived fun after a brief time.

From the time I left my home in Westbury, around 1962 until 2008, I neither had the time nor permanent space to even contemplate my train hobby. However, once I finished the attic in the Queens Village house, I decided to begin a train board. I had saved most pieces of the Lionel set from the old days, but elected to use "N" scale, due to its size advantage. I began to build the layout, as I seem to do all my projects, with no plans. My dad would have been very disappointed in my approach, as his would have been the complete opposite. When I was a boy, he built a wall unit to separate the dining room from the kitchen in our Westbury house. It turned out great; however, he spent more time calculating the amount of wood the project would require, attempting to buy the exact quantity than the actual time it took to build the unit.

Constructing a layout at 64 years old is definitely not the same as when I began one under my father's guidance at five or six. Being an avid model builder all my life, I felt this would be a piece of cake, and I thought I would not have to research it before starting. Of course, following this philosophy, I would have to toil several times on something to finally complete it correctly. Only God knows how many hours it took to properly lay tracks, so the train would not derail. I will be the first to warn anyone contemplating this hobby to be prepared for a million anxiety attacks. "Why do I continue?" It's great to have the challenge and rewarding to stand back and see something created.

An Apple a Day...

I never inquired as to the VA benefits offered to veterans. I felt guilty due to the fact that I left Vietnam with all my pieces intact, and although I went through "survivor's syndrome" as most do, it did not permanently affect me mentally. Note: Some people would dispute the latter. The Miami VA hospital had an excellent reputation, and after leaving Vietnam almost 45 years earlier, I inquired regarding benefits due to Karina's insistence. I was eligible and about a year into the routine of regular checkups, I was diagnosed with prostate cancer. Although the doctors said I had been carrying it around probably for the past 20 years, it was time to act. It really didn't bother me, since I heard it wasn't a matter of *if* a man will get this form of cancer, but *when.*

My dad had it, Dahl had the woman's version, and so I simply looked at the situation as, "Well, it's my turn." Karina immediately took charge, and we went to a recommended specialist for a second opinion. We all concluded that the best course of action was to get the damn thing out. At 63, I certainly didn't need it to have any more children.

Karina said, "Daddy, if you had another child, you would *wish* you had cancer, as opposed to what I would do to you." Her doctor gave me a book to read, *Guide to Surviving Prostrate Cancer,* before I did anything. After reading 450 pages, I knew nothing more of great importance than before starting to read. One section did say that the VA took full responsibility for people serving during the Agent Orange period, regardless of family history. Because I was "in-country" during that period, they would take it out, so I had two places to get it removed. Although Rita and Karina were not too encouraged to have the VA perform the operation, I felt an obligation to give the chore to them; it's difficult to explain if you are not a vet, but they accepted.

The next six weeks were supposed to be a recuperation period during which I'd more or less do nothing. However, I had to make a living and resumed teaching in Trinidad three weeks later. I think that in most cases you can safely cut the recommended recovery time in half because doctors usually double it to cover their butts. After more than seven years, I am still cancer-free. It upsets me when I hear derogatory remarks about the VA and "socialized medicine." I have benefited enormously from the programs and possibly would not be around today without them.

Karina was stung by a bee when we were roommates in Miami and decided to go to the emergency room at a local hospital around 10:00 p.m. due to the swelling. After being asked the routine question "What insurance do you have?" we waited into the wee hours of the morning. Extremely irritated, I finally inquired as to what was taking so long to be seen. "Someone died, sir," was the response, and my reply was, "This is a hospital, people are supposed to die here!" My comment did not help our situation, and approximately two hours later, we were paged. To cap a less-than-perfect evening that was now morning, Karina had run out of underwear and was wearing a pair of mine, which was discovered when she had to get a shot in her rear end.

At this time, the Miami location of Academics of Flight was becoming quiet, due to several Angolan airlines downsizing and then going bankrupt. It became obvious that I would be spending the majority of my time in New York. As a result, I continued my association with the VA hospital in The Bronx. The ambience is quite different compared to Miami and can be very entertaining.

Initially, I would ride the VA van from the Queens clinic to The Bronx, and some of the co-riders were characters. One such fellow was a marine corporal who apparently felt like becoming a self-made captain for the weekend. Everyone has the right to upgrade, but when he was busted being drunk while wearing his new uniform, the Marines didn't agree with his promotion process; they gave him the choice of jail or Vietnam. He chose the latter. Karina, being the wise-ass she is, asked if they gave me milk and cookies during the van ride.

The hospital conducts business consistent with the New York lifestyle: very direct with no time wasted. I was lying on my back on the table for a checkup and was told to move farther down. The instruction given from a Jamaican nurse was, "Keep moving down until your ass touches my hand." I got the point.

In 2011, I had to have a minor operation, and instead of being wheeled, I had to walk to the operating room. Thank God I found the right room and did not interrupt someone else's surgery.

The following year, I went for a routine checkup at the Queens VA branch, which has its office directly across the street from the Academics of Flight office in New York. The visit resulted in a lifetime benefit that has nothing to do with health. Arlene, the receptionist at the clinic, handed me a flyer that contained a list of all the companies giving anywhere from 10 to 20 percent discounts for purchases at some of my favorite stores: Home Depot, GNC, Dunkin' Donuts, and several others. So far, I have had complete success from all the retailers I've visited and I regret not being aware of this offering sooner. By now I could have saved several thousand, probably at Home Depot alone. One of the cashiers at Home Depot asked if I fought in the Civil War when I showed him my military ID.

Most people thumb their noses at VA hospitals in general; however, an experience I had with a non-VA medical center could not compare to the VA. I had a throat problem: nothing serious, just a lump that seemed determined to stay. I went for an exam by a specialist. After placing a camera in my throat through my nostril, he gave me antibiotics, and I was instructed to have a follow-up the next week. The only problem the doctor could confirm was that the throat was swollen, but nothing to worry about.

On the day before the follow-up, I called to cancel, due to work. When I requested the change, the receptionist said I should come due to an emergency with my test results: the doctor *had* to see me. After a sleepless night I arrived early the next morning, prior to the scheduled appointment. Within a few minutes, I was escorted to an exam room to wait for the doctor. Alone, I glanced over my shoulder and saw a disgusting image on the computer screen of a round object that could be compared to an apple that was half-eaten by worms.

I thought, "Oh God, I am not going to live long enough to see Karina and Chloe!" Karina was planning a visit with her daughter at the end of the month. When the doctor came in and I questioned him about all my anxieties, he couldn't understand why the receptionist had claimed there was an emergency and assured me that the image I was viewing was that of the previous patient. It reminded me of the boy who was running through a cow pasture when his foot landed in cow manure. Looking at his foot in the middle of the cow shit, he said, "Oh God, I am melting!" I was relieved, to say the least.

During all the post-care periods, Rita was by my side taking care of the aches and pains. However, when a woman finds herself in a shopping atmosphere, it takes precedence over all other thoughts, which I was faced with when we lived in an apartment during our first year of marriage. Once when I had the "runs" and couldn't leave the bathroom, I bid Rita farewell as she left for a drugstore a few blocks away to pick up the needed medicine. I waited and waited in anticipation of getting back on my feet to resume normal duties.

One hour went by and coming up on two, when she finally entered, she had a new pair of red shoes, instead of the medicine. There happened to be a boutique between the pharmacy and apartment, and she forgot her primary mission. On another occasion, I was barefoot and stepped on a sewing needle that went into the bottom of my foot about a quarter of an inch. After pulling it out, to a chorus of many choice words, I showed it to Rita. Instead of getting sympathy, she said, "Oh good: I have been looking for that needle for a week. Where did you find it?" I was very clear in stating how and where I located the damn thing.

Rita had her own turn. The first was a hot summer night years ago when in bed, I was restless and decided to crawl over Rita to the other side of the bed. Before making my leap, I threw the pillow to my new location and caught a picture hanging over the headboard. Down came the work of art, striking Rita on the side of the head and opening a cut over her eyebrow. The blood ran down to her ear and in the dark, it looked like a large gash. As she started to moan, asking for a mirror that I would not provide, I called 911.

As I was giving directions, Rita was alert enough to interrupt informing me that I was giving the address of the office. When EMS and two cops arrived, the looks I received when I explained what happened were those of disbelief; they were convinced it was a "domestic violence" situation involving a knife. All of us, with Rita holding her eye, Karina in her pajamas, and me feeling guilty, were led to an emergency room where we were met by a Puerto Rican intern who would close the wound. He was amusing to watch, since prior to starting his task, he had to turn on a radio to listen to salsa music as he stitched. He never missed a beat and did a beautiful job.

The last time Rita went to the hospital, I felt for sure I was on my way to jail. I got a call in the office from Karina, who said that Rita had gotten very sick or fainted and was on her way to the emergency room. Before leaving the house that morning, I had given Rita a couple of painkillers since she had a headache. I bought them in Miami, where they were obtained without a prescription. I remember driving home before going to the hospital to throw the remaining pills away, so if her condition turned for the worse, there would be no evidence suggesting I may have intended foul play.

Everything turned out fine, and Rita was back to normal by the end of the day after being diagnosed with temporary low blood pressure.

Freight Dog

I met a guy named Paul, who owned two C45/D-18 airplanes that he used for nightly cargo flights out of JFK to Buffalo, Rochester, Boston, and anywhere else he could obtain a contract to fly. He asked me to join as a pilot, and since unemployed, I jumped at the offer. Had I known the condition of the airplanes at that time, I would not have been so willing. I don't think Paul intentionally tried to cut corners on maintenance, but there always seemed to be a problem.

The airplanes were single-pilot authorized; however, at night we carried restricted cargo, so the company flew with two pilots. The flights were scheduled to depart JFK at midnight and return around 5:00 a.m. It hardly ever happened, due to maintenance issues and/or the weather. Delays were also encountered on landings. At Rochester, the FAA car would be driving alongside one wing tip, while the Port Authority car was on the other as we taxied to the ramp. The Port Authority wanted their landing fee on the spot because the company had fallen out of its graces by not paying previous invoices. The company now had to pay by cash after each landing.

Once we finished with them, it was the FAA's turn. As per regulations, each flight had to have a proper weight and balance form completed indicating that the aircraft was loaded properly, plus a list of restricted articles on board. This was rarely done, and limiting the amount of radioactive material to a certain quantity was never observed. We carried so much radioactive material that I'm sure our flight path glowed at night. After each inspection, the FAA always shook their heads in disbelief; however, we somehow were allowed to continue flying.

On my first night, I reported to the office and made small talk with the captain, John, waiting for the aircraft to arrive. I began to hear the sounds of airplane engines coming from around the hangar corner: backfiring, misfiring, farting, and every other noise no one could describe. The captain, seeing my expression, started laughing and said, "Yes, that's ours for the night." All I could think of was, "My God, I will never see sunrise!" Had cell phones been available at that time, I would have called Rita to say goodbye. Prior to going out on the plane, I asked the captain whether I should check the weather since it was raining with poor visibility. His response was "Why? We have to go anyway."

After climbing into the cockpit from on top of the wing and settling in, I noticed a few empty spaces in the instrument panel where certain instruments were supposed to be. I didn't say a word. After takeoff, we turned toward LaGuardia's airspace, on our way to Buffalo. We were requested by Air Traffic Control (ATC) to report our altitude since the airplane did not have the proper equipment, a mode C transponder, to indicate our altitude on the radar screen. The plane was supposed to have this, but the owner always got away without it.

I was reaching for the microphone to report the altimeter reading of 2,500 feet when John took the mic and reported 9,000 feet. He saw the confusion on my face and later explained that 9,000 was the minimum to enter LaGuardia airspace. If not, the airplane would have to fly into a climbing holding pattern until reaching that altitude. Of course, putting safety aside, it would take additional fuel and time to follow this procedure, which was unacceptable to the company. The other possibility was to have a midair collision by stating an incorrect altitude, but if the captain wasn't worrying, why should I?

My old friend, "Mr. Cold," returned to my life, and ever. The C-45 is an absolutely rugged airplane that will take you anywhere. It was made for the military, and the designers never gave much thought to a heating system; we flew literally wrapped in army blankets. Flying around the northeast over the winter in a C-45 to places such as Buffalo would make you freeze regardless of how many layers of clothes you wore. The woman who took care of Karina, Esther from Argentina, used to cross herself as I was leaving for these flights, due to my multilayer clothing. Snow and ice were another serious problem encountered on a nightly basis, especially the JFK–Buffalo leg, due to the distance. The highest we would fly was 8,000–9,000 feet, making the plane a prime target for icing. The two systems in use were "anti-ice" and "deice." The deicing system used hot air from the engines along the leading edge of the wing, the vertical and horizontal stabilizers that run through rubber channels called "boots." You would allow a little ice to build on these areas and then turn on the boots. The hot air would expand these surfaces, and the ice would pop off. It was great for the wings, but by the time the air got to the tail section, it was cold and did nothing to remove the ice. Air speed would start to decline, indicating that it was time to come down and deice on the ground. We would deice the airplane at an airport in Elmira, New York. Seldom did we make it to Buffalo without first stopping in Elmira.

The crew would beg Allegheny Airlines to perform this operation. I can still picture one of the captains, Paul, standing on the ramp with his beard frozen, ice crystals hanging down. He was a great pilot, as were the others, and I am sure later flew with a major carrier.

The anti-ice system was simply a bottle of fluid with a low freezing point. Flipping a switch would spray the windshield and propellers, coating them with the fluid. It is the same as a driver cleaning his windshield with bug spray. The system worked fine, but a few times we would activate the switch and nothing would come out. Was there a mechanical problem? No. It was a mental problem because one of us had forgotten or thought the other pilot filled the bottle prior to takeoff. It seemed Buffalo was always buried in snow, and many times the runway sides had piles of snow plowed higher than our airplane.

Flights to Boston meant a short night. During one approach, I had snow accumulating on my shoulder, due to a cracked side cockpit window. During another, one of our customers was transporting white laboratory mice back and forth to JFK. On this particular night, after loading the mice, one of the boxes came open, and the cockpit was mouse hell. Every time one of us used the rudder pedals, we caught several mice between our boots and the pedal.

I don't know how many we lost by the time we landed at JFK, but I know there were quite a few.

The company had just purchased a DC-3, and we were delighted to advance to a larger airplane. To the disappointment of all, the company went bankrupt a week later, and once more, I was unemployed. From this point on, beginning in 1976, Academics of Flight came into being.

Cóbano, Costa Rica: 1990s–Present

Soon after a trip to Nicaragua, an opportunity surfaced to realize my desire to become a farmer. Academics of Flight had a Costa Rican secretary, Alba, who introduced her brother, Fernando, during one of his visits to New York. He had graduated with his doctorate degree in forestry from the University of Maine and managed several farms in the Alajuela area on the northern border of Costa Rica. With an invitation to visit and possibly invest, I packed my bag and headed south. After several trips, I found myself the owner of 20-some-odd cattle that were grazing on the property I leased.

It took a few years to build from the original three in the herd, with the assistance of the first bull doing a damn good job. I purchased a second bull to share the workload, but he turned out gay and was not interested in being "snuggly" with the female cows. With the gay bull, and the coincidence that during the holidays, I would always receive a call, informing me a cow or two died, which most likely wound up on the Christmas dinner table of a local, I decided to sell the herd and use the funds to buy property on which I'd grow Gmelina and teak trees. In 2011, we owned approximately 60 acres in a pueblo named Cóbano, approximately an hour drive north of San Carlos, situated along the Nicaraguan border.

Going to the farm over the years has been an experience because of the local people and the area's history of participating in the Contra War. The only way to describe the terrain is an area hacked out of the jungle. The canopy was as I had seen in Vietnam, where you could not tell if it was day or night when underneath. The earth is red clay with all the tropical creatures present: large snakes, wild boars, cougars, and panthers. During the Contra War, the U.S. Army constructed dirt roads for easy access to the area. The problem is that the roads have not been maintained since that period, and during the two annual rainy seasons, the only plausible mode of transportation is on foot or by horseback. If someone suffered a wound that resulted in significant bleeding, he would most likely bleed to death before reaching a hospital or aid station.

The locals I have seen are tough as nails, yet with a warm heart, and many at one time or other, "slipped" across the border from Nicaragua. Fernando had a crew foreman, Mund, who everyone called "Robert Redford." He never stopped talking. As is true with most people in that part of the world, he enjoyed his booze and would pack up and leave without giving notice. I had been to his house on several occasions, and Mund's family told me that one day he went out for cigarettes and didn't come back for two years. After being gone, he simply returned as though he were only gone for a few minutes. Apparently, he had gone to live with a girlfriend in El Salvador. Fernando and I agreed that it was probably the only time his family had any peace and quiet. I had a real nice pair of cowboy boots from Arizona and Mund asked if he could try them to see if they fit. I never got them back and had to settle for his worn-out boots as an exchange.

The Contra War period provided lessons in diplomacy. Most of the workers are from Nicaragua. At that time, an American would make a weekly trip to the area to give the local Contra force leader money for his troops as payment for fighting the Sandinistas. The United States failed to realize that although there were two sides, the fighters were from the same region, naturally having mutual ties to family and friends. The paymaster would not go on patrol with the "good guys," so the guys would head to the jungle without him, sit and drink with their Sandinista friends, firing their weapons in the air to pretend they were engaged in a firefight against each other. They would then split the money. One of them told me the worst thing that happened was the war coming to an end. The U.S. government was the country's best source of revenue.

Karina joined me on two occasions during trips back and forth. The first was to come and hold my hand while I had a little "cosmetic work" around the eyes. A few acquaintances ridiculed me for my "nip and tuck," and I responded with the story about the soldier who got caught by a few of his buddies masturbating while taking a shower in the barracks. He explained: "It's my soap and my penis, and I will wash it as fast as I want." In Costa Rica, such procedures cost half what they would in the United States. Academics of Flight had another secretary from Costa Rica, Kathy, and the night after the procedure, Kathy and her husband, Paul, took Karina and me out to eat.

I believe we drove on every road in the area that had holes and ruts, which made for a painful ride due to the stitches put in that morning. The following evening, we got together again and went to a nightclub. Paul had a few too many and started to provoke the people at the next table. It started to look as though it was going to have a physical conclusion, and Paul kept telling his foe that I knew karate. I told him to shut up, that I wasn't about to tear the place up, and besides, I could hardly see because of the surgery: I wouldn't know who I was kicking. Karina had already prepared herself by grabbing a bottle of beer off the table as a weapon, and all I could think of was us having to call home to tell Rita that we were both in jail.

God was with us, the emotions settled, and we left without incident. I did get to take Karina to see a banana plantation that belonged to one of the large American companies. I thought Karina would find it interesting, but she said the main reason we went was so I could flirt with the girls. We left the next day and all in all, it was a successful trip.

On our next venture, the mission was to resolve some legal matters concerning the farm. We always have a good time traveling together, and my only complaint is the television shows Karina chooses to watch while I am trying to sleep. She engulfs herself with murder mystery programs that are quite morbid.

While on this trip, the farm lawyer and husband took us to visit a volcano that had an elevation of approximately 10,000 feet. While they were detailing the area's history, Karina and I were slowly getting hypoxia as a result of a lack of oxygen; we weren't sure that we would come down alive. Up to that point, Karina had not been to the farm but did make a solo trip approximately a year later, when an urgent matter arose. Her debriefing events of the trip were quite comical, one concerning traveling on the back roads. Apparently, her boobs got quite a workout, as the car went over every bump in the road. It was the rainy season, which made the roads almost useless.

At that time, a portion of Karina's sales territory for Telemundo/ Universal included Central America. One of her contacts was Zaida Jimenez, the program director for Televisora de Costa Rica S.A. in San Jose, the capital of Costa Rica. She is married to Bernal Vargus, a prominent lawyer, who is well known in that area. Karina and I became displeased with our current lawyer's performance in 2010 and decided to have Bernal take charge of the farm's legal matters.

Rita also made a trip with me and was impressed with the country. We visited the farm belonging to Lilliana and Jorge Paris, the family who own the house we rent in Miami. Previously, they had a house on a hilltop that overlooked all of San Jose. Unfortunately, it was destroyed during an earthquake and was never rebuilt. When walking up the hill to see the house, Rita and I would stop every few minutes to point out something interesting; we really didn't care about the item but were just trying to catch our breath. It was a long way up, and Jorge, who is our senior by at least 20 years, was like the energizer bunny: he just kept "ticking," not slowing down once as we ascended. We also visited Kathy's father's ranch, and it was absolutely beautiful. Don Jose, a real gentleman, raised prize bulls, and I heard later that the ranch was sold.

I have been growing trees for the past 10–15 years and in 2011 returned from a short visit and meeting with Bernal and the farm manager, Hugo. Hugo has been running the everyday chores for the past 10 years, and he has proven to be very prudent. It was agreed that since there had been two tree cuttings with the next and last due within a two-year period, we would restock with cattle. Although I am sure there will be problems, it is better than immediately replanting trees; the land needs a few years to recuperate.

In 2012, the future of the farm was still uncertain. When I was in my mid-forties, I felt by the time I was 60, I would enjoy retiring and sitting on the front porch watching the cows. However, although the farm is located in a beautiful area, I am presently 68 and have no intention of packing my bags to live in Costa Rica. Maybe in a few more years!

The Next Generation

I believe that it's difficult for parents to pay tribute to their children as they watch them grow and meet life's challenges. When a child is on the way, people often ask, "Do you want a boy or girl?" I think that's such a shallow question. Although blessed with a daughter, I think gender is unimportant. After many years as a father, I would like to include a prayer that General Douglas E. MacArthur wrote as a spiritual legacy to his son Arthur during the early days of World War II, which was made public after MacArthur's death in 1964. I want Karina to know that in my eyes, she has met every one of MacArthur's wishes.

> *Build me a son, O Lord, who will be strong enough to know when he is weak, and brave enough to face himself when he is afraid: one who will be proud and unbending in honest defeat, humble and gentle in victory. Build me a son whose wishes will not take the place of deeds; a son who will know Thee—and that to know himself is the foundation stone of knowledge. Lead him, I pray, not in the path of ease and comfort, but under the stress and spur of difficulties and challenge. Here let him learn to stand up in the storm; let him learn compassion for those who fail. Build me a son whose heart will be clear, whose goal will be high; a son who will master himself before he seeks to master other men; one who will reach into the future, yet never forget his past. And after all these things are his, add, I pray, enough of a sense of humor so that he may always be serious yet never take himself too seriously. Give him humility, so that he may always remember the simplicity of true greatness, the open mind of true wisdom, and the meekness of true strength. Then I, his father, will dare to whisper, "I have not lived in vain."*

I once saw a bumper sticker that read "Be nice to your children, for they choose your old age home." It made me aware of how nice I should be to Karina.

On July 14, 2007, the day that many fathers live for became a reality; Karina married Andres Castano from Colombia, South America. The wedding was an unbelievable event, and of course, Karina and Rita went all out with the ceremony taking place at St. Patrick's Catholic Church in Miami Beach. The reception was at the Four Seasons Hotel in Miami.

Shortly thereafter, Karina was offered an executive position with NBC in Madrid, and being a true "Etchison," the bags were packed and off they went, residing in the beautiful area known as Salamanca. Although I have only been there twice, the first for Chloe's birth, and the second to celebrate Christmas, Rita seemed to find several reasons for Madrid-bound flights. While she spent time becoming acquainted with the museums and other points of cultural locations, my main interest was the local hobby shops. Karina treated me to business class on my flight with an Iberia Airbus A340. Although I had walked around this type of airplane countless times when instructing in Trinidad for Caribbean Airlines, I never realized how large it was inside. It was a great flight from JFK, and I entertained myself almost the entire seven flying hours trying to figure out how the seat worked with all the buttons. It was very frustrating because a single button would send my leg one way, while another would put me in a horizontal position. I am sure I provided amusement to the flight attendants, as they observed this "pilot" who couldn't figure out the mechanics of a seat.

Two years later, almost to the day of Chloe's birth, November 21, 2009, Olivia entered the world on November 24, 2011. Of course, Rita *had* to travel to Madrid at the beginning of November to "get things ready." I remained in New York to instruct, but e-mails sent that night kept me updated. I left New York on December 20, 2011, to join them for Christmas and meet the new family member. Chloe has now passed her second birthday and recognized me as "papa" throughout my stay. She picked up the habit of moving her eyes from Rita, which illustrates Chloe's awareness at such a young age. I never noticed this characteristic in 40 years of knowing Rita. I was proud of Karina's ability to multitask between the two girls and just as impressed with Rita's never-ending energy in keeping the show on track. In addition to all her domestic endeavors, Rita learned Madrid as though it was the back of her hand; she even knew which ATMs throughout the neighborhood gave the best exchange rates.

More than once, Karina has come to me concerning her fear of not being loved by her children due to her obligation to discipline them when necessary. I came across the following letter concerning this subject that I once read in a philosophy class:

> *The river is limited and confined by its banks but these same banks permit it to move onward freely to the sea. Without its bank's the river would collapse into a swamp: Only through limitations, can it reach its goal. Man, similarly, needs limitations and discipline before he can find direction.*
>
> —Undated Letter

In addition to the immediate family, Karina had several other family members as guests.

Madrid is a very clean and beautiful city. They left Madrid in the summer of 2012, bound for Miami, Florida. Spain's labor laws allow a non-citizen to work in the country for a maximum of 4 years. Karina's time was up; therefore, she had to leave and work from the company's Miami office.

PART TWO

You can give a man a fish and he can feed his family for a day, or you can teach a man how to fish and he can feed his family forever.

—Proverb; origin unknown

By listening, one will learn truths.
By hearing, one will only learn half truths.

—Proverb; origin unknown

11

ACADEMICS OF FLIGHT IS BORN

THE BEGINNING

I guess there was no escaping my fate to fly. Although I never really had a passion for it like my father, it was meant to be my destiny. Even though I enjoyed my time as a banker and claims adjuster, I returned to aviation.

The day I decided to create Academics of Flight is as clear as if it were yesterday. While we were in the kitchen, I told Rita that I was going to start a school. I was tired of being at the mercy of a company, and I wanted to control my own trials and tribulations through life. The power in the apartment lights had been shut off for nonpayment of the electric bill, and we were living solely off Rita's salary. Karina was approximately six months old, and the family was literally living from day to day. I told Rita in no way would I blame her if she divorced me, knowing that starting a business from the ground up would be a monumental task consuming my time, day and night.

However, I did ask her for a $35 loan to acquire a business certificate before she left. She didn't leave, and she lent me the money, and on March 22, 1976, Academics of Flight became a reality. At that time, I didn't realize how it would influence the lives of so many people around the world. The name was selected with the help of our friends Ray and Felicia Calasabetta. Our intention was that it might appear as the first listing in the yellow pages, the main source of advertising during that period. Ray also considered becoming a partner; however, being employed with Pan Am maintenance, he rightfully declined. Felicia was the school's primary secretary for the next 14 years.

With everyone's help and cooperation, the school's first location was the apartment. Students would appear for individual instruction, which I would attempt to schedule while Rita was working. Felicia would temporarily convert the dining room table into an office desk, and we were off and running. The only person resisting the operation was Esther, not out of spitefulness but for her love for Karina. Esther was the mother of Rita's friend, Gloria, and Rita made arrangements for Esther to be Karina's nanny. Over the years, she became part of our extended family. When the phone rang for business, she would start making unnecessary noise in the kitchen, banging pots and pans, making it difficult to concentrate on the call. Esther also couldn't understand why Felicia had to use the noisy old typewriter that was the only office equipment we owned. I couldn't convince her all this was necessary to make a living.

Felicia took control of the school's operations, especially the accounting. Everyone was instructed not to touch her books when she would be gone for a few days. When we were having a disagreement, she once told me "If you don't like it, *you* can leave!" She came from Catania, Italy, approximately 20 years prior, but spoke as though she had just arrived. Felicia was a cornerstone, and the school hated to see her leave after all those years.

Karina's love for Esther had no bounds, and on Esther's passing, Karina wrote her feelings in a letter to Gloria; the following are excerpts:

> *I, as well, am extremely sad at the passing of Abuelita and finding it a difficult time . . . I consider myself very lucky to have had Abuelita in my life and always felt her as a mom and true grandmother. Most of all, she was the person that had the most influence on me as I came into this world.*
>
> *When I was little, I have so many stories that I could sit here for days and write, but I can say, I never met someone so dedicated to her family . . . Even though I wasn't blood-related, there was never a moment I didn't feel her love.*
>
> *As I got older I remember loving the weekends when she would sleep over. Although I was getting bigger, we would sleep on a*

twin-size bed. I would tell her she was sleeping and to put her magazine away and she would insist that she was still reading.

Like I said, I could go on for days with her stories. Her love for tango, tequila, and Fernet Branca. I had a speech class in St. Johns that I hated. After lunch before class she would give a tiny shot of tequila or Fernet Branca and say, "Che no pasa nada!"

Needless to say, I received an A in that class . . . I loved her yesterday, today, and forever. We are very blessed to have taken part in her life, but I know she is watching over us and will always watch over us . . .

Out of the Apartment

After a few months of trying to keep everybody happy, I found an office space a few blocks from the apartment that was rented by an automobile insurance club on 43rd Street in Sunnyside, Queens. The owner was willing to share a portion of the area on certain days, and due to a lack of business for the insurance company, within a year the school took over the lease.

Nina Claremont was an English woman who owned her own airplane tied down at Republic Airport on Long Island. Nina could write a book on her flight adventures, and I am sure it would be a best seller. She was a radar specialist during WWII who emigrated to the United States. Nina, who was maybe five foot two, had to fly sitting on a phone book to see over the instrument panel and had the rudder pedals extended so she could reach them. She would think nothing of taking her plane across the United States plus Nassau and the Bahamas at the drop of a hat; she was truly a "free spirit."

She was very active in the aviation community and held a position with the Wings Club located at the Roosevelt Hotel in midtown Manhattan. The club was very prestigious, with several CEOs of the major airlines as members. Nina arranged for Academics of Flight to teach a private pilot session at the club, and on May 3, 1976, Academics of Flight conducted its first formal ground school class.

The group comprised approximately seven or eight students; only a few paid.

A few of the people present were Rita; Enoris, her friend; Mac Elliot, her boss; and Wava, another friend of hers, plus a few others. I think the only ones taking the class seriously were Mac and the others. I still remember holding the first check for the class in my hand, and it was an encouraging moment. At one point during the lecture, I intercepted a note written to Rita from Enoris; it read, "Jim is getting fat!" This illustrated the effectiveness of my ability to keep them focused on the lecture topic.

I had a conversation with a prospective student not long before or after intercepting the note. Rita and I had gone to Arizona on a visit, where I purchased a very nice set of cowboy boots that I wore daily after returning to New York. I was sitting at my desk with my feet up, showing off my prized footwear, and during our talk, the person asked if I was from Texas. "No," I replied. "Are you asking because of my boots?" I was elated at the question, thinking he was impressed with my Western attire. "No," he answered. "Because of your big belly!"

For the first couple of years, Academics of Flight concentrated strictly on ground training, leaving the flight portion to established schools around the area. At that time, there were no computer-based training programs, online courses, and so on. If people wanted to learn, they had to do it the old-fashioned way by going to a class with a teacher. Academics of Flight was finally beginning to stand on its own two feet, and I even offered to pay Rita back the loan for the business certificate, but she refused.

Citibank was not as generous when I requested a loan to buy a tabletop simulator, which was needed to expand training. I went to the bank early in the morning to speak with a loan officer about a loan of $6,000. He gave all reasons why the bank couldn't comply, and I replied with reasons why the bank should. I told him I wasn't going to leave until the request was approved, and I sat in the waiting area all day; every once and a while he would walk by to see if I was still there. Finally, at closing time, he came to me with the approval, shaking his head. He said if I ran the business with the determination as I had demonstrated in asking for the loan, he was sure I wouldn't default. I walked out with the money, and the bank was paid back in full.

Most flight schools had their investment solely in airplanes; therefore, their efforts went toward keeping the planes in the air, having little interest in conducting ground school. I made a joint venture with Cliff Rice, owner of a flight school next to LaGuardia Airport. His school finally closed due to continual runway flooding and conflicting traffic between his students and airliners flying in and out of LaGuardia. Cliff was a rough speaker, but a good guy, and we continued to do business when he moved his operation to Suffolk County Airport on Long Island.

The Drug Trade

With the office adjacent to Roosevelt Ave, Jackson Heights, it was guaranteed sooner or later the school would be requested to get involved in "transporting." At that time, Jackson Heights was well known as one of the main distribution points for the Colombian cartels. Surprisingly, in all the years in that location, I was only approached about drug running once or twice. I am sure a few of our graduates chose drug running instead of becoming airline pilots. One day, a man approximately my age came for some simulator instrument training. It was obvious that although somewhat confused about a few techniques, he had flown before. He liked to be called "Negro" and was the type that you couldn't help but like immediately. After a few sessions, I was introduced to his girlfriend and was invited out for dinner and drinks one evening.

Negro had a farm in Colombia where he raised horses and grew what one might call "cash crops." He put so much trust in me that he played a video of the property showing the horses, family, and the *plants*. This type of exposure is rare except among very close friends and family; I was honored. Negro had a Cessna 402 and a *plan*.

His plane was based in Miami, and we would fly to his farm somewhere in Colombia, load it with *cargo*, and then fly to a small dirt strip in Mexico. The field would be protected by the Mexican military as we off-loaded, conducting a high-speed taxi, and then back in the air. From there, we were to go to Bermuda, disconnect the fuel line to make it appear as if there was a maintenance problem, and take Eastern Airlines back to New York. The payment was to be $75,000 up front and another $75,000 when I got back to New York.

Although the compensation was great, I was more interested in the excitement and was to give him my answer in a few days. Many of Pan Am's initial pilots were "rum runners" between the United States and Canada during prohibition, and I felt it was more or less the same, just a different time and product. Also, during the Contra War, our own government turned their backs on drugs entering the United States, as long as the dealers diverted funds from their profit to arm the Contras, since the United States officially stopped funding the war.

I toiled and toiled with the offer and finally decided not to go in fearing that once I started, I'd be unable to get out. My biggest concerns were Karina and Rita. It was not uncommon for the cartel to execute family members. I never got to see Negro again to give him my answer. At that time, the George H. W. Bush administration went all out with the aid of Colombian officials to eradicate the drug problem. Although I hope it was not the case, I believe Negro's operation was targeted. I guess I have Karina and Rita to thank. Nevertheless, I do wish I had done it at least one time.

The Goodfellas

When people think of the "mob," metropolitan New York is always their first association due to John Gotti and his social clubs. The area around Academics of Flight certainly had its group; they were always great to me and very respectful to my family. Of course, I reciprocated and allowed them to use one of the classrooms.

"Jimmy" ran the Merry-Go-Round, a strip club around the corner from the school, and he was the one you went to if you had serious business such as wanting someone to disappear or permanently injured. He had a price list for services that included everything from complete disappearance to broken arms, legs, and so forth. I asked him if there was a discount for more than one item disassembled during one visit, and his answer was "We can work it out!" Frankie, with his ghetto blaster always nearby playing Frank Sinatra songs, was the loan shark. Harry was the loan collector, and Mike was the runner for the other *company* executives. They added color to the neighborhood, especially during hot weather, sitting in lawn chairs in front of the Merry-Go-Round with their big cigars and gold chains.

In 2012, I was still having coffee with Harry, a member of the group, at the local doughnut shop once in a while and would still see Mike running to and from God knows where. Harry always complains that he can't hit a winner at the track and misses the "good old days." Everything sort of disappeared after Jimmy had a heart attack and died in prison, where he was serving time for murder. It was said that he took the blame for someone higher up in the organization.

The boys assisted me with several problems. The first involved the mob's control over garbage collection in the city. For years, I would take it home two nights a week and combine the pickup with that of the house. One day, someone came to the school and asked how I disposed of the trash. After explaining the procedure, he stated it was not the correct method and the school needed a "sticker" on the door. With this sticker, for $30 a month, his organization would collect the garbage. I asked him what would happen if I didn't become a member of his "sticker club." He changed the subject immediately, which told me it would be advisable to join the club. When I told Jimmy about this unnecessary expense, he placed his hand on my shoulder and told me not to give it a second thought. From then on, I lost my membership and took the garbage home as I had done in the past. Jimmy was angry that I had not told him sooner.

The other assistance had to do with one of the secretaries from the "old country," Rosemary. She was middle-aged, high-strung, and a pain in the ass. I hired her to give FAA examinations that at that time were administered on paper. About a year later, the FAA upgraded to computer-based exams, and everyone had to go to an FAA class to learn the new procedure. A test was given after the seminar, and if you failed twice, you could not perform this function. Rosemary failed twice, I fired her, and she took the school to labor court.

Rosemary won, as I did not give her a job description of her duties in *writing* when she was hired. It was a lesson learned. Since I had to pay her unemployment, it was costing the school money in unemployment tax. Rosemary lived by the school in Jimmy's "district," and I gave him her telephone number. I never heard from her again. She apparently *volunteered* to stop collecting unemployment.

Jimmy assisted many other people in the area as well. A woman had her apartment broken into and jewelry stolen. Jimmy somehow located the missing items, and they were returned within a few days of the crime; he was much more effective than the local police.

In Karina's eyes, the boys were made up of Frankie and Jimmy, and I'd imagine there was a Vinnie somewhere in the mix. They would greet me every afternoon as I got off the Flushing line, sitting on their milk crates listening to Frank Sinatra and smoking cigars. Their attire was straight out of a mob film; 1970s tracksuits, tinted sunglasses, and slicked back hair with sideburns. Karina described an exchange she had with the boys:

> *Hey kiddo, your dad's upstairs . . . Ask your old man if we can borrow the back room for a poker game . . . kid, who's the gentleman you were talking to?*

Years later, I was describing to a middle-aged Italian student how the mob controlled the school's neighborhood during the late 1970s and 1980s and that I missed interacting with them. As I mentioned, they were great to me and very respectful to my family. The woman I was reminiscing with was from Staten Island, a favored residential area for several crime families and their associates. Her first comment was, "Oh, you mean the gang that couldn't shoot straight." She further told me that many of their methods have changed over time and that they get fewer calls for "eliminations." For example, everybody knows that in the past, if a husband wanted to get rid of his wife, he would usually make a telephone call. Nowadays, he gives her three items: first, a big SUV since chances are she can't drive it safely; second, a cellphone because she will be talking on it while driving and not paying attention to the road; and third, a credit card to get her out on the road to shop. This triple combination appears to have proven fatal many times over.

I can't discuss the Merry-Go-Round without describing an episode involving a girl. I didn't know who was more embarrassed, the girl or myself. I had finished teaching a private pilot class one evening that had six or seven students, one being a very shapely young lady who would sit in the front row. My initial contact with Pakistan

International Airlines was through a senior captain, Captain Afaq Rizvi, who was staying with me as a houseguest at that time since PIA was a client. He was observing the class, and after completing post-class paperwork, we both agreed that it would be a good idea to end the evening with a nightcap at the Merry-Go-Round to watch the girls expose their wares dancing to the current songs of the time. After entering, and not yet placing my attention on the stage's activity, I heard a loud, "Oh no, I knew this would happen." There she was, my future pilot from the front row of class. I said, "I always wondered what you really look like, and I am certainly not disappointed." The student/dancer graduated with high honors.

For many years, the Irish Republican Army has had a strong foothold in the neighborhood. Several Irish local students learned to fly with the hopes of returning to their country to take up the cause as gunrunners. The Irish presence is felt the most on St. Patrick's Day; the local pubs are overflowing with business by 10:00 a.m.

Ground to Flight

> *For once you have tasted flight you will walk the earth with your eyes turned skywards, for there you have been, and therefore long to return.*
>
> —Leonardo Da Vinci

I never wanted to own an airplane due to a common belief that "The best two days of your life are the day you buy an airplane, and the day you sell it!" Over the years, Academics of Flight owned seven. With the school's Pakistan International Airline contacts, several of the captains requested that I train their sons for the commercial pilot certificate. The more I said, "No," the more they said, "Yes." The pilots won, and the sons started arriving. Cliff Rice had moved his operations to Suffolk County Airport, on Long Island. The airport was originally a military base, and he converted the barracks into student housing. The plan was to do the ground training in Queens and then send the students to Cliff in Suffolk for flight training. During the ground portion of the program, several students had local relatives with whom they stayed. Rita and I would find housing for the others in need. One of our neighbors converted their basement into an apartment, and we mainly housed the students there.

Rita and I became the adoptive parents for the future pilots, with Karina as a sister, and to have them in class was the easy part. When they ventured to Manhattan after class was when the challenges began. For many of them, this was their first taste of independence from their parents, of which they took full advantage. This kept us on our toes 24/7. They knew Rita was not as strict as me and would come across the street when they knew I wasn't home. She was to speak on their behalf as to items they felt were a necessity: a car, an increase in their allowance, and so on. The parents had absolute trust in me, and the following is an excerpt from a letter from one of their fathers dated 1980:

> *In Karachi if you have stay with someone else I shall mind it. You are my brother and it would be to my greatest pleasure to serve you and your wife all through my life as you have changed our fortunes. You know well that—is our only son and you have yet to play a great role in guiding him and making a man out of him. He is just like your own son and we have entrusted him to you. Even if you beat him to blue black or kill him we shall not ask you for the same but we wish him to turn out to be a man of honor and dignity and must achieve a name in flying. Now there is no difference between us. I am a Pathan and man of words about whom you may have read in the books also. We die but the friendship and brotherhood continues for generations.*

I didn't beat or kill him, and he is now a captain flying for Pakistan International Airlines.

Cliff passed away during the students' flight training at Suffolk, but there was a rumor he was, in fact, still alive. The airport is situated at the eastern end of Long Island, an ideal location for bringing drugs into the country. Some believed Cliff was an informant for the Feds. Apparently, he was rushed to the hospital with pneumonia, died there, and had a closed casket during his funeral. After he left for the hospital, no one actually saw him again.

I attended a "flyby" using the training aircraft that the boys performed in honor of Cliff, which illustrated their respect for him. He was a very militant individual, and I have no doubts that the story has merit. This is especially true since a few years later, Rita and I were in a Florida supermarket, and I stopped short due to seeing a man shopping who looked exactly like Cliff. While he was running the flight operation, the planes were flying so frequently that a representative of Piper Aircraft (the manufacturer) paid a visit to record his modus operandi.

After Cliff "departed," one way or another, the flight training was relocated to Caldwell (now Essex County) Airport, in Fairfield, New Jersey. The location was adequate for local flight students; however, it was not suitable for the foreign group that required housing at a cost comparable to flight schools in Texas and Oklahoma. Therefore, Carolina Air Academy was created in North Carolina.

Academics of Flight purchased a beautiful four-seat Piper Warrior that everyone wanted to fly from the moment it went on the flight line at Caldwell. It didn't last very long. The plane had flown only for a few days when I received a call from a scheduled student informing me that he was at the airport for instruction, but the airplane wasn't there. I told him that no one was on the schedule before him and that he should wait a while, as I was sure it would show up. It was common for an instructor to go on a flight and complete scheduling paperwork after the lesson instead of prior to the flight as requested.

The plane never returned to Caldwell. I called the FBI, and they assured me they'd do all they could to find it. I would get the same response when I'd call every few days. A month went by. I then received a tie-down bill for the plane at an airport no more than 10 miles from Caldwell Airport and raised mortal hell with the FBI concerning their efficiency. The airport where it was tied down also got a taste of my frustration for taking so long to inform me that the plane was at their location. By then it was a closed case, the insurance company had the plane and sent me a check, with no one arrested for the crime. A few weeks later, Felicia showed me a bill from Republic Airport, for a landing fee a day before the student first called concerning the missing plane. I remembered that one of our instructors had mentioned that he was going to take a flight check with the FAA at Republic to upgrade his instructor certificate.

I checked and confirmed with the FAA that on the first day the aircraft was missing, the instructor had gone to them for a check ride. I informed the FBI, and at that time, the instructor had gone to Oklahoma City to attend the FAA Academy to become an air traffic controller. They questioned him but couldn't prove that he hadn't taken the plane back to Caldwell after his check ride with the FAA. He claimed the tower was closed before he landed, which may have been true as it closes each night. He said that the plane must have been stolen after he landed.

The FBI bought his story, but I did not. I knew that to fly in that area's airspace, he would have had to be in contact with ATC. These transmissions are recorded, along with flight paths. Through a friend in ATC, I got a copy of the transmissions for that particular day and listened to them for hours until I heard the plane's call sign and the conversation between the controllers and the pilot. It was clear the instructor did not return to Caldwell but to the field where the plane was found. After reporting the findings to the FBI, they went back to Oklahoma City and arrested the instructor. I was never informed of his trial date but felt that by terminating his aviation career through his actions, he paid the price for his stupidity.

On July 17, 1996, TWA Flight 800 fell out of the sky from 13,500 feet off Long Island's south shore shortly after takeoff from JFK on climb out. To this day, there is a dispute as to the cause, much like the Arrow Air Flight 1285 disaster. Two hundred thirty people were killed when the TWA B-747-131 disappeared into the waters of the Atlantic Ocean; some say it was an electrical discharge in a fuel tank, while others say it was a missile strike by our own military. An article concerning the accident reported it as follows:

> *The government of the United States, despite the embarrassment of having been caught in court rigging lab tests and lying in its reports, still officially attributes the disaster to a spark in the center fuel tank, while government people insist that the witnesses who said a missile hit the jumbo jet are all drunks.*

I was engrossed in an office project, and although Karina told me that I had a phone call, my mind was elsewhere. After her third request for me to pick up the phone, informing me that it was the FBI, I answered and was greeted with, "Hello, Mr. Etchison, this is Agent Jones from the FBI. Do you own an airplane, N32559?" I knew damn well that he was aware I did, and all I could think was, "What's in store for me now?" Apparently, N32559 was picked up on radar as to being in close proximity to TWA Flight 800 when it went down, and they wanted to interview the pilot, a guy named Jim from Spain. Jim claims he saw the whole incident and was visibly shaken by the occurrence when he realized what he was watching. We never heard from the Feds again after they spoke to Jim.

That was not the first time I received a call from the FBI requesting a meeting. I was awoken one morning around 7:00 a.m. requesting a "get-together" in my office later that day. It concerned an old New York State license plate set from one of our cars, which I had thrown away when I exchanged them for North Carolina plates. Anytime New York State plates are no longer used, they are to be returned to the Department of Motor Vehicles. That, of course, I didn't do since the garbage can was a lot closer. Throughout the meeting, I swore I surrendered the plates in the proper way but finally confessed to my sin. The plates apparently wound up on a car driven by someone who attempted to assassinate a diplomat in front of the United Nations building in New York. The FBI had traced the plate number to our car, but since the shooter's vehicle was a different make and model, they realized the plates were the only evidence that connected me to the diplomat's problem. It was my turn to call the Feds several years after 9/11, concerning a prospective student from a country in the Middle East who was applying to the school. The paperwork received from the person didn't seem proper; I had a sixth sense. I must have been correct since I received a cash "gift" from the government and was given a code name for future communications.

Regarding 9/11, at that time, Academics of Flight had been deeply involved in training pilots from Saudi Arabia and aircraft dispatcher students from Kuwait. After the attack, the school seemed to be a collection point for the FBI, resulting in my day being totally consumed by meetings with them. I once had seven agents in my office at one time. They were going through the student list, and one commented, "Holy shit, these are all Arabs!" Apparently, the main hijacker, Atta, had called the school several times but only left a message on our answering machine; it was enough to require many question–answer sessions. The dust settled after a few months, and I was able to return to a normal routine. It was absolutely amazing how uncoordinated the FBI was in their investigation. They were "stepping on each other's toes" and seemed not to have a clue as to how to proceed in an efficient manner.

Actually, the FBI and I developed a relationship many years prior to 9/11 when I was around 12 years old. I had been sent to summer camp at Camp Greenkill in Huguenot, New York. It was great, with all the activities that a camp is expected to offer. The occupants of our cabin, approximately eight, had an overnight hike when we camped in the woods. It was located close to railroad tracks, and prior to turning in, a freight train happened to pass. What are 12-year-olds supposed to do in such a situation? Of course, throw rocks at it. We did, and the next morning, a gentleman with a badge visited the camp and had a long conversation with our counselor. He didn't tell us much except that the man was from the railroad and took our names. Years later, I applied for employment with the FBI and the fact that I had thrown rocks at a freight train when I was 12 years old came up during their background investigation.

After approximately 25 years of providing worldwide flight training, I sold the flight portion of the school to Bill Thomas, the school's second in command. Bill's operation did not endure; therefore, N32559 was returned. I did not jump for joy, since I had already distanced myself from providing flight training at the private, commercial level and was heavily involved in our new Miami branch. I also began teaching in Panama and Trinidad several times a year. It was the same scenario as when you receive a gift that you have absolutely no use for but that is going to cost money and will not go away. After the plane was returned, I had one of the flight instructors, Marina, ferry it to Miami. Prior to her departure, she called to advise that the brakes were not working but that she would fly it anyway, with the hopes they would not have to be used. My life was coming around full circle.

After a period in Florida, with N32559 pretty much doing nothing, I received a call from one of the pilots flying for AirNet. AirNet is a company based in Columbus, Ohio, that flies bank checks around the country. The pilot planned to start a flying club for the company and wanted to lease N32559. Financial arrangements were negotiated, and the plane headed north to Ohio. The club got off to a good start, and for approximately six months thereafter, the plane made a profit. Then came the phone call, "Mr. Etchison, do you want to sell your airplane that's in the field?" "Field" is often used to replace the word "airport," so I asked at which airport the plane currently was located. "Mr. Etchison. The plane is in a farmer's field, not an airport. It made an emergency landing there approximately three weeks ago." The old days returned in a flash.

One of the club members, with three passengers aboard, apparently decided to fly to LaGuardia Airport in New York. En route, the engine seized due to a lack of oil. Luckily, the pilot was able to bring it down without any further damage or injuries to the passengers. When I asked the club president why I had not been informed of the occurrence, he claimed to have had a mental breakdown and that the situation was too much for him; this is a Learjet pilot.

The FAA conducted an investigation, and the pilot received a violation for not doing a preflight check when it would have been found that the oil level was low, making the plane ineligible to fly passengers. In order to fly with passengers, a pilot has to make three takeoffs and landings within a 90-day period, which he had not done. In addition, there was no way in hell he could have been headed for LaGuardia because the airport would not have allowed the landing of a small training airplane such as N32559 unless it was an emergency. I asked my longtime friend, Phil Segal, a lawyer who is also a former judge in The Bronx, to assist in suing all parties involved. He did; we went to Ohio to file and won against all three. One party settled out of court. Of course, winning means nothing without collecting, and we still have not collected from the pilot. One day, he will have his guard down, and I will be there. The plane was eventually disassembled, removed from Farmer Brown's field, and sold. N32559 was like a yo-yo; every time I thought I'd gotten rid of it, the plane would come back. But not this time.

The Academics of Flight Staff

The Academics of Flight staff is as diversified as the students, and not until I started writing, did I realize how many different countries they represent. I am sure I will miss one or two, but the following list will give the reader an idea as to how Academics of Flight depended upon international teamwork to survive. To name a few:

Office Staff	*Country of Origin*
Felicia	Italy
Norma Denise, Rhoda	Puerto Rico
Fabiola	Haiti
Gladis	El Salvador
Ana Marie	Colombia
Carol, Alba, Kathy	Costa Rica
Nubia	Honduras
Cynthia	Venezuela
Nadia	Morocco
Rosie	Dominican Republic
Mila	Russia
Tariq	Pakistan
Irene Liao	Taiwan
Karina, Bil	USA

Instructors	*Country of Origin*
David	Russia
Marina	Bulgaria
Shawfak	Turkey
Frank	Greece
Rod, Frank	Dominican Republic
Vlada	Yugoslavia
Alex	Ecuador
Aymee	Cuba
Irene Liao	Taiwan

The surnames are omitted intentionally because I cannot remember many of them, and even if I did, there is a good chance the majority would be misspelled. The list does not include those who assisted with the Florida location, which existed for approximately 15 years. They were as representative of different countries as the New York group. The school employees (I prefer the term "co-workers") were great, and they contributed to Academics of Flight's longevity, even though many may have left years ago. When I encounter past students, inevitably a previous school staff member's name is mentioned. I could not be completely honest without saying that in every barrel of apples, a few bad ones will surface. Some of the bad spots included stealing the company's airplane, teaching students on the side for personal financial gain not school revenue, and stealing money, cash, and checks from the school. For the years of ongoing operations, it is understandable that there will be a few rough bumps along the way, as with any company. Academics of Flight is no exception.

Karina matured around her assigned duties at the school and was a strong pillar in the workforce. After finishing high school classes, she would come to Academics of Flight to work and never let anyone treat her as "the boss's daughter." I did have a problem one day due to workload pressure. Instead of diplomatically handling a situation where she was talking on the phone to excess, as any high school pupil does, I fired her. When I got home that night, Rita barred me from entering the house until Karina was rehired. Rita also threatened me with no more amenities bestowed upon a husband. Having no choice, I rehired Karina and was rewarded by Karina sticking her tongue out at me when I passed her bedroom that night as if to say, "I am the *boss's wife's* daughter."

One afternoon, a girl from Bulgaria in a waitressing uniform came in and simply said, "I want to learn to fly." I tried to discourage her, but as life will have it, she eventually turned out to be the school's chief instructor for several years. Marina, while still a student, was going through simulator training one day with another student practicing a navigation session. I was called away to the telephone, and they did not see me return. In my absence, she took command of the simulator session on her own initiative, explaining the procedure in a very impressive manner. I offered her the opportunity to teach certain subjects and eventually conduct a full program.

Marina is a born teacher, and I depended on her to instruct in Ohio, Pennsylvania, and Florida, in addition to the New York classes. As was true of others, Marina left to become a captain with an airline that flew around New England during the summer, transferring to the Caribbean Islands for the winter. We still stay in touch, and she is the proud mother of two (Megan and Nicholas) and married to a pilot, Chris, who conducts a flight school at Republic Airport on Long Island. The history of Academics of Flight will always be indebted to her contributions. In 2012, she became an FAA-designated flight examiner, and I couldn't be prouder.

Nadia, from Morocco, was another student who joined Academics of Flight without a clue as to the aviation environment. However, step by step, she became familiar with the technical aspects and received her FAA aircraft dispatcher certificate. Nadia was also extremely computer literate, along with being highly patient. Because of these skills, she was hired by the school as an instructor for the aircraft dispatcher program and developed computer-based course material.

At the end of the 1980s, when Nadia was working with the school, I was spending a good deal of my time driving back and forth from Queens to Sterling, Massachusetts. I would drive the airline pilot candidate to Sterling to work with Dick Backu for training and a flight check once I had completed the ground portion of the program. At that time, the course was extremely popular with foreign pilots. As a result, I was always on the road between both locations and never spent much time in the office. Nadia liked to drive, and after taking her on one trip, she took over the majority of these ventures.

Returning from one trip, she handed me a summons for driving 80 mph in a 60 mph zone. Her explanation for the ticket was that it was a hot summer day and that the passenger was riding in the front seat, with his arm draped over the back of her seat. Apparently, he had not bathed for several days prior to their journey resulting in a bad odor throughout the car. Nadia's only solution was to open the windows and travel at a speed that would air out the car. Unfortunately, the highway patrol officer felt that her solution was outside the tolerance of Connecticut's speed-limit laws, and hence, she was rendered a traffic ticket. Nadia relayed this story to me with a straight face.

I am fascinated with Cuban history. In 2011, I instructed a young woman from Havana, Cuba, Aymee Armenteros, who was employed by Cubaña Air, Cuba's international carrier. We spent more time discussing her home country than we did on course subjects. It is absolutely incredible how the Cuban locals can make a living with such low salaries and the continual rationing of basic goods, things we take for granted. Aymee has become a school instructor since graduation, and she has gained a tremendous amount of respect from everyone with whom she has had contact, both students and FAA inspectors alike.

When I introduce some of my staff to Rita, I have to laugh when she says, "Where do you find these people?" I purposely recruit secretaries from fast-food restaurants such as McDonald's or Roy Rogers because they have been trained to interact with people and to handle cash. I don't make a habit of patronizing these establishments; I do so only when necessary. I am amazed how the cashiers patiently take orders that change several times before being finalized, especially when the customers are ordering for their friends via cell phone.

One of the women I was impressed with was Gladis Gomes from El Salvador, who came to the United States when she was a teenager to live with her mother in Los Angeles, California. The family was brought up in a rough neighborhood where drive-by shootings were common. The area was controlled by two Mexican (Chicano) gangs that were always dressed in their representative colors, the "w/s 18" and "Venice 13." She relocated to New York and began working at Roy Rogers. Karina and I used to eat breakfast there, and soon after, I asked Gladis to work for us part-time, after observing her positive relations with customers.

I was unaware at that time that she had a baseball accident while playing in Los Angeles. Although it was not severe enough to bleed, it did form a blood clot in her brain. There were no indications until approximately 10 years later when she began to experience blackout periods that interfered with a normal life, such as driving. Several of these occurred at AOF, but since they were short in duration, there was no danger. I learned the symptoms and would simply hold her head upright while she was sitting until it was over. Once when I was interviewing someone, I saw it coming, casually walked over, and held her by the back of her blouse while she was sitting at the reception desk. She went through her routine without the people even knowing. After many years of the physicians simply giving her pills as a cure-all, one doctor took interest, and after a seven-hour operation, Gladis came out smelling like a rose. She is living a normal life, back to driving and holding a regular job without any symptoms of blackouts.

I mention Gladis due to her loyalty toward the school, which she displayed famously. A few untrustworthy co-workers appeared over the years, and I had one in my office for a "showdown" that resulted from ongoing instances of missing cash. Gladis came into the meeting, and the girl tried to have her confirm that she was not the thief. Gladis turned to the accused and said, "You know what you have been doing." The girl confessed and was discharged. The incident shook our family, since Rita and I had financed her last semester in Catholic high school.

When Karina had surgery, she spent the night with her in the hospital as a sister. I never blamed the employee directly, since I felt she was following her aunt's instructions on how to embezzle. I always expected her to approach me years later to apologize. To date, this hasn't happened; however, I learned a legal procedure from the incident.

When it was confirmed that she stole the money, I called the police to arrest her for larceny. Prior to being picked up by the police, her lawyer came by the office. He did not deny what she had done, and he told me he would give me a certain amount of cash immediately, and the rest would be paid in installments. I agreed, but with the stipulation that she would have to go on some type of program that would teach her the seriousness of her actions.

I felt if it were Academics of Flight now, who would be next? Future crimes could result in years of prison time for the girl. The lawyer promised and when he did not follow his word, I called again to have her arrested. Here's the lesson: since I had agreed on a solution with her lawyer, it was no longer considered a criminal offense but a civil case, and I could not have her locked up until she was convicted in court. I had never taken her to court. Things you learn in life.

In late 2011, I received a call from a young woman, Irene, inquiring about the private pilot program. Academics of Flight had more or less discontinued this course after the school opened its Miami branch. I always attempted to terminate these conversations as quickly as possible by telling the caller they should call another school. For some reason, this particular conversation with Irene went on and on. When I informed the young woman of the cost, she said she would have to ask "Daddy" for the money. Of course, I thought immediately of Karina when she used to ask me for favors which led to loan requests. The monetary amount would increase proportionately according to the length of time she said the word "Daddy." When "Daddy" went to "Daddddddddddy," I knew I was in trouble, especially when she would end by saying, "I love you, Daddy!"

As it turned out, Irene decided to join Academics of Flight, enrolling in and completing the aircraft dispatcher program. She received the FAA aircraft dispatcher certificate. The relationship didn't end there. Irene was born in Taiwan and came to the United States to complete her master's degree in computer science, which she did. From there, the college began to sponsor her on a work permit.

It would be difficult to find someone less computer literate than I am, and Irene, along with her friend Dennis, was a blessing that resulted in the school beginning to come out of the "dark ages" with their knowledge of today's technology. Dennis taught me a new phrase to use when I become overloaded trying to accomplish many tasks at one time, "It's like putting an elephant up a rat's ass." Being Chinese, he also explained why it takes years for a Chinese person to show signs of aging when compared to other races. Their philosophy to life is simple, "If there is a solution to the problem, why worry? If there is no solution to the problem, it does no good to worry since nothing can be done about the situation, so again, why worry?"

The Students

The students who comprise a typical class are as demographically varied as New York itself. I've taught everyone from strippers to doctors to lawyers and everything in between. I often feel world destruction results from politics when I observe how well everyone works together in class, regardless of their home region. Yet, in many cases, if they went back to their country, they would be killing each other.

Karina and I experienced the low end of the financial spectrum one evening coming home from a night class. A young man in his mid-twenties with impeccable manners always attended class dressed in a suit and tie. He paid in full the first night, and he was a pleasure to have in class. One night, Karina and I closed the school about half an hour after class, came out of the parking lot, and turned onto 45th Street on our way home. We saw the back of someone dressed in rags pushing a shopping cart full of bags. It was the same well-dressed boy from class, and I don't know whose jaw dropped lower, Karina's or mine. I never mentioned this sighting to him in future sessions, and I don't know whether he saw us. He graduated, and I sincerely hope his efforts got him off the street. Actually, he was not the only student in a similar situation.

Laszlo was a student from Hungary who came to the school to continue a flying career that began in his native country. At that time, he held a job and flew regularly until making a bad landing with one of the school's airplanes, bending the prop to approximately a 90-degree angle. He didn't have the money to pay for the damage, even though I took him to court and won. In any event, he disappeared from the neighborhood for years after his school attendance.

In 2012, approximately 20 years later, as I was rounding the corner in the neighborhood of the school, there he was, pushing a shopping cart full of items that could only be classified as "junk." His attire completed the picture of a homeless person. We spoke for a while, and he said he'd gotten into an argument with his roommate and severed his arm with a butcher knife in a heated exchange.

After completing his time in prison, he came back to the neighborhood and has walked the streets ever since, rain or shine, regardless of the season. In her book *Child of the Dark,* Carolina Maria de Jesus describes raising her children in the favela of Sao Paulo. It's very descriptive of the survival of the extremely poor on the street. After reading this, I view Laszlo's situation differently.

I don't know whether any of Academics of Flight's students were "illegals," but prior to 9/11, nobody really cared. I had a cop from the local 108th precinct, Milton, as one of my students. He used to come by the school in uniform on his breaks to pass the time. When I looked around, about half the class would be missing, and they would only return after Milton had gone. They thought he was an immigration officer, and I jokingly told him to come see me only in street clothes. I had several street cops and detectives enrolled for one course or another, so I was well protected when the need arose and given an honorary shield to show to an officer if pulled over.

I was too timid to use the shield except for one occasion when I received a call from one of the employees who happened by the school one afternoon when it was closed. He apparently happened on a robbery in progress, overheard items being turned over, and ran out to give me a call at home. I jumped into the Corvette and headed for the school via the Long Island Expressway. Seeing a cop sitting in his car on the side of the road, and after giving him a quick briefing with the shield in sight, I asked him if he could escort me to the school. He said it was not allowed, but he was going *in a hurry* in that direction and for me to keep the Corvette close to his car. Also, there would be another police car waiting for me at the exit on Queens Boulevard, which I would follow to the school.

There I was, roaring down the LIE in the Corvette with a cop in front; it's usually the other way around. I was passed onto the waiting cop car when I reached Queens Boulevard, as team runners pass the baton in the Olympics. I am sure many drivers thought the Corvette was an unmarked police car. By the time we got to the school, there had to be half a dozen police, but the intruder escaped. Nothing of great importance was taken, and actually, I had a very entertaining afternoon.

The "student–instructors" relationship grows in proportion to the length of time the class lasts, with the goal being to achieve a meaningful end. I have had students who I couldn't wait to finish due to our lack of chemistry. However, on the other side of the coin, I have had tears in my eyes as I've watched a student graduate. These are tears of joy, knowing that I have in some way assisted in providing a new beginning that will bring rewards not only to the student but also to their family down the line.

You get to know the whole family. Although you may have never met their mother, father, sisters, or brothers during break times throughout the course, the student has told you all about them. You begin to know the good and the bad about the country they come from. In several cases, I have made it a point to travel to some of these countries, such as Pakistan and Nigeria, if I have had several students from that area and expected more.

The better you know their country, the more familiar you'll be about the students coming to you seeking knowledge. You become aware of whether they really want that career in life or if the desire comes from the parents, who want that profession for him. Sadly, I had a student from Croatia come to become a pilot, and during conversations outside of class, I learned that he really wasn't interested in that career. When I spoke to his father, who was an airline pilot for that country, the son's wishes were ignored. Out of respect for his father, the student worked hard, received his pilot certificate, went home, and *committed suicide.* The technical books written on the correct instructor–student dynamic advise that the instructor cannot become too friendly with the student. I agree that there is a line that cannot and should not be crossed. However, an instructor without compassion for those that have come to him/her is not an instructor. A case in point is illustrated in an e-mail I recently received from Jade, a student who came to the school from Korea to complete the aircraft dispatcher program.

She was having an interview with Asiana Airline for employment:

> *Here is a story I would like to tell you about a question I answered during the interview. "When was your hardest time in your life" I did not expect they would ask me this question, and I should answer in three seconds. I told them I had a hard time while working with Alitalia Airline and studying in New York, so my teacher, Jim, took me to the doctor's office for a blood check. He always told me I looked too tired. I received a favorable response and the interviewers all laughed. It reminds me that you cared for me a lot. Thanks again, Jim.*

As time went by, I began teaching operations personnel from Kuwait Airways, and they were a great bunch of guys. It was a long-term noncontractual arrangement between Academics of Flight and the airline, which resulted in the aircraft dispatcher certification of about 20 students. The contract would have continued, but the first Gulf War in 1990 brought it to a close. I kept in touch with several of the students, and the following is an excerpt of a letter from Iraq concerning the invasion:

> *Dear Jim,*
> *It was nice talking to you over the phone after a long time. Nice to know your wife and your daughter are well. We left Kuwait on the 2nd Sept '90, a month after the invasion. By road through Iraq and Jordan we managed to escape. The situation at the moment is terrible. Women are being raped, no food, babies being removed out of their incubators and sick people are taken off their life support machines, so that they can take the machines to Iraq. All is lost, fourteen years of our savings, all what the company owes us, house, car, but most of all by the grace of God, we are here safe.*
>
> —Letter, September 29, 1990

I was elated to receive a call from the sender toward the end of 2012. He emigrated first to England and then to Canada with his family and became a well-known contemporary artist.

Sissy, a student from Rwanda, was employed by the United Nations in Manhattan. He was also a tenant in one of the school's apartments. Rwanda was dominated by three tribes: the Tutsi, the Hutu, and the Twa. The Tutsi were in power; however, the majority of the population was Hutu. On April 6, 1994, a rocket hit the Hutu president's plane, killing two Hutu presidents from different regions, one from Rwanda and the other from neighboring Burundi.

This action began what became known as the Rwandan Genocide campaign. In a 100-day period, between 500,000 and 1 million Tutsi and moderate Hutu were slaughtered. Many Twa were also killed, despite not being directly targeted. International response to the campaign was limited, with the major powers reluctant to participate due to already overstretched UN peacekeeping forces. The number killed represented approximately 20% of the entire population. It was the worst instance of genocide since World War II.

Sissy was a Tutsi and was sent a telegram from Rwanda, by now ruled by the Hutu tribe, demanding he return home to be executed. Naturally, Sissy did not accept the invitation, and he went to work with IBM, located in Armonk, New York. An enlightening movie concerning this dark period in history is *Hotel Rwanda* (2004).

Through the years, Academics of Flight has always felt the repercussions of international disputes and policies. A longtime neighborhood friend, Joe, once said, "I never had to watch the news to see what countries were having political problems. All I had to do was watch where the students attending your school were from." To this day, he swears I was involved with the CIA, calls me "Sir," and salutes me when we meet.

True long-term friendships materialize very infrequently in life. One such relationship began when Academics of Flight had only been in operation for a short period of time. I was sitting in the front office, and in walked three teenaged Russians. None of them spoke very good English, and the one who to this day is part of our "extended family" relied on the other two to translate. His name is David Chubalashivili. I still can only get through about a third of his last name with the correct pronunciation, although Rita can say it without missing a beat.

David had no money, but a hell of a story as to how he escaped from Russia through Switzerland, sleeping on park benches, and through other countries before settling in New York. While attending Academics of Flight, his mom and dad, Lea and Soso, arrived with his brother, Mike. They lived in a very nice apartment off the Long Island Expressway around 108th Street. Rita, Karina, and I were guests for many dinners, and once there, between Lea's cooking and Soso's vodka, they became great evenings.

Lea's English was not particularly good due to her recent arrival, and her favorite word, which she pronounced perfectly, was "eat." When she told you to "eat," it was not an invitation, but a command. You not only ate at the table but also left with an armful of wrapped food. They opened their hearts to us, and unfortunately, Soso passed after a long illness, and everyone in both families missed him terribly. Lea was the "boss," and what she said was law. To illustrate, she felt it was time for David and Mike to get married to begin raising a family. Since neither of them was seeing anyone at that time, Lea went to Israel and came back with two young women. Before the boys could turn around, they were married. Lea passed in 2017.

In all the years of training students, there have been many who succeeded in securing a rewarding future; however, I would place David at the highest pinnacle, while certainly not taking away anything from the others. He knew what he wanted and didn't let any obstacle that could sidetrack him remain in his path. He maintained a straight course and overcame every potential deterrent. He was short on funds, and I needed a lot of work done around the house. This resulted in David trading his labor for flight training. Also, Lea babysat Karina. In time, he overcame his language barrier, completed every course the school had to offer, and became the school's chief flight instructor. He was a natural for teaching, and the students flocked to him.

I knew there would be a day when I would lose David due to the dream of all pilots to become an airline pilot. That day came in 1981, with a call from Provincetown–Boston Airlines (PBA), to fly as captain on several aircraft. In 1984, he was hired by Eastern Airlines on the B-727 and left in 1991, after an incident. Apparently, David was in the simulator with a very unpopular instructor, and a dispute erupted between the two as to a flying technique. David settled the argument by "cold-cocking" the hell out of the instructor right in the simulator.

Although the pilots praised him and felt the instructor was long overdue in receiving his just reward, David was terminated. Later, he met a very wealthy oilman from Russia who hired him as chief pilot on the company's corporate jet, a B-727. To date, he has accumulated 19,000 hours of flight time flying six different types of jet. Every time I meet someone who starts with a long list of why they can't achieve a goal, I sit them down, explaining that I am here to help only if they stop giving excuses; I cite David Chubalashivili's achievements as an example.

The fact that Academics of Flight is located in New York has led to several well-known international students attending the school at one time or another. Such was the case with a Formula One race car driver, Ian Ashley. He experienced a terrible accident on the track in a Canadian race, which resulted in several broken bones starting at his head and ending at his feet, in addition to severe burns. Having a type A personality, he decided to learn to fly during his convalescence period. He literally threw himself into the endeavor and not only became an instructor for us but a good family friend as well, spending a lot of time at the house. Rita had a family from Brazil that was well versed in car racing staying with us, and they couldn't believe Ian was coming to spend an evening.

The school also had a member of the group Earth, Wind & Fire as a private pilot student. I also administered two FAA written examinations to Christopher Meloni, the actor who played Detective Elliot Stabler on *Law and Order*, and he is a very down-to-earth guy. I was the only one in the office who didn't recognize him and asked him what he did for a living.

You can learn from everyone. Recently, I was educated in stabbing someone with a pen versus a pencil as seen through the "eyes of the law." One of my female students lost her temper during a heated discussion with her spouse and terminated the difference of opinion by stabbing him in the back with a pencil. The police were called, and my honor student was hauled off to jail. The "detainee" was told she should have used a pen, since the charge would have only been a "misdemeanor." However, because the weapon was a pencil, it was a "felony." The lesson is obvious, if you are going to lose it, choose your weapon carefully.

Over the years, I have heard countless amusing stories from students, including one from a dispatcher, Scotty, who I was training in Orlando, Florida, for Capital Air Cargo. He had a neighbor who, suffering from erectile dysfunction, had his problem solved by having an electronic device implanted, a procedure that required a frequency that would be activated by a push button to function. Hearing the neighbor complain that throughout the day and night he would get an erection without pushing the button, Scotty soon realized that his garage door opener was on the same frequency. Every time Scotty activated the door, the neighbor would be ready "for action," which of course was not always desirable due to timing, neighborhood pool parties, mowing the lawn in his shorts, and so on. Scotty, not being very neighborly, would activate the garage door mechanism for sheer amusement. After a week or so of having fun, Scotty changed the chips in his automatic door remote.

One of my most memorable students, Ivona, came from Cubaña Air, where she was a flight attendant for the company and later transferred into operations. Ivona described how the pilots would smuggle contraband for the black market on their flights. The cockpit would be filled with cans of gas and other highly flammable items as the pilots lit one cigarette after another.

Ivona had a light-skinned friend who was an air traffic controller for the Cuban government. She once brought two aircraft closer in the air than standard separation practice allows. The woman disappeared for six months, and when she returned to her job in Havana, she was almost black. As a penalty for her mistake, she was sent to a farm in the country to grow vegetables for six months. At least she wasn't fired.

In 2011, I trained a student from Brazil who was a loadmaster for Southern Air Transport (SAT) for the aircraft dispatcher certificate. SAT is a well-known CIA carrier that flies "cargo" to all the godforsaken parts of the world. Once when on an approach in a B-747 to an airport in the Congo, the crew requested clearance from the tower to land but did not receive an acknowledgement. With no response, the airplane landed and parked on the ramp by the tower. The tower cab was in sight and confirmed to be empty. However, three or four people were bent over collecting grasshoppers in a field close by. It had rained the night before, an infrequent event at that time of the year, and due to the rain, the grasshoppers were plentiful. Since these are a favored dish for dinner, the tower operators felt it was more important to collect their meal than to sit in the tower and direct airplane traffic. Everyone has a priority in life.

Then there was Johnny, a private pilot student who had heard another version as to how hurricanes are created and their method of reaching the United States. I finished a half-hour lecture on the subject of explaining how the storms ride the trade winds (wind flows from east to west beginning at the equator, north to 30 degrees north latitude). As the air mass travels, when the ocean is warm, it accumulates a tremendous amount of moisture through convection by the time it arrives in our part of the world.

John, very seriously, raised his hand after my explanation and asked if I would write what I had just talked about on paper and give it to him so he could present it to his wife. When he was in Africa, he had been accused of being a "bad boy" by his wife. His wife uncovered evidence of his misadventures and believed that his African partner in crime was sending the hurricanes to her as harassment. The power of love.

Mr. Blaze was another student who arrived at the school from the Congo with the hopes of becoming an airline pilot. He was a nice guy but had a problem understanding that there were rules and regulations pertaining to the correct time and place for each step of training. His Ecuadorian instructor, Alex, was a bundle of nerves, but a good instructor. I received a call from Caldwell that a plane was missing, this time from Alex, who had an appointment with Blaze. I had not heard from Blaze, and in the back of my mind, I said, "Oh God, I hope he didn't take the plane and go fly by himself." Before a pilot can go solo for the first time, they have to be signed off by their instructor. Alex felt Blaze was far from that level of proficiency.

My fear became a reality. Blaze felt it was time to solo, so he simply took the plane, not waiting for a sign-off from Alex, got clearance from the tower, and took off. I knew the controller and called the tower. Before letting the controller, Frank, know the circumstances, I asked how Blaze was doing.

> "Great. His landings are perfect, especially with this strong crosswind."
>
> "Frank, He's not supposed to be there. His instructor didn't sign him off!"
>
> "Shit."
>
> "You bet. Tell him to make a full stop and have him call me after he ties the plane down."
>
> "No problem. Let's keep this between ourselves. There will be too much paperwork if it goes public."

Alex hit the roof when I told him the story and that Blaze would be arriving shortly. Another plane landing in front of Blaze ran off the side of the runway due to crosswinds, so I guess Blaze was correct when he felt he was ready. I am sure Alex gave him both barrels, but

I don't think it lowered Blaze's self-esteem over his accomplishment. When he called me, he said, "Mr. Jim, I just soloed," as if he just became a proud father. After I congratulated him, I told him to come to the office for a meeting. He did, and I dismissed him from the school. He was a good student, but I did what had to be done. I am sure he joined another school, and most likely, he is flying as an airline pilot somewhere in the world.

There was another student who went to another planet with the school airplane, or so he thought. The secretary passed on a call from the student, who up to this time had been a pleasure in ground school.

"Hello, Mr. Jim, I am here on Jupiter with N32559, and I am being hit by *cosmic* rays." This went on for several minutes as if he were in an outer space situation. Realizing, he firmly believed his predicament, I tried to be as helpful as I could. "Take the credit card from the airplane, refuel, and when you land back at Republic Airport, give me a call."

"OK, Mr. Jim, I hope they don't shoot me down." The next day I called him at home and suggested he come in with his father for a "chat." He had a medical condition, had forgotten to take his medication at home, and started to hallucinate that he was flying. Naturally, I had to dismiss him from flying on medical grounds. He was a good student, and it was somewhat difficult for me to end his desire to become a pilot.

On another occasion, I got a call from an officer at an air force base in the Washington, DC, area. Academics of Flight had an Italian student, Sergio, who was a nervous wreck, could hardly speak English, and stood about five foot two. He was on his way from New York to North Carolina on a cross-country with one of the school's planes and became engulfed in bad weather. Taking the correct course of action, he diverted to the nearest field. Taking the wrong course of action, he taxied past a sign that read, *"Restricted Area, Do No Enter."*

As soon as the nose wheel crossed the line painted on the taxiway, he was surrounded by military police pointing enough guns at him to start a war. After shutting down the engine, he was thrown into a spread-eagle position on the ground. The more he tried to explain, the more English he forgot, reverting to his native tongue,

Italian. This made matters worse, since none of his detainers spoke Italian.

After an extensive body search and being interrogated all night while standing, they realized Sergio was harmless. I convinced the officer who called me at 5:00 a.m. that Sergio was only a danger to himself. Satisfied he didn't fly into the base to commit an act of sabotage, Sergio was given the all clear and took off, returning to New York instead of continuing to North Carolina. We had a meeting after his return, and he claimed that none of his captives were less than six foot four. Sergio's problem started when he did not understand what the sign meant.

One way or another, Academics of Flight would get involved in international politics without trying; it just seems to happen on a continual basis. One afternoon, without an appointment, a gentleman dressed in a suit identified himself as a government official, FBI, CIA, or State Department—God only knows what—entered the office and introduced two individuals, George and George. Without hesitation, I was told that this conversation was not taking place, and my task was to convert their current Romanian Airline Transport Pilot certificates to the U.S. certificate.

Naturally, after George and George attended class for a while, they began to trust me, and their story unraveled. They flew for the Romanian airline and had a routine turnaround flight to Berlin, Germany, from Bucharest, Romania. They were to be on the ground for approximately an hour. This flight was conducted during the period when Berlin was divided by the wall and communism was in full swing.

Apparently, George and George plus a flight attendant, who was the wife of one of them, had planned to defect to the West for a long time. To do this, they arranged a flight to be together as part of the operating crew. After landing in Berlin, the three disappeared into the terminal building, instead of returning to their airplane to fly the return trip. They threw their uniforms away in the airport bathroom and put on civilian clothes as the announcements to return to their plane could be heard over the terminal's public address system. As the time to their scheduled departure grew closer, the announcement went from a reminder to a stern tone and, finally, ended in a plea. They were eventually transferred to safe houses in Berlin until they made their way to New York. I've lost contact with them, but I assume they've continued flying with a company on this side of the world.

These are but a few of Academics of Flight's stories involving its students. I wish that each one could be mentioned.

Flight Engineer

In the beginning, Academics of Flight's programs were pilot-oriented, and I felt there would be a market to conduct a turbojet flight engineer program because there were only a few schools offering such a course in the United States. Two requirements were a simulator and a large transport airplane. Frank Berry was in charge of outside sales for Pan Am. One of his functions was to sell time on the company's simulators housed at JFK when the Pan Am crews were not using them for training. The school was also able to lease time on their B-707 aircraft.

Frank and my dad put together a fantastic teaching staff. Many of the instructors were retired flight engineers from Pan Am dating back to the flying boats and ending their careers on jets. The program was so successful that at times, the school was using the simulators more than Pan Am to train its own crews.

All the instructors threw themselves into the course 100%, and it was great therapy for them, since they missed the flying environment in retirement. My dad called Jim Maloney, an ex-Pan Am flight engineer, to see if he would be interested. His answer was "Why didn't you call me sooner?"

From that point on, Jim more or less ran the show. He had approximately 20,000 hours at the flight engineer panel from the B-314 flying boats to the B-747. He was in his early seventies, short, Irish as hell, and hardly ever without a stinking cigar in his mouth. Jim was like a runaway train you couldn't stop, and we were together day and night. Many times we would run to the house to get a few hours of sleep between simulator sessions, since we were training on a 24/7 schedule. He had keys to the house and would come in and make tea while waiting for me to get ready to leave together.

During a simulator session, we had two students with serious body odor, which wasn't a very pleasant experience, since we were enclosed in a small space. One night during a session, he had enough of the smell and laid a bar of soap on the engineer panel as a hint.

Many times, Jim called me the "son that he never had," and when he passed away, I sat with his family during the funeral. It took me a long time to get over his death, which was very quick and without any symptoms of illness. He told his wife, Alice, he was going to lie down because he wasn't feeling well. He went upstairs to his bed and died.

The students were as colorful as the instructors. We had a pair from Switzerland, Paul and Bernard, who were mechanics and wanted a seat in the cockpit. Approximately halfway through the program, they ran short of funds, so they lived at the school, converting a classroom to a bedroom during the night and coming to the house on weekends to do laundry and shower. I assigned them chores around the school, including painting the classrooms.

I watched for a while and noticed that Paul was doing all the work, while Bernard didn't move from a desk, consumed with reading the newspaper. I asked Bernard why he was not helping, and his reply was, "Actually, I am—Paul is putting on the paint. I'm drying it."

Bernard was color-blind, and Paul could hardly see without glasses, which he couldn't afford at that time. Color recognition is very important in the cockpit because the different colors of the various lights on the panel signify different conditions. Maloney came up with a solution by putting them together during training sessions. This way, Bernard would point to the light, and Paul would tell Bernard what color it was. By the time of the FAA check ride, the two had it all worked out, and sailed through the check ride with flying colors.

They slept so many nights in the school that Bernard knew the building's layout better than I did. He would explore at night and felt he could become rich with very little work but with a whole lot of luck. The school and local bank were in the same building and attached to each other. Through his nightly explorations, Bernard found a way to get into the room where the bank stored its money. All he had to do was crawl through a large ceiling duct beginning in one of the classrooms and venture through a maze of turns to reach his jackpot. It took a lot of effort to talk Bernard out of his plans, and he looked like a child being told by his parent not to go out and play.

After graduating, they went to fly in Africa as gunrunners with a company employed by Oliver North. They later returned to Europe. Bernard is currently with a major European carrier, visiting us as often as possible during his New York layovers, and he came with family to Karina's wedding. Paul is flying on a private jet owned by an oilman, and last year, he returned to the school for a course 33 years after his flight engineer program.

On one of Bernard's visits in 2011, he reminded me of a day that we were sitting at the B-707 paper mock-up ground trainer in one of the classrooms when someone from the street came in and sat with us. The visitor started asking a lot of questions concerning how a plane flew and was getting rather determined to go to Baltimore in the mock-up. The situation got to the point where we were about to get hijacked. Bernard and I looked at each other as to which one of us was going to restrain our "passenger" friend. I told him that we would love to take him; however, the ground crew was on strike, and we wouldn't be able to refuel. The guy accepted the scenario, left the school mumbling, and possibly went to the bus or train station to go to Baltimore as we suggested.

Then there was Louis and Hamlet from the Dominican Republic. Again, they were a pair, with Louis the "wheeler and dealer." He was living temporarily in Elmhurst with his relatives, not far from the school while going through the program. During off-school hours, he frequented local gambling spots. He came one day and wanted to clear his account with air-conditioners. Louis had a problem on his first two check rides, and I told him he was not serious enough to continue.

Naturally, he absolutely had it in him, and I wanted to redirect his outside activities to flight engineer studies. It worked, and later, Louis told me he was so pissed at my statement, he wanted to prove me wrong, and he did. On Lou's second or third attempted check ride, I was flying in the first officer position, with John Griffin as captain. As soon as the FAA inspector informed him that he passed, Lou threw a pencil in the air that he had been using to do calculations at the FE panel, and it took about 10 minutes to come to rest. The pencil hit John and me and bounced off every part of the simulator, including the inspector.

Lou disappeared rather abruptly after obtaining his certificate, and months later, I received a call from him in Santo Domingo. After graduating, he acquired a substantial amount of money, terminated his employment, and returned home to Santo Domingo. Rita, Karina, and I visited Lou a short time later in Santo Domingo, and we were treated lavishly. Lou became chief flight engineer with Falcon Air in Miami, Florida, and I would see him quite frequently having many laughs about the "good old days."

Hamlet was the program's first graduate. After the candidates passed their simulator check, if they were not commercial/instrument-rated pilots, they had to go up on a flight and extend the landing gear. This was accomplished by using one of Pan Am's B-707s when it was on a training flight in the New York area. I knew when the plane was going to land and went up to Pan Am's terminal rooftop at Kennedy. From there, I had a panoramic view of the runways, and the roof was equipped with devices that allowed me to listen to the conversation between air traffic control and pilots landing and taking off.

As the flight got closer to touchdown, my emotions intensified, and I wouldn't have been able to speak if spoken to. I remained on the rooftop long after the flight landed with a feeling of achievement at a level that I've only experienced once or twice. I was so proud of everyone for making that day possible.

Hamlet subsequently became a pilot and later went to a Miami-based airline. After the company went bankrupt, he flew as captain with another company. I was told that he was making an approach with his first officer flying and got too low, taking a portion of the approach lights with them to the runway. Although Hamlet wasn't flying, he was the captain and was discharged. However, I am sure he is still in the air flying for someone.

Tragedy struck on December 12, 1985, at 4:15 a.m., New York time, when Arrow Air Flight 1285 crashed on takeoff at Gander, Newfoundland. The trip was bringing back mostly 101st Airborne troops from Cairo, Egypt, to Fort Campbell, Kentucky, and all passengers plus crew perished. There remains a dispute as to the cause. Some people said it was due to icing on the wings not removed prior to flight, while others claim an explosion of "an undetermined nature" occurred. Mortar shells were found at the site, and the next day, Islamic Jihad, a wing of Hezbollah, claimed responsibility. The U.S. government denied their statement. Evidence also suggested a strong connection between the weapons being carried on board and the Iran–Contra affair. Many believe the statement regarding the "icing" as the probable cause was a cover-up. I saw the report of the accident on the TV news and said to Rita, "I have a feeling the captain was John Griffin." This was confirmed in minutes after calling his home in Florida. He was 40 years old. John always came to see us at the house on layovers, and I can still picture him in our family room watching television with us. I acquired a tremendous amount of flying skill while in the simulator when I flew with him as first officer supporting the school's flight engineer program. John was more than an exceptional pilot. There is absolutely no way he would have taken off with ice on the wings. He flew C-130s in the military, B-707s with Pan Am, and then DC-8s with Arrow Air. Being in aviation, these accidents are expected but never accepted without great pain.

The third pair that came through the program was from Nigeria, Joe and John. Joe never made it through the program and went to another school in California. While attending Academics of Flight, he would sit in the classroom all day with books open but just couldn't absorb the material. Karina, approximately six years old, would come in and yell at him for his bad study habits. John had been in the Nigerian army as an officer and having been involved in one of the country's civil wars, had been shot in his forearm. They never took the bullet out, and you could feel it when you touched his arm. He went on to become a pilot, and I believe he flew for Nigeria Airways.

When Rita and I were visiting Germany, we purchased a cuckoo clock that Esther was cleaning one day. The clock had stopped working, so she sat staring at it while praying to Saint Anthony to fix it. Saint Anthony must have been listening, since the clock started ticking again. A few months later, I was in the simulator on a check ride for one of the students on his third attempt to pass the FAA check ride. As the session was in progress, I prayed to the saint.

"Saint Anthony, you don't know me, but I am a friend of Esther's. Please get this guy through his check ride." The student passed and received his flight engineer certificate. I thanked Saint Anthony.

Pan Am transferred its training facilities, including simulators, to the company's new center on NW 36th Street in Miami. With this move from New York, Academics of Flight's flight engineer program came to an end. For every beginning, there is an end.

GOVERNMENT AGENCIES

New York State Rehabilitation Agency/Veterans Administration

During the early days of Academics of Flight, I received a call from the New York State Rehabilitation Agency requesting a meeting concerning a guy named Charlie, who wanted to become a pilot despite missing fingers on one hand. The cost to the State at that time would have been about $35,000 for Charlie's dream to come true. They didn't want to pay, but since an FAA medical waiver would allow him to proceed with the training, the agency had a dilemma on their hands.

The requested meeting was conducted with both parties present, and I was able to negotiate a compromise. If Charlie was still interested in becoming a commercial pilot after successfully completing the aircraft dispatcher program, the State agreed to pay. The dispatcher course, similar in curriculum to the pilot course, was a fraction of the cost; it was now in his hands to prove himself. Charlie did complete the program, receiving the FAA aircraft dispatcher certificate, and to the delight of the State, he didn't want to proceed any further. Due to the positive outcome between the State and Academics of Flight, the school was given permanent New York State approval for its educational courses. Shortly thereafter, the school applied for and received Veteran's Administration approval for several of its programs.

Federal Aviation Administration

Aviation industry leaders believed the airplane couldn't reach its full commercial potential without federal oversight to improve the safety standards; thus, the Air Commerce Act was passed in 1926. In 1938, President Franklin D. Roosevelt signed the Civil Aeronautics Act (CAA). In the aftermath of several subsequent accidents, Senator Almer Stillwell "Mike" Monroney introduced a bill to create the independent Federal Aviation Agency to provide for the safe and efficient use of national airspace. On August 23, 1958, President Dwight D. Eisenhower signed the act, and the FAA was born.

The history of Academics of Flight would not be complete without mentioning the FAA. Since 1976, the two organizations have worked, sometimes "battled," side by side in a relationship that is at times difficult to understand. Most of the programs offered by the school require the agency's endorsement prior to allowing a student to enroll in the course. The FAA can be characterized the same as all bureaucratic conglomerates: slow-moving with an endless chain of command.

However, after a while, you realize it is composed of individuals with different traits and work philosophies. Approximately every two years, Academics of Flight is assigned a new inspector, and the school has to "hope for the best." Some inspectors feel that if a school's requested procedure is not authorized in writing, the request cannot be approved. Others feel that even if it isn't in writing, the request can be authorized. Naturally, I would always hope for the latter, but unfortunately, the school would seldom be assigned an inspector with this philosophy. No matter how well the program is written and presented for approval, a request for a few changes will always be required by the FAA; if not, the inspector's job security will be threatened.

In the 1970s, course writing was more difficult than later years, since there were no formal guidelines and approval depended a lot on the opinion and disposition of the inspector. Today, it is easy to find a program template. This degree of automation allows the school to demonstrate to the inspector that all items are covered. With a little luck, approval is pretty much assured without a lot of resubmissions.

My first encounter under fire came when I was writing an air taxi manual for an on-demand charter service. The manual had to explain all the policies of the company. I had labored day and night compiling the manual, known as *Operations Specifications,* and the day came for reviewing my "work of art" at Farmingdale Airport's FAA office on Long Island, with its senior inspector, who everyone feared. We sat at a large conference table across from each other, and the session continued for what felt like forever.

The inspector reviewed the manual page by page, grunting and groaning with each change in his facial expression. After what seemed like a lifetime, he slid it across the table and said, "Make changes and resubmit, I cannot accept it as is." Out of frustration, I slid it right back and told him to be specific on what he wanted. My action took him by surprise, and for the next hour, I had one of the most productive sessions I have had with the agency.

Years later after the meeting, he passed away, and until that time, he was a tremendous help to me when I had questions. His name was Charles Walters, he was an icon in the FAA. As is true with most inspectors, he had flown for an airline and, I believe, for the military. He then retired to the FAA. Someone had mentioned that Charley owned a lot of land with his brother in New Hampshire and financially speaking, didn't actually have to work. He remained with the FAA well into his seventies or eighties. I don't think anyone knew his real age.

Knowing that there would be a lot of flying required as a result of a new contract from Pakistan, I had to get my own flight medical report renewed. This is always a "situation" due to being color-blind. I was born with it, and the condition requires a medical waiver to be able to fly. Usually, you will be on the ground with an FAA inspector, and the tower will direct different color lights toward you. In turn, you have to tell the inspector the color, and hopefully, you are correct. I had a good relationship with the FAA due to constantly being in their office for the school certification process. The inspector assigned to do my color test, felt it was too nice of a day to do the exam on the ground, and elected to take one of Academics of Flight's airplanes and conduct it in the air. On takeoff, we took a runway heading that flew us over Jones Beach, and his first question was, "Etch. What color is the sand?"

"Light brown."
"Good."

We then took a heading that brought us over a cemetery alongside the airport, and his second question was, "What color is the grass?"

"Green."
"You're doing damn well."

Turning on the final approach, we were over the Long Island Expressway with his last question, "What color is that blue car off your wing tip?"

"Blue."

"Hell, Jim, there's nothing wrong with your eyes!"

After landing, he signed my waiver, and I was good for another year!

I wasn't always as lucky and had many moments of extreme frustration with inspectors. One afternoon, I was sitting in Bob Osinski's office at Mid Island Air Service with Ron Hughes, an FAA inspector. We were wasting the afternoon with small talk, and at that time, Ron and I had never had any interrelated business, and it was the first time we met each other; Bob was a mutual friend. In the middle of the conversation, Ron jumped out of his chair as though a snake had bitten him in the ass. He ran outside to the ramp to stop a pilot taxiing a plane by the office window. This could only mean bad news for the pilot and the airplane owner. Unfortunately, Bill was the pilot working for Academics of Flight, and I was the aircraft owner. The school had just received a contract from Nigeria to train and certify nine flight instructors; thus, it needed another airplane to add to its fleet for the required additional flying. I wasn't afforded a great amount of time to pick and choose, so I took the first offer on a plane for sale that was based at our North Carolina branch in Mount Airy. My dad felt it was a great deal; I made the purchase arrangements, and the pilot–owner flew it north. Upon arrival, I had Mid Island maintenance make a "pre-buy" inspection, and after their "thumbs-up," the plane belonged to Academics of Flight.

It was only a week later that Ron stopped the airplane. Observing an external item that he didn't like, the aircraft had to go through another maintenance inspection, but this time, with an FAA inspector present. The outcome was a lot different from the pre-buy inspection. Among the issues was the fact that the airplane was fitted with automobile circuit breakers instead of those approved for an aircraft. By the time the last item on the list was corrected, the maintenance bill was close to $10,000.

Prior to having the items repaired or replaced, Bill and I were invited to the FAA for a meeting concerning my new purchase. All I received was double-talk. It became a real dog and pony show. I finally told the FAA (more or less) "Go to hell. Either ground the airplane or leave it alone."

One of my staff, Marina, increased her aviation skills through the years and applied for an FAA-designated flight examiner position in 2011. Ron was still with the FAA and was one of the people in the meeting. He was reviewing her résumé and stopped when he saw Academics of Flight and began to laugh with the other inspector, Steve Tromkin. Steve was also one of the inspectors assigned to Academics of Flight more than 25 years prior to the meeting. Ron said, "I will never forget Jim saying, 'Ron, you're killing me with this damn inspection.'" All this was reported to me by Marina when she left the meeting.

An FAA inspector named John Aterberry was assigned to conduct the flight engineer check rides for the school's B-707 program in New York. The first rule of administering a check ride in the simulator is to not give the candidate more than one problem at a time. Not only would John give more than one problem simultaneously, but he also had no idea how to operate the simulator's instructor panel to the degree that not only the crew didn't know what was going on, but the simulator itself seemed confused. I had had enough and demanded a meeting with the FAA chief. The conference was only to include all parties involved; however, when I walked into the meeting room, there had to be at least 10 FAA personnel. One slept through the entire conference. After going back and forth like a ping-pong ball, a course of action was agreed upon. Another inspector would check the three candidates that Aterberry had failed. The inspector did, all passed, and Aterberry no longer had any authority over Academics of Flight. The last time I saw him was approximately three months later, being asked to leave the simulator next to the one we were using at that time, when he was giving a check ride to an Eastern Airlines flight crew. It was anything but a polite request to abandon the check ride by the pilots, and I thought to myself, "Poor John, he will never learn."

I think the reward for complete incoherence would go to an inspector named Jorge, who was assigned to Academics of Flight from the Miami FAA office. It was his task to oversee the school's aircraft dispatcher program, and he had no clue as to the scope of his duties. Prior to being assigned to monitor, the inspector is supposed to attend an FAA seminar/workshop in Oklahoma City to become familiar with the FAA regulations and procedures governing the school's program. If in fact Jorge did attend, he must have slept through the whole course.

The FAA has an explicit outline listing the course topics to be included in the program; this is an attempt to maintain a level of standardization for all applicable schools throughout the country. This outline is called a *Technical Course Outline* (TCO), and Academics of Flight's version comprises about 19 typed pages. I had two meetings with Jorge, listening to him explain his interpretation of the FAA regulations governing the aircraft dispatcher program and what he expected from the school. The relationship between us terminated when he told me I would have to submit the TCOs as one-sided pages, since it confused him to read a page with printing on both sides. I asked him if he ever read a book.

Around 2008, Academics of Flight in New York was assigned a new inspector, Robert, for its pilot ground programs. Bob was great as an inspector, and I moved ahead with several new programs, taking advantage of his philosophy that if a request did not violate any written policy, it could be placed into effect. Although given a new inspector in 2010, Bob and I have remained good friends, and he continues to advise me as I encounter "bumps along the way." We have dinner now and then, and during these times, I have discovered that he himself could write a book on his life, which no doubt in my mind would be a best seller. One chapter would concern his time flying as a Navy pilot over Vietnam. He would fly in after bombing runs and take pictures to assess target damage. On one mission, he didn't make the round trip back to his aircraft carrier due to being shot down and became a "guest" of the North Vietnamese. The U.S. government believed he knew a lot, and since they were fearful that he might become talkative during a torture session, the Navy sent in a team and extracted him from his "hotel room." Bob said he was grateful, but he was clearly pissed. He said the guys who came in and retrieved him were more physically abusive during the extraction than his captors were during his captivity.

Carolina Air Academy: Mount Airy, North Carolina

When my dad retired to North Carolina, Academics of Flight needed a small airport away from high-density aircraft traffic to provide housing and flight training for its foreign students. Therefore, the school bought a trailer and began operations at Elkin Airport, North Carolina, with the permission of the airport operator, Dave. He was an ex-air force F-4 fighter pilot from the Vietnam era. He would leave Elkin on selected weekends, fly a fighter from somewhere, drop bombs on the Sandinistas in Nicaragua, and be back for work Monday mornings at the airport. The new branch of Academics of Flight was named the Carolina Air Academy.

Elkin was adequate for a while, but the school soon outgrew the airport, and it moved to Mount Airy Airport, North Carolina. North Carolina is not the Deep South; however, there were concerns as to whether the local people would accept our foreign pilots. Johnny Sadiq, a captain for Pakistan International Airlines, made a special trip to Mount Airy to give a formal presentation to the local business club members on behalf of the students from Pakistan. It helped tremendously. For the most part, the pilots were accepted, because they were contributing financially to the small community. But, on the other hand, when they began to mingle with the local girls, I am sure several parents began to have second thoughts about the flight school.

To save money, I used to ferry our New York airplanes to Mount Airy for required annual maintenance inspections, which was less expensive compared to having similar work done in New York. On one trip, I took along Junior, a black training pilot from Nigeria, who was going to spend a month flying at Mount Airy. He had been in the United States long enough to know that there were still pockets of racial discrimination, and he was somewhat apprehensive.

After landing in Mount Airy, while I was tending to the airplane, Junior went to the trailer to meet the students he already knew from when they were together in New York. A local was visiting with the pilots who were sitting in the living room of their trailer. In the midst of the conversation with Junior and the others, the local took out his oversized pocket knife and started whittling a stick while looking at Junior. Junior took this very personally and returned to New York with me the next day when the inspection on the plane was completed. He never returned to Mount Airy.

While in New York, I received a call from a Charlotte-based FAA inspector who started the conversation with "Hello, Mr. Etchison, this is Jim Bruton from the FAA. Do you own two Tomahawk airplanes, one blue and white, the other red and white?" I knew he was aware they were ours and couldn't guess as to what trouble I was in now. I answered, "Yes, sir."

Apparently, two of the pilots decided to do contour flying, which means flying in formation as close to the ground as possible without hitting it. They were following a river and came around a bend two or three feet above the water, wing tip to wing tip. This type of flying is dangerous but, more importantly, illegal. The regulations allow you no closer than five hundred feet from a surface or any obstacle in an unpopulated area. All this aside, the pilots were having a great time, and when they came around the bend, they were headed directly for a man and woman in a rowboat, who were enjoying a quiet Sunday afternoon fishing. Their tranquility came to an abrupt halt, as the couple dove into the water, with the planes passing a few feet over their boat.

After the inspector explained the incident to me, he commenced with a very stern lecture for the next 15 minutes or so, while I thought to myself, "How much am I going to be fined for *this* violation?" Every now and then, I would interrupt by saying, "That's terrible!" By now, we were on a first-name basis, and he ended by saying, "Jim, since the people didn't get the registration painted on the side of the airplane, I don't know for sure if it was yours. I realize there are a couple of other schools with Tomahawks." I could have kissed him: he was giving me a way out. I went to see him a few weeks later. He explained that his retirement date was around the corner and that he didn't want to get involved in an investigation. God bless the FAA's mentality.

The debt collection process at Carolina Air Academy needed improvement, and one of the students I had sent down for flying was a cab driver from Brooklyn named Ishmael. As he flew, he kept promising my dad his money was on the way. Of course, the funds never materialized before he returned to New York. His last promise was that he was going to send the money owed to the school after returning to New York. By this time, the amount was quite substantial.

Although my dad believed him, I knew there was no way we would see it unless some of my "friends" visited him back in Brooklyn. By this time, the "Goodfellas" had pretty much left the neighborhood in Queens, but I had a tenant in one of the Queens apartments who gave me a contact number. After making a call, I was told to drive out the next day to Howard Beach, Queens, to meet a guy in a parking lot who would be driving such and such a car. Not knowing exactly what would evolve, I told Felicia that if I didn't call her by a certain time, she should call the police and tell them the location of the meeting.

On time, my contact and I started strolling along the beach, making small talk about flying, blah, blah, blah. It was hot as hell, but the guy was wearing a windbreaker zipped all the way to his neck. I thought, "This isn't good." He was either wired or concealing a weapon or both. We finally got around to the subject of "collection," but he was more interested in discussing transporting drugs with the airplanes. I would come back to the debt owed, and he would return to his subject. We went back and forth three or four times, and I wasn't getting anywhere. I told him that after he collected the debt, I would talk about drug running. He never collected the money and I never ran drugs. I still don't know if he was with the FBI and trying to set me up or an actual drug dealer.

There was no one who enjoyed Carolina Air Academy more than Karina. The pilots would run from her, but she couldn't be stopped. Her whole day was spent up in the air with the student pilots. When they pleaded to end the flight, she would have no part of the request. After approximately five years of operation, my dad felt it was time to terminate Carolina Air Academy. Although I did not share his opinion, the school was closed.

AirNet: Columbus, Ohio, 2000s

Around 2000, Academics of Flight received a call from AirNet. At that time, the company owned approximately six Learjets and twice as many prop airplanes. They even had Willie Nelson's jet after Willie lost it to the IRS, and it ended up on the auction block. The airplanes were used to transport bank checks to various Federal Reserves scattered throughout the United States because if a bank got their checks to a Reserve bank before a certain hour, it would earn interest for that day. One of the most impressive sights I have ever witnessed would occur around 11:00 p.m. while standing on the ramp at Air-Net's home base in Columbus, Ohio. Approximately 20 Learjets, not to mention the props, would start turning their engines for flights to predetermined destinations. I simply watched in awe as the operation was conducted with military precision. Walking across the ramp at this time could only be compared to crossing a busy street in Manhattan at rush hour. These flights are conducted nightly, while most people are sleeping.

Dave Newman, AirNet's operations representative, had asked me to participate in a bidding to teach an FAA-approved aircraft dispatcher program for the company. The classes would be conducted at Columbus three days a week, and the instructor would be transported back and forth with the company Learjets on their nightly runs. I flew out from Teterboro, New Jersey, arriving at Columbus after midnight with Dave meeting me upon landing. He gave me a company car with directions to the hotel that had been booked for the night.

Dave's directions meant nothing to me since I had no idea where any of the interstate highways were. To make matters worse, it was snowing. Somehow, I found the hotel.

His directions reminded me of a section in a book that my neighbor, Edward, wrote about his diplomatic life with the UN and OPEC. Ed, born in Nigeria, is a natural storyteller. When he was flying with a pilot in a small UN plane looking for a village in Nimbi, Africa, they didn't have adequate directions to locate the village and landed when they saw several children on the ground in hopes they could direct the pilot to their destination. Pointing in a direction, one of the children came forward and said, "You go, go, and go some more. Then, you turn right, and go, go and go some more until you get to the village." They took off and, believe it or not, found the village.

The next morning, after a few schools made elaborate proposals for the contract, I came in with a napkin on which I had written calculations during a quick breakfast at the hotel. I translated what was on the napkin to Dave, Bob Gatto, and a few other AirNet representatives. Bob Gatto was a Long Island boy, and by the end of the morning, I had the contract. He told me if I had the *cujones* to make a presentation off notes on a napkin, I was their man. During the next few years, I acquired a tremendous amount of aviation knowledge from Bob, and to this day, I include that information in my lectures. Unfortunately, he passed away a few years back but will be remembered by all for his contributions.

Throughout the years that I flew with AirNet in the jumpseat as a passenger, I have nothing but the greatest admiration for the pilots. They flew in weather that would ground airline flights. It would be unfair for me to write about AirNet without a special thanks to pilots Glenn Dorries and Ed Knap. They were the crew that flew the Charlotte, North Carolina–Fort Lauderdale, Florida leg, and their professionalism combined with humor made every flight enjoyable. The company allowed me access to their system for transportation between Academics of Flight's two locations in New York and Miami, Florida. Karina even had the pleasure of flying with them on a couple of occasions including one flight through pretty rough weather. She lived to laugh about it.

The relationship and contract ended several years later due to 9/11. I had just started a new class in Ohio, and during the first hour of the first day, I was called to their operations room to watch the disaster unfold on television. We were watching the ATC radar screen, and I was amazed to see how international flights were being diverted to airports north of the United States. It reminded me of a line of ants marching in columns to a hole and disappearing into the ground. Within no time at all, the radar screen that had thousands of targets now had only a handful of military aircraft images in the air.

Rita was home in New York, and since all communications were cut off in and out of New York, I lost contact with her for two days. Also, AirNet's aircraft were grounded indefinitely, resulting in my not being able to return home on their planes.

The company had a contingency plan of transporting the checks by ground, and it was obvious that this would be the only way home. The first leg, from Columbus, Ohio, to Pittsburgh, Pennsylvania, took approximately eight hours, and the driver, a nice guy, had the nickname "Radar" after the TV character from *M*A*S*H*. Radar was known to be a conversationalist, and he didn't stop talking from the moment we left Ohio until we reached Pittsburgh.

We arrived around midnight: tired and hungry, with my ears ringing from listening to Radar. The relay truck and driver were waiting for us for the second leg at a predetermined location, and after a few minutes of transferring the checks, we were off to Philadelphia. It was obvious during the first few minutes, after going around the first turn at approximately 60 mph, that the driver had been called out on the spur of the moment and must have had a "few" or, actually, quite a "few," prior to being appointed to take the trip. I suggested that he pull over so we could discuss how we would make it *alive* to our next destination. The driver very quickly claimed that he had a "cold," and that it would be better if I drove, while he "rested." I had no idea how to drive the truck, but it was a better option than having my passenger continue to drive. Little by little, mile by mile, I got used to driving and was a pro by the time we pulled into the Philadelphia office. My friend only woke briefly once to get his "cough medicine" under the seat. His only comment walking into the office was, "God sent you to me."

By now, I had been up for two days and slept most of the way on the third leg by truck from Philadelphia to Teterboro Airport, New Jersey, where I had left my car. As we came up the NJ Turnpike parallel to Manhattan, we both silently watched the smoke billowing from where the Twin Towers had once been. The sight was hard to digest, and all I wanted to do was get to my car and get home to Rita.

The 40-minute drive from the airport, over the George Washington Bridge, through The Bronx, and finally into the driveway seemed like a lifetime. Walking through the door, it was as though I were a ghost, and Rita couldn't talk through her tears. For everyone, it was a very unsettled period, with many life changes that are still felt more than a dozen years after the attack. I came across a song by Alan Jackson that I believe describes the mood that transpired from the tragedy:

Where were you when the world stopped turning on
that September day?
Were you in the yard with your wife and children

Or working on some stage in LA?
Did you stand there in shock at the sight of that
black smoke?

—Alan Jackson

Apartments

With the influx of foreign students, the time spent in securing housing was becoming time-consuming and frustrating. Hotel prices in New York for students taking courses longer than one week in duration were considerably higher compared to other hotels across the country. Academics of Flight searched the area to find rooms in local homes, but that had its own set of problems. Jews didn't want to live with Arabs, whites didn't want to live with blacks, and vice versa, etc. Therefore, I bought three co-op apartments within a two-year period. When I couldn't keep them occupied with students, I would lease them to other tenants. This was the case after 9/11, when the U.S. government tightened the restrictions on foreign students. As of 2012, we still had two apartments. The third was sold in 2000 to raise funds for expanding the farm in Costa Rica.

Being a landlord is not an easy task, and I am not sure if the investment is worth the overall returns; there are periods of vacancy, plus ongoing maintenance expenses. While I have been fortunate with my tenants overall, after 25 years of ownership I have had my moments. Only twice have I taken tenants to court for nonpayment. I found it easier to force an individual to vacate on a non-lease agreement than if they had signed a lease. Since there is no formal agreement, the tenant can be legally required to leave in 30 days. If a lease is in place, it can take up to six months or more.

One memorable incident was the day I went to evict tenants who were obviously wheeling and dealing drugs. I had a student from the islands requesting that I lease an apartment to one of her relatives or friends. All was fine for the first few months, but then rent checks started arriving late and then stopped altogether. There was no lease involved, and I simply knocked on the door and told the tenants that they had 24 hours to vacate the premises. There were three guys, not one less than six feet or under 250 pounds, plus two women holding babies sitting on the couch. I really didn't know which one was the tenant, but they all got up and simply walked out.

I couldn't believe it. No bad looks, threats, or anything derogatory. When they left, after closing the door, I slid down it like you see in the cartoons. I hadn't planned on making such a bold stance, it just came out. Rita and I were amazed at the number of sneakers and leather coats plus other brand-name clothes they left behind. I must say they were very well-dressed individuals. I laughed at their sneaker sizes; none were under 13. We never found the actual drugs, but cutters, scales, baggies, and other related items were scattered throughout. I filled three plastic construction refuse bags with the clothes and gave them to the girl who had originally requested the rental. I did keep the TVs and the VCR.

There was a second case of suspected drug activity in an apartment, this time involving students from the Middle East. Karina and I were cleaning the apartment after their departure and in several places found what I thought to be crack cocaine. I had never seen it except in pictures, but being a good citizen, we took it to the local police station. The police were very appreciative of the concern, and as each officer examined the evidence of my war on drugs, the cop would smile or laugh; it was rock candy.

One of the tenants from our Flushing, Queens, apartment had to move his accommodations to Riker's Island, one of New York's penitentiaries, due to committing a felony. He is from Jamaica and is one of the most soft-spoken individuals you will ever meet. He came to Academics of Flight for flying, but naturally, with his situation, it had to be postponed. During his period of incarceration, I took his phone calls and listened as he revealed his life story. My accepting his calls was a blessing to him, since most of the people he called turned their backs. I am not one to condemn, and as far as I was concerned, he was and still is a nice guy.

He had every opportunity to lead a life of crime, as a great percentage of inmates do once out of jail, but he refused to take this path. He bought an 18-wheeler and became a trucker. He subsequently moved some items for me from the house in Florida to New York. I attempted to pay for his services; however, he refused, bringing back the past as to how I took the time to listen to him. "What goes around, comes around" applies in this case. He still calls me once in a while when he is out on the road, and I consider him a good friend. I will always answer his phone calls.

In 2010, I completed payments for a two-bedroom, approximately 1,000 square foot apartment in Panama overlooking the city. It is presently rented to a Panamanian lawyer from one of the local banks.

12

DOMESTIC TO INTERNATIONAL

Considering Academics of Flight's location in the melting pot of New York, it wasn't long before the school received foreign recognition, nor surprising when it did. These days, most flights are usually turned around in 24 hours, with the crew staying in a hotel close to JFK. In the 1970s and 1980s, however, most foreign airlines had crew layovers for a few days in midtown Manhattan. Since Academics of Flight is 10 minutes from Manhattan, the Queens location was and still is convenient for conducting classes for foreign airline pilots who either wanted or required the U.S. airline transport pilot certificate. The school is a short subway ride away.

From the late 1970s until the mid-1990s, most pilots wanted a U.S. rating due to its acceptance worldwide. Many of the pilots were already captains flying large aircraft; however, their licenses from their home countries were of limited use outside their own country. There were at least four instances when I taught one pilot at our facility in Queens and then found myself in that particular pilot's native country teaching for their airline: Belgium, Morocco, Nigeria, and Pakistan. There were ongoing trips to these countries, which obviously led to a wide variety of experiences. I was fortunate to have the school during that period of time, since today, the stature of the U.S. rating has declined because the European Union now has its own recognized certificate. Also, since 9/11, the training of foreign-born pilots has been greatly reduced in the United States due to stricter screening requirements.

Pakistan

Pakistan International Airlines (PIA) had ordered a few B-747s that were "N" registered. Every country has a registration letter prefixed to its aircraft assigned number; "N" is the letter for the United States. As per FAA regulations, in order to fly as a captain in an aircraft with this letter, the pilot must hold a U.S. airline transport pilot certificate. Afaq Rizvi, one of the senior captains for PIA, was the first from this airline to undergo the program offered by Academics of Flight in Queens; he was soon followed by one or two more. Under the coordination of Captain Rizvi, within a few months, I began conducting the program in Karachi, Pakistan.

The first class had 10–15 senior pilots attending, representing a tremendous amount of hours flown. I remember thinking to myself during the first few hours of teaching class, "My God, I don't have the experience to teach such a group." I was only a commercial pilot with no international experience, and the youngest class member was at least 10 years my senior. The class went well, and I was called back for two more sessions.

The first flight to Karachi was an evening departure, and earlier in the afternoon, I received a call from the captain who would be taking me on the first leg to Paris. It was Captain Johnny Sadiq, who I had never met, and he was welcoming me for the flight. As the flight changed crews along the way, I was handed off to new captains and couldn't have been treated better if I had been a diplomat. Johnny and I became very good friends. (I have also mentioned him in the sections "Flights" and "Carolina Air Academy.")

I stayed with Captain Rizvi and his wife, Zaquia, and their three sons while teaching. Again, I cannot properly describe the kindness bestowed upon me. The Eastern hospitality far outweighs that of the West. As an example, an evening is spent dressing up and getting in the car to visit without prior notice. In New York, you would think of this as an intrusion, since the visitors were not invited. But in Karachi, it is looked upon as a privilege for someone to spend an evening in your company, even without an invitation.

To illustrate the hospitality shown to a friend, I had a Pakistani ex-dispatcher who said that he had been visiting one of his friends in the tribal area north of Islamabad, near the border of Pakistan and Afghanistan, when a feud erupted between the villagers he was visiting and another settlement. Since he was not involved in the disagreement, a representative from both sides met and agreed to render him free and safe passage from the area. Once he departed, the war continued until both parties felt retribution had been achieved.

On the second trip, Rita and Karina accompanied me, again as the guests of the Rizvi family. While I labored in the classroom, they spent the day gossiping and visiting with the other women. One morning, they woke up to find a pair of horses waiting for them to ride. Karina was so into it that she insisted that I buy her a camel on our return home. I don't know how she went from a horse to a camel; however, I don't think either one would have worked out too well on busy Queens Boulevard. Thank God she got over it. Also, Afaq had a personal servant for her, and to say the least, there was an adjustment period required when the trip was over: no more camel, no servant, and so on. Rita and Karina both had a problem adjusting to the hot, spicy food while in Pakistan and requisitioned cookies from the kitchen as often as possible when no one was looking.

On one of the trips, I had just arrived, and Afaq instructed me to get a few hours of rest because he wanted us to attend a "parade"; I went to sleep thinking I was going to see Pakistan's version of Mickey Mouse. When Alfaq and I joined the spectators, it seemed that I was the only Westerner in the crowd, and it only took seconds to realize this was not a parade, but more or less, a bloodbath. The marchers were lined up in rows, approximately six or seven to a line, naked to the waist. Their backs were covered with blood from self-inflicted wounds. The participants had a chain with several different styles of knives attached and would take several steps forward, stop, and whip the ornament over their shoulder, striking their back. They would continue this self-flagellation until they passed out or were too weak to stand. At one point when they stopped, it appeared they all stared at me, and I shouted to Afaq, "Run, Afaq, they are after us." I ran and cannot remember how I found him, but when I did, he could hardly stand due to laughing so hard at my paranoia. On our way home, he confessed that this was the first year he had gone to the event since nobody would go with him in the past.

The purpose of this gathering was to celebrate the Battle of Karbala in 680 AD that involved the Shia Muslims. During the battle, Ali al-Asghar ibn Husayn, the six-month old grandson of Prophet Muhammad, and several family members were killed. Traditionally, the dead are regarded as martyrs by Muslims. This "parade" was part of the commemoration held during the annual 10-day period that culminates on the tenth day, Ashura. In her book *Inside the Pakistan Army*, Carey Schofield describes this procession:

> *Men and boys parade, stripping to the waist, singing and chanting. They slash at their backs using chains with razor blades, or knives until their flesh is raw, with blood pouring down their legs. They are bewailing that they were not at Karbala to save Husain and his companions.*

On my third visit, I stayed with Captain Johnny and was again treated at a level that is, in my experience, unattainable in the West. For the entire week, when taking a shower, I had a three-legged lizard share the tub. On the last day, the lizard was nowhere to be found, and I actually missed seeing the creature. It was time to go home. A friend of Johnny was Gigi, an arms dealer who was less than legitimate at times. Rita and I took him shopping at Macy's in Queens Center when he was our houseguest. Gigi was spending so much money that the store had to open his own private register to ring up his purchases. The items were all for his daughters, and the salesgirls assisting Gigi at Macy's begged to be adopted by him.

During a Christmas dinner with Luther Regina and his family, he described an incident during one of his flights. He was one of the younger captains, and while flying a B-707 on his return to Karachi, the nose gear wouldn't extend. He was flying in circles over the airport to give the fire brigade time to foam the runway to cushion the impact of the airplane's landing with the nose gear retracted. Unfortunately, the ground crew foamed a section of the runway that the plane would not be using on touchdown. Luther couldn't wait and made a beautiful landing, reducing the speed so that the nose came down very gently. After disembarking, the ground crew came out with a crane and hoisted up the nose with a chain. While towing the plane to the hangar, the chain snapped, and the aircraft nose came crashing down to the ground, causing a considerable amount of damage. Luther was mad as hell and said, "Why did I go through all that trouble, since the ground crew busted the airplane up anyway?"

Years later, many of the captains visited us in New York, and we have stayed in touch with quite a few. They began asking me to train their sons for flying, and with great reluctance, I took on the challenge. As the seniors retired, many of the sons trained by Academics of Flight became captains; it is a good feeling to have trained both generations. I have been invited back to Pakistan to visit several times; however, considering the global situation after 9/11, and Pakistan's location, I don't think it would be a good idea.

Alvin Tariq came to Academics of Flight in the mid-1980s wanting to be a pilot. At that time, he was a flight attendant with PIA. Not only did Alvin complete his pilot certification, but he successfully finished several other FAA-approved programs. Tariq then became an instructor for Academics of Flight when his flight schedule allowed, and most importantly, we have remained good friends ever since. He came to see me over the Christmas holidays in 2012. I was very happy to hear that for the past three years, Alvin has been flying as captain with Pakistan International Airlines.

The political deterioration between Pakistan and the United States was the major topic of our conversation. Tariq is a strong believer that Pakistan was unaware of Bin Laden living in Pakistan; however, he did feel the CIA had been watching him for a long time and knew his exact location. When Pakistan jailed one of our CIA agents for murdering two locals in their country, the CIA felt it was time to retaliate and conducted the operation code-named "Neptune Spear" on May 2, 2011, at Abbottabad, Pakistan. Bin Laden was shot in the brain by a Navy Seal. Most people classified the mission as a "political assassination."

We both agreed that the United States would never win in Afghanistan, since it is a "tribal country." History has proven that a lasting peace is nonexistent in such a society.

Tariq gave the following illustration of the tribal mentality of these regions:

> *Two individuals from different tribes would be friends having tea together. After an afternoon of*

pleasantries, and at some point in the conversation, one would turn to the other, informing him that he would have to kill this person since that person's grandfather had killed the speaker's grandfather fifty years ago. This cycle continues without end.

Morocco

As my connection with Pakistan began, Morocco quickly followed. I trained a pilot named Badouwi in New York and, soon after, found myself on a plane to Morocco to train pilots for Royal Air Maroc (RAM) in Casablanca. Badouwi was a wheeler–dealer and made sure he was compensated from the revenue earned by Academics of Flight. He would routinely change the terms of our agreements to his benefit, and his explanation was always the same: "You misunderstood me." I had to live with it, because nothing got done in Casablanca without his approval. A few years later, he retired to Miami and married an ex-Pan Am flight attendant. He has been living in Homestead, Florida, where I visited them in 2000.

Not only were there Moroccan pilots, but also several pilots from Belgium and Yugoslavia flying for RAM on contract. Jim Maloney traveled with me to teach RAM's flight engineers while I was in class with the pilots in Casablanca. One night after class, we were walking in the Casablanca street market with its narrow paths, jammed with vendors, more or less putting their wares in our faces in hopes of a sale. I think Jim and I were the only non-Arabs in the area. Jimmy kept walking beside me, with his shoulder touching my forearm as though we were one. When I turned to the left or right, he never left my side. I asked, "Jim, why in the hell are you walking attached to me?" "Because if someone hits us over the head, since you're taller, they'll hit you first." He was dead serious.

The flight engineers loved his simplicity and stories of his early days with Pan Am. They treated him as a father. Most teachers use a fancy laser pointer when lecturing to highlight items on the board. Not Jimmy, he found an old coat hanger in the classroom and unraveled it, and that was his pointer. If the United States had used him as a goodwill ambassador, the country couldn't have found a more appropriate person. We were taken to a club one night to see Casablanca's version of a strip club. Jim kept saying all night, "I am going to tell your mother."

Through the efforts of George Mercovic, one of the contract pilots and a legend himself, I returned for one more teaching assignment, accompanied by Rita and Karina. While I was teaching, Rita and Karina toured Casablanca and Marrakech. At night, we attended several dinners hosted by the European pilots and sampled couscous. One of the most memorable pilots was Helmut from Germany. He was explaining that if I wanted to be a registered "baron," he could arrange the paperwork through his brother. The only stipulation was that his brother was hard to find, since he was always running from the authorities.

During our stay, we were told a story about a king who owned an island off the shore of Morocco and loved aviation. He was so fascinated with airplanes that he built a runway, taxiway, and tower. None of the locals on his island flew; however, he had so much influence with the Moroccan government that RAM had a weekly flight to his island. Approximately a half hour prior to a scheduled arrival, he would go to the tower and wait for RAM to request landing clearance. Once requested, the king would read a weather report for the local area and airport that was actually the same report he had been using for years. He would then give the clearance to land. One time, he was late getting to the tower, and the plane had already landed and was taxiing to the ramp by the time he reached the tower. He saw the plane taxiing and insisted that the pilots request clearance to land. The pilots appeased him as they would a child, and the king responded, "RAM, Cleared to land."

Years later, I had the pleasure of training Mercovic's daughter, Kookie, and son, George. "Little George" is now a captain with Air France. When Yugoslavia split up into rival countries, Serbia and Croatia, resulting in a civil war, it was sad to see these pilots take sides, since they had worked so closely together in Morocco. One of them told me how he would sit on his rooftop, watching the military planes on bombing runs. Politics can lead to destruction in a very short period of time.

I was requested to make one more trip to have a meeting with Morocco's top military advisor, General Kabah, who was interested in having Academics of Flight establish a flying school to start the Moroccans on a flying career. My friend Badouwi was right in the middle of negotiations to ensure he wouldn't be ignored financially if and when the program got off the ground. It didn't. The round trip, including the meeting, took 36 hours, and I didn't have time to get jet lag.

On the trip back, I was in the cockpit when the flight had to report to New York ATC, since the airplane was crossing the boundary between U.S. and international (oceanic) airspace. All aircraft were in a line spaced approximately 10 minutes apart, and unknowingly, PIA was in front of us. As the Pakistani captain reported, I recognized the captain's voice as that of someone I knew, Captain Burcheed. After his transmission to ATC, I called on another frequency and told him I was right behind him. He replied that I was flying more than a line pilot.

Nigeria

It is absolutely impossible to describe Nigeria to someone who has not been there. My only advice would be to throw the rulebook away upon landing and be ready for anything. My introduction to the country occurred when a few captains from Nigeria's national carrier, Nigeria Airways, came to me for the airline transport pilot program. The ground portion was conducted in the office in Queens and the flight training in Massachusetts with Dick Backu. Dick was an FAA-designated examiner and, often as not, closed one eye during the check rides. He moved his operation to Florida where we continued our long-standing business relationship, as noted in the section called "Miami, Florida, 1997–2012."

My initial contact with Nigeria Airways was Captain Udom, and after the Airways went bankrupt, he formed his own company, Aviation Development Company (ADC), in 1984. On October 29, 2006, ADC Flight 53 crashed on takeoff, killing Nigeria's Muslim spiritual leader, Muhammadu Maccido; his son, Badamasi Maccido; Dr. Nnennia Mgbor, the first female West African ENT surgeon; and Abdulrahman Shehu Shagari, son of a former president, along with many more. The company also had a previous crash on November 7, 1996, when 143 people perished when the B-727 tried to avoid a midair collision near Ejirin, Nigeria. ADC shut its doors in 2007.

I was required to fly to Lagos to meet certain government aviation authorities in order to be an approved school recognized by Nigeria.

Once Academics of Flight began teaching for Nigeria Airways, the school began as a snowball rolling downhill and became the default trainer for most of the country's other airlines, plus the presidential fleet. I was told by one of the inspectors in the meeting that I would have to pay for round-trip airfare, plus $200 per day in expenses per individual for an inspection of Academics of Flight by five government officials, but that I should not expect them to come. I told the inspector to go to hell. Over 30 years later, the school is still doing business with the country.

I was once Udom's dinner guest at his sister's apartment in an upscale section of Lagos. The doorbell rang continuously, and certain visitors would go and hug the telephone in the adjacent room as we ate. I kept hearing them repeat in a low voice, "The hammer is strong." I have been known to participate in home construction, and there were no renovation projects being done in the apartment. It finally dawned on me what was happening, and I said, "Look guys, whatever you are planning, can it wait until tomorrow, since I am leaving on the morning flight to New York?" They chuckled, and that was the end of the discussion.

Sure as hell, when I got seated on the plane in the morning, I opened the newspaper with the headline, "Government overthrown." Due to my ongoing traveling to "hot spots," I was somehow thought to be on the CIA's payroll and said to myself, "Oh God, how am I going to explain this one?"

I had to make another trip for the United Nations with a representative from the International Civil Aviation Organization (ICAO) and a local Nigerian government official to determine the validity of funding an aviation college in Zaria, close to Kaduna. I was the team leader and was naturally requested by the Nigerian representative to give a good report continuously. In return, he assured me that I would be very *comfortable* during my stay. Since I had previous experience with Nigerians, I was aware of the true meanings of his requests, and when we were finished, he said, "Damn, Jim, you are more Nigerian than me."

For the first few years, Zaria College was very prestigious and highly regarded throughout Africa. However, as the years passed, it became a means of diverting money that had been budgeted for the school's expansion into the pockets of a few. When we arrived, the school had deteriorated to being almost extinct; pilot training was close to being nonexistent. Upon returning to the UN, I wrote a formal report that went straight to the point: "Burn the college to the ground and forget it ever existed!"

The pilots themselves were great, and to this day, I am very fond of a guy named Ode who now holds a high-level position with the aviation branch in the Nigerian government. Ode always wanted to be a pilot, but his parents wanted a doctor as a son and sent him (or so they thought) to medical school. He diverted his funds and became a first officer with a local airline. One day on landing, the weather was bad, and the plane crashed, killing several people. Ode was lying on the ground barely alive when the news crew came with cameras to cover the accident. Apparently, his mom had the TV news tuned in; yep, there was her son, covered with blood from head to toe lying on the ground. Only because he looked (and was) half-dead did his parents accept the fact they had a pilot for a son and not a doctor.

Then there was Sammy. He and a friend took off from Zaria, landing in a swamp due to engine failure; although shaken up, he and the other pilot were not seriously hurt. His flying partner left to seek assistance, not returning for the rest of the day and night. Sammy spent the time holding on to a piece of wing that separated from the airplane during the crash. Naturally, the swamp was filled with snakes, crocodiles, and other not-so-pleasant creatures, and Sammy, weighing approximately 250 pounds, would have made a nice dinner for all of them; however, they left him alone. The rescuers came in the morning and he said, "It was the longest night of my life!"

Academics of Flight became a household name among the aviation community in Nigeria. I learned that the school had trained 95 percent of all airline pilots from that country. I don't know if that's good or bad. While walking on the ramp in Lagos after returning from Zaria, I noticed five or six airplanes away from the terminal on the ramp in various forms of boarding, with a few already running their engines. I wandered over and was honored by the captains shutting down engines, disembarking to come and say "hello." Again, it was a feeling that has only been duplicated once or twice in my life. I was their "father," like it or not, and even with all the problems, they were my "boys." To this day, I'm referred to as "the white Nigerian."

On the final trip, I was contracted to return to Zaria to train a group of pilots for the U.S. flight instructor certificate. Ground training for the written exams was conducted over two weeks at the college campus in Nigeria, with the flight training done in New York. Nigerians have their own method of forgiving after a dispute, which I witnessed firsthand. A few years prior to this trip, I had trained a pilot who went back to Nigeria, and approximately a year after his return, he ran off the runway on takeoff at Kaduna. One of the senior pilots with the government blamed Academics of Flight for the faulty piloting. I was unaware of his exact comments; however, many of my previous graduates kept me informed and went to my defense. The pilot had been a military jock flying MIGs (aircraft manufactured by the Russian company Mikoyan) before being hired by this particular company. It was revealed that he hadn't flown for almost a year after receiving his rating from Academics of Flight and naturally lost what little proficiency he had to begin with.

I had approximately five boxes of material for the class at Zaria and had my pockets stuffed with $10 and $20 bills ready for a customs shakedown, as I had encountered during previous trips to Nigeria. I breezed right through the formalities of immigration and prepared for customs. Zaria had sent down a pilot and plane for me to go from Lagos to Zaria, and the pilot, Jim, assisted in placing the boxes on the customs' table. The official said, "Sir, that's not necessary, you are free to go." I couldn't believe my ears and stood there for a moment in shock.

After his comment registered, Jim got a trolley for the books, and as we were walking out, a man I had never met before came forward, shook my hand, and walked off without saying a word. He turned out to be the captain who had attempted to ruin Academics of Flight's reputation in the aftermath of the aircraft accident. To bury the hatchet, he arranged for customs to leave me alone.

In a conversation with one of the pilots, the subject of neighborhood security was mentioned, and I learned that the Nigerian punishment for a burglar is significant. The locals know where the airline pilots live and are also aware that they carry U.S. currency. For this reason, these pilots are constant victims of home invasions that are usually coordinated with the housekeeper of the home. The captain I knew had been a victim; however, he caught the thief. While detaining the culprit, the captain's neighbors came, surrounded him with tires, and threw gas on him so that the local kids could light him up. Jungle justice can be very effective.

Once more, I was caught up in the country's turmoil in 1993. During that period, the president was a military man, General Ibrahim Babangida, who had taken power by a former coup d'état. Due to growing pressure, he promised free elections. The candidate running against him, Chief Moshood Abiola, was a very wealthy businessman and a well-known philanthropist among the people. Elections were on, Abiola reportedly won by capturing 58% of the vote, but the results were annulled by Babangida. Rioting began, Babangida stepped down, and Abiola left the country to gain world support for himself as the legitimate president.

Another military man, General Sani Abacha, subsequently assumed power. When Abiola returned to Nigeria against the advice of many, Abacha had him arrested, and the Nigerian high court accused him of treason for claiming to be president. Abacha sent 200 police vehicles to take him into custody. He was imprisoned and later died under suspicious circumstances on the day he was due to be released, July 7, 1998. Although the official autopsy report stated that he died of "natural causes," Abacha's chief security officer al-Mustapha alleged that he was beaten to death. His outspoken wife was shot and killed while being driven around Lagos. I met Abiola once or twice on previous trips since he owned Concord Airlines and Academics of Flight trained most of the company pilots.

Stories associated with him were numerous, and apparently, he assisted many of the poor financially. It is said that he would write an amount for an individual on a leaf and the person would take it to any bank to cash. Nobody knows with certainty how many wives he had, and many women came forward after his death with their children, proclaiming he was their father. The young girls would go before the number one wife who would inspect the child. If she felt the child resembled Abiola, the mother was given a certain amount of money. Nigeria always has a system to settle such matters.

When I was teaching at Zaria, the country was a mess due to the political turmoil. It was very difficult for me to call home and speak with Rita and Karina. Over the course of three to four weeks, I believe I got through on only one call. Obviously, the family was worried due to the news coverage and lack of contact with me. One day while teaching, the headmaster of the school interrupted my class and told me very casually to follow him. He took me to a utility closet and told me that it "would be best" if I stayed there until he came for me. The room had a window covered with blinds, and when I peeked out, I saw several soldiers running around with machine guns. I thought to myself, "Oh well, my life is going to end in a closet in Nigeria. This is going to be a hard one for the family to accept."

On my last day at the college, I prepared for my departure and that night went to eat at a local restaurant. I saw a dish on the menu called "pepper soup," which I ordered. The waitress apologetically told me they didn't have it. Just as I was about to change my order, she came back with, "But sir, we do have soup *with pepper*." After dinner, I got my travel items together and asked the pilot who was going to fly me to Kaduna at what time the plane was going to depart from Kaduna for Lagos. From Lagos, I would then fly to New York.

"Well. They start arriving at Kaduna around midday and leave for Lagos when the pilot feels he has enough passengers to make the trip worthwhile." This was an airliner, not a small plane. The next day, sure enough, around 12:00 p.m., several B-727s started landing. The captain stood at the foot of the airplane steps and collected cash from the passengers for Lagos. There was no established price, and the fare was whatever the pilot and passenger agreed upon. When the captain felt it was time to go, he would simply wave off the passengers that had not yet boarded, although there were plenty of seats left, and fly away. I later read online that a particular Nigerian airline was banned from flying in Europe because the company used lawn chairs as seats in one of their planes. I knew that I would miss that country.

The students are great, and they do what it takes to survive, since no one else will take care of them. A few of my previous pupils from

Nigeria have been killed in aviation accidents over the years, and it always hurts.

El Salvador

I made a trip to Usulután, El Salvador, in the mid-1980s, the period of civil war between the conservative right (primarily ARENA) and the liberal left (primarily FMLN). From 1979 to 1992, the government-supported military targeted anyone they suspected of social and economic reform. Usulután, located in the southeast part of the country, was one of the most violent battlegrounds during the war due to its agricultural importance. At that time, the country was said to have been owned by 12 families, all residing in Florida. The United States was deeply involved, siding with the military.

Being picked up at the airport, the driver crossed himself, and we drove by jeep to Usulután. His gesture of crossing was not out of habit but due to the area being a hotbed of recent guerrilla activity, with the latest instance of a cotton mill being blown up. Due to my nationality, I was a prime target for kidnapping to collect a ransom. It was absolutely Vietnam all over again with the helicopters, Hueys, and low-level flights, combined with constant search-and-rescue missions by the Salvador military. In general, the country was simply "war-torn," with atrocities committed by both sides.

The sight that turned my stomach the most was to see four or five men with weapons in a Bronco SUV on their way to execute an individual who happened to get his name on the "wrong list." I was happy when my departure day arrived. Introduced to the crew with a seat in the cockpit, we taxied for takeoff; I thought to myself, "Only a few more minutes and all this will be behind me." I was wrong. During our taxi to the runway, the airspace was suddenly closed without warning due to *Operation Just Cause*. It was December 20, 1989, and the invasion of Panama by the United States to oust Noriega and his thugs had just begun. We sat for hours in the plane on the taxiway prior to finally becoming airborne.

Nicaragua

I went to Nicaragua in an attempt to spread the word about Academics of Flight's desire to expand the school's market in Central

America. As I was writing this book and trying to determine what year this took place, I asked Rita. "Call your Nicaraguan girlfriend and ask her," she replied. I said that I didn't have one, but that if I did, it wouldn't be a good idea to call her, since she'd likely want 20–25 years of overdue support money. That reminded me of what my dad told me more than once, "If I had 10% of the girlfriends your mother accused me of having, I would have been a happy man."

The Contra War had officially ended in 1987, and the country, unfortunately, had been in the direct path of Hurricane Joan in 1988. I arrived a couple of years later, around 1990. Between the two events, Managua was still in a state of devastation when I arrived at the InterContinental Hotel. The hotel was built on a hill overlooking what used to be the city. Managua's deteriorated condition was mainly due to most of the hurricane relief money going into the pockets of a few, feeling their income was more important than rebuilding the city and the surrounding area. Although Daniel Ortega was in office during this period, the history books claim Anastasio Somoza (1967–1979) as the worst offender in terms of the misappropriation of funds. He had a two-year break from power from 1972 to 1974. The United States supported him in return for favors. Karina has traveled on business to Managua over the past few years and told me that as of 2010, construction was still at a standstill.

I felt like a millionaire when I got my breakfast bill in the morning: the total was 12 million Córdobas (Nicaraguan currency). There was a park at the bottom of the hill with a basketball court, and with nothing to do for the moment, I secured a basketball and began shooting hoops one evening. As I was playing, it was turning dark, and out of the corner of my eye, I saw a demonstration coming around a bend that bordered the park. They passed within 50 yards of me and shots began to be fired. I didn't want to run for cover, since it might look as though I was involved, especially being from the United States, so I just kept playing, feeling that if it was my time, it was my time.

It wasn't. After things quieted down, I returned to the hotel, not running, but as close as you could get to it. It was absolutely amazing how warm the people were to me, even though the United States had mistreated the locals for years and years. Not knowing anyone,

I headed for the bar in the evening and started talking with a local businessman named John Pastora. After a few drinks, we went into the dance area and settled at a table with three ladies: a lawyer, a school teacher, and a doctor for the Sandinistas. John had to leave, and I entertained the ladies for the evening dancing and, of course, buying the drinks.

When I left, the sun was coming up. John picked me up later that day, and we drove all over the country: Chinandega, Masaya, plus many places in between. He insisted that I stay with him at his home instead of rooming at the hotel, and he was a great host. I am certain he wanted to keep an eye on me, not sure of what my true reason for the visit to the country might have been. Although John was apprehensive regarding my request to visit a pilot military base, we went. I was greeted very warmly, and when I explained that I owned an aviation training facility, the pilots gave me a grand tour.

They showed me their Russian helicopters. When I told them I was a helicopter gunner in Vietnam, I thought John would collapse on the spot. I explained to him and he later saw that flight crews have a special bond despite the fact that politics can force us to shoot at each other. I kept in contact with several of the pilots after my visit and sent a few headsets to them. After returning to the United States, I discovered John's surname, "Pastora," is the same as Eden Pastora, a commander of over two thousand Sandinistas. This coincidence may have had something to do with him not wanting to lose sight of me during my stay. I left the country very respectful of the people.

Guyana

Guyana Airways requested that Academics of Flight conduct two crew resource management (CRM) sessions in Georgetown, Guyana. Until then, I only knew the country was on the Atlantic Coast of South America and was once an English colony where Jim Jones's cult achieved notoriety with its mass suicide. His location was buried so deep in the jungle that the people I spoke with didn't know it existed until days after the event occurred. Georgetown is sleepy: it has one main avenue, with a few side streets. The buildings are made of wood, which sets your imagination back one hundred years. The locals are a mix of blacks, Indians, and Chinese. It is a rich country with gold and many other resources, but the wealth is in the hands of a few.

Of all the CRM classes, I think the most "active" was the Guyana crew. One of the primary themes of the course is communication between the cockpit and the cabin staff. The subject is a common sore spot since the cockpit crew is perpetually cited for deficiencies in this area by cabin crews. But there are always two sides to any story. The Guyanese flight attendants are a "spicy" group and started on the pilots with a no-holds-barred approach citing one incident after another to prove their point.

The B-707 has a peephole in the cockpit door, allowing the flight deck crew to look out into the cabin. It is similar to those installed in apartment front doors. Since the flight attendants felt they weren't being kept abreast of events in the cockpit, they simply removed the peephole. Any time they felt they were not being informed properly of a situation, they simply looked into the flight deck through the open hole in the door. They were a great group, and although working very hard, we had productive fun.

Aruba

The most memorable class was an in-country CRM course conducted for Air Aruba. The CRM concept was initiated by the FAA for all airlines after it was determined that most accidents were due to human error. The jet age arrived, resulting in the vast improvement of airplane systems that led to a major decrease in accidents. However, it was found the majority of airplane crashes were due to inappropriate flight crew actions.

Therefore, the FAA imposed a management program taken from big business and adopted it for aviation. After further research, it was proposed that the program should be expanded to most of the operational departments, due to the many accident inputs that are created not only from the flight deck but outside the cockpit as well. I developed a program, had it approved by the FAA, and taught it to several airlines, both stateside and abroad. As time went on, most airlines developed their own course.

While working at Pan Am International Flight Academy, I became friends with a fairly high-level official in the Aruban CAA, John

Koolman, when he was pursuing a B-747-type rating. He is currently flying in Bangladesh, and to this day, we stay in contact. I call him "Son," while he addresses me as "Pa." Naturally, when the Aruban government required their airline to include the program, I was on the top of the list for the contract. Off I went with books in hand to conduct the course for their pilots and flight attendants. I was most likely one of the few that left Aruba without a suntan.

Class began with approximately 12 crewmembers plus one Civil Aviation Authority (CAA) representative. There were three classes in total, each three days in duration. As in any class, while most participated continuously, a few remained silent unless encouraged to speak. There was a flight attendant sitting in the rear of the classroom, and without contributing up to that point, she raised her hand and requested to come in front of the class to speak during the last hour of day three. I was delighted; however, you could hear a pin drop and cut the air with a knife. I was the only one unaware of what was about to evolve.

Apparently, the girl's husband had also been a flight attendant for the company and decided to become a pilot, which he did. The next step after certification for any pilot is to find a way of accumulating hours in order to meet airline entrance requirements. This is a period of, for want of a better term, pure prostitution. You will fly almost anything with wings, night or day, to achieve the required hours. Most become flight instructors, while others fly cargo (freight dogs). Her husband only had the chance to run freight at night between Aruba and Venezuela. Naturally, it was an overwater route, and as luck would have it, he had an engine failure one night, went down, and was never recovered. The company had a very poor maintenance record but was allowed to remain operational.

The reason for her presentation was to put the authority's representative attending the class on the spot, emotionally demanding an explanation as to how the government could allow this company to fly with such a poor operational record. Government responsibility is one of the course topics, and I must give her credit for knowing when to strike. I felt very sorry for her as her story was told but also felt sorry for the CAA representative attending the class. For a petite young girl, she could pack a mean punch: it seemed she had been waiting an extended period of time, long before the class, to air her feelings. The recipient of her questioning was very diplomatic, and although they were not leaving the class as friends, their relations improved.

Aruba is always pictured as a family-oriented vacation spot with mom, dad, and the kids on the beach swimming and building sandcastles. Also, at any time during day or night, the cruise ships are docked, while the passengers stroll around town eating at the many fine restaurants and shopping. There is an area in the southern part of the island, facing the Caribbean Sea, named St. Nicholas. The pilots, ensuring that I saw the complete offerings of their homeland, felt it would only be appropriate for me to take a tour with them to this area. The inhabitants are mostly beautiful young ladies from Colombia who have been given a strictly monitored 60-day visa to provide entertainment to eager tourists who venture to that part of the island. I could understand why the Air Aruba pilots' favorite flights were between the island and Colombia to transport these women to and from their work assignments.

Trinidad

I always laugh when telling people I have to travel to Trinidad to teach a course for Caribbean Airlines. Immediately, the listener pictures sandy beaches, bikinis, and rum. Their mind is tuned to the resort area on Tobago, the smaller of the two islands that make up the Republic of Trinidad and Tobago. Unfortunately, my obligations require me to be at Piarco Airport for classes and in downtown Port of Spain during my off time, both a far cry from Tobago. I did get there on one trip when I took a familiarization flight with Tobago Express. It was a 17-minute flight from Trinidad, and I never left the cockpit since it was a turnaround. The contract began in 2003 and is currently still in effect. I was becoming such a familiar face around the airport, that it was suggested that I obtain a permanent ID card. Karina accompanied me on one of the trips that is mentioned in the section "Flights."

Trinidad is an oil country with several other resources that have combined to afford it a considerable amount of wealth. Unfortunately, as in similar countries, the wealth is in the hands of a few; many inhabitants are without. The continual construction in Port of Spain, the capital city of Trinidad, is ambitious, with office buildings and new hotels constantly being erected. I watched the city grow from the balcony of many different hotel rooms over the years when I stayed at the Crowne Plaza Hotel, located by the "Port." During the early days, I could see the ocean from the third or fourth floor; however, as time went by, I would have to stay above the eighth floor to have a similar view. Unfortunately, crime is rampant in Port of Spain, with a very high murder rate. Most of the problem is drug-related due to the close proximity of the island to Venezuela. Trinidad is a primary drug traffic route from South America northbound. There is also a considerable amount of kidnapping for ransom. With these local problems, unless being taken out by an acquaintance, once in the hotel after work, I remained there. Also, the city is not "shopping friendly." The stores at the mall (some claim the largest mall in the Caribbean) close by 7:00 p.m. and only open for half a day on Sundays.

Socializing can be expensive, as I discovered on one trip when I should have stayed in the hotel. I had taken a flight that arrived in the morning, and during the trip, being one of only a few passengers in business class, I chatted for a while with one of the flight attendants. Arriving at Piarco Airport, Caribbean Airlines always hired a company called R and R Transport to take me to the hotel. As I was getting into the car, the flight attendant I had been talking to on the flight asked if I would share my ride to town, since she missed her crew transport. I had no objection, so off we went, chatting some more.

She suggested we have dinner one night at a restaurant of *her* choice, and I thought it was a great gesture. Well, I should have done my homework and inquired about eating places; we went to the hot spot known as The Prime, and our (actually *my*) bill came to approximately $250. I cried for a week. On subsequent trips, all the flight attendants would give me the royal treatment, and I am sure the word was passed around, "If you hit it off with this bald-headed guy that teaches classes for the Systems Operations Control department (SOCC), he will take you to The Prime." "I am sorry ladies, never again." When I told Rita, she had no sympathy for me and told me that's what I get for thinking I am a stud. You know, sometimes she has a point.

As in Guyana, the locals are a mix of blacks, Indians, and Chinese, and although I am sure they have their racial problems, it is well hidden, and they seem to work in harmony. During the entire time I was there, I never heard a derogatory racial remark. Politely, I was told that Indians ("red skins") are holding down the blacks, but this is a natural feeling. As for the Chinese, well, they just keep making lots of money.

The people I came in contact with, from taxi drivers to airline employees to hotel workers, were all very humble and accommodating. You learned early that although a person would say he would do something at your request, it may not get done. They would rather not fulfill their commitment than refuse. Instead of offending you, they will, for example, agree to meet you at a specific time and place while having no intention of keeping the appointment. Also, forget your watch. "It's the Islands, man!" Their smiles are wide and genuine. Just because Trinidad is an English-speaking country, don't think that you will understand a conversation they are having between themselves, especially if they are talking fast. A good deal of my time spent in the classroom was asking the students to repeat themselves.

An example of how hospitable the people are was illustrated on one of the trips when, after arriving, I was met, as usual, by R and R to be taken to the Crowne Plaza Hotel around 10:00 p.m. The reservation was either not made or lost in the system, and due to a celebration period, the hotel was overbooked. The driver, who I had not met before, drove to almost every hotel in the city searching for accommodations.

At one hotel, claiming they had rooms, I was handed a key and headed for a room that turned out to be a utility closet. After accepting apologies from the receptionist, I was given another key, and down the hall I went, the driver at my side. We returned to the front desk explaining that the key was not necessary, since there was no door on the room. We left and, in a last-ditch effort, returned to the Crowne Plaza to see if any reservations had been canceled. We were in luck and I finally got to sleep around 2:00 a.m. The driver would not leave me until he was sure I would find a room and even told me if I couldn't, I would come to his house to sleep. Can you imagine a New York cabbie being so concerned?

By mid-2012, Caribbean Airlines was in the process of purchasing two B-767s to conduct flights between Trinidad and London. The company had flown this route previously with an Airbus A340 and later discontinued the flights for several years. I returned in 2012 with the assignment of teaching the dispatch staff a familiarization program to prepare them for the new aircraft. It was about my ninth year of conducting various training programs for them, and they are a very humble group, always appreciative of learning.

A few years ago, we were assigned a classroom close to a neighboring company that provided flight service to several offshore oil drilling platforms surrounding the coast. Many of the helicopters used for this service were the type with which I became familiar in Vietnam. While teaching, I would break out in a cold sweat hearing the "popping" of the rotor blades. After watching me and being familiar with my role in Vietnam, they moved the classroom location for the afternoon session without any request.

On July 30, 2011, Caribbean Airlines' Flight 523 attempted a night landing during a heavy rainstorm at Cheddi Jagan International Airport, Georgetown, Guyana. The B-737-800 had 157 passengers and 6 crew on board. Upon runway contact, the airplane lost control, slid off the short runway, and broke in two. Fortunately, it missed a ravine by approximately 200 feet, which would have been catastrophic. Although there were several injuries, there were no fatalities. Captain Fareed Dean was the aircraft commander, and due to company policy, he was relieved from flying until the investigation was completed; as of August 2013, it was still ongoing. In the interim, he has been assigned to the Systems Operations Control Department. During a teaching assignment in November 2012, Captain Dean was assigned to my class, and in the beginning of the three-day session, I was somewhat apprehensive, since discussing accidents was included in the curriculum. As it turned out, he was a great participant and a very personable guy. I hope he is cleared of any contribution to the accident when the investigation is finalized.

At one time or another, although many people will not confess, they have had thoughts of having had a previous life. I am no exception. If there was such a life, I believe it was in the Caribbean along the coast of Trinidad. Every now and then, I picture myself in a swordfight, ankle-deep in water at a beach. I am dressed in pirate clothes really going at it with my attacker, or maybe I attacked him. There was also a beautiful bare-breasted young mulatto girl with long black hair to her waist nearby observing the confrontation; therefore, we were probably fighting over her. Some things will never change, no matter what life you live. I don't know who won, but I am assuming that I lost, which ended my pirate days.

These thoughts are no big deal, because many people have them. But here is the interesting part. While training Caribbean Airlines on one of my days off, I was taken to a beach representing a cove. Walking around I felt very familiar with the area and was able to pinpoint certain landmarks before I actually saw them. Life contains many secrets without explanations.

My trip at the end of 2013 was quite unusual compared to previous ones. I had dinner with a pilot flying for Caribbean Airlines and his wife, and while eating, I asked if Trinidad ever witnessed earthquakes. "Once in a while" was the response. I don't know why I even asked the question since during the 10 years plus being associated with the country, I neither felt one nor even heard the subject discussed. No more than 30 minutes after returning to my hotel after dinner while packing for my flight home the next morning, the room began shaking side to side, up and down, with pictures coming off the wall, and items I had yet to pack striking the floor after falling from a table. All I remember thinking was not who I won't see anymore, but simply, "Fuck off, I am going to die in a Trinidad hotel minding my own business, after being in a war zone for three years in Vietnam." It didn't seem logical, but I accepted the fact. It was a 6.1 on the Richter scale, far from being in the group of most powerful recorded but strong enough to scare the hell out of me.

Jamaica

A few years after conducting training for Caribbean Airlines, the airline took control of Air Jamaica (JAM), headquartered in Kingston, Jamaica. Due to my years of friendship with Mr. Thomas, who is from Jamaica, I always had hopes of visiting the Island. The time had come: CAL was flying the B-737-800s with JAM operating the AB-319/320 airplanes, and I was asked to go to Kingston in 2011 to standardize the Jamaican dispatchers with CAL's policies and procedures. The group, as all others I met, was great with a gift of laughing at adversities and not taking life too seriously. It was one of the few places traveled where from the moment I landed, I didn't want to leave. Maybe that's what they call *island fever*.

One of Academics of Flight's first pilot and dispatch students was Basil Ferguson, who was born in Jamaica. He had initially attended the school in the late 1970s or early 1980s. I was aware that he was a captain with JAM, and after many years passed, we made contact. I could not have asked for a better host while in Jamaica. Nightly, we patronized various restaurants and watering holes. He introduced me to one of the Jamaican pilots flying in Nigeria, and we spent a good deal of time discussing mutual friends from that part of the world, which in aviation is very small.

I had previously read a considerable amount of material concerning Jamaica from the pirate days, through the earthquake that almost put Port Royal off the map, to the recent extradition of the drug lord and gun trafficker, Christopher "Dudus" Coke, to New York. He controlled his turf and business from Tivoli Gardens, a section of Kingston that no one claimed, except himself and his soldiers. It was a country within a country. During his capture, several law enforcement officers were gunned down as they finally apprehended him dressed as a woman, hoping to use the disguise to escape. I found an article that expressed the atmosphere in Tivoli Gardens at the time of his arrest. A portion of the article is as follows:

> *"If I go out, they kill me, I am sure," she says by phone. "The soldiers are everywhere. They are shooting everywhere. All the men have disappeared. They take them away. The women and the children are here but we have no food. There was so much shooting, my daughter, she is terrified. There are guns. There are bombs."*

Being white, I was told to avoid the area, especially since I didn't belong there. It was absolutely true, I didn't have any business going, and it is also absolutely true that I did go. I was not old enough to be in Jamaica for the previous historical moments but was not about to miss out on this current piece of history. The driver Air Jamaica assigned me was also in the security business; therefore, I could not find a reason not to go.

The whole area had been surrounded by barbwire and barricades with the entrances controlled by police checkpoints. The only analogy I can think of is putting a rope around parts of the South Bronx, or areas of Brooklyn, checking the ID of people coming and going. Moving out of the zone is forbidden, since the unofficial controllers tax residents based on their income. Therefore, if they move, income is lost. Also, the owners of the buildings rely on the group to gather rent, since it is too dangerous for anyone else to enter the complex. Of course, a fee is paid for this service. After leaving, we rode to the right side of the tracks, and the homes were beautiful, overlooking the Caribbean Sea from surrounding hills. It's amazing how within a 15-minute drive the island's economic status changes.

When I told my students about the adventure the next day in class, I found that none of them had ever gone to Tivoli Gardens and didn't approve of my "wandering." I didn't tell them we had also gone to Denim Town, which has a reputation similar to that of Tivoli Gardens. It was an education that could not be equaled simply by reading about the events. At times, to find the true story of life, chances have to be taken.

Antigua

While training for Tobago Express, which later became part of Caribbean Airlines, in Trinidad I met the airline's manager of systems control, Dhanash Ramdath, who entered aviation from the oil platforms off the country's coast. When Tobago Express was taken over by CAL, he left Trinidad and became the manager of systems operation control for Leeward Islands Air Transport (LIAT), Antigua's national air carrier. LIAT's previous SOCC manager had sent a few students to a school in Florida for their aircraft dispatcher certificate in anticipation of the island requiring a future certificate from an ICAO country; Antigua did not have its own certification process.

For several reasons, none of the five employees satisfactorily completed the program, and Dhanash invited me to Antigua to discuss having the employees attend the course with Academics of Flight. Upon interviewing the individuals and being briefed on LIAT's operations, I accepted the challenge. To date, three have come to New York and successfully completed the program.

I was very impressed with the island's cleanliness plus being so green and lush; however, the economy has taken its toll with a present rate of 25% unemployment due to the downturn in tourism from 2011 to 2012. The Saladoid people who migrated up the island chain from Venezuela were the early inhabitants, with the Arawaks at a later date being the first well-documented group of Antiguans. The island was settled by England in 1632, becoming basically a "sugar colony," with all the associated problems of slavery and uprisings. It gained its independence in 1981.

St. Johns, the major city, is small with narrow one-way streets lined with tourist shops made of wooden structures, which, I would estimate, were constructed at the beginning of the 1900s. There are several movie houses, which are simply guys sitting outdoors with laptops on tables and a selection of DVDs for the customers to watch: our version of a drive-in theater.

It reminded me of several trips to rural areas in the Third World, where the house with a television set was the focal point of the evening throughout the neighborhood. After dark, a small crowd would congregate outside the window, watching whatever the homeowner had tuned in for entertainment.

I took a second flight to Antigua to assist in establishing an in-house course for their employees, so the company would not have to outsource the training. I departed JFK for San Juan, Puerto Rico, and from there, I took a LIAT flight into Antigua, V.C. Bird International Airport, St. Johns. The arrival in San Juan, via Luis Muñoz Marín International Airport, is one of the most impressive arrival paths I have witnessed. Most island flight approaches refrain from bringing the aircraft too low over populated areas; they are routed from the water directly to the runway. However, this procedure takes you a few thousand feet directly over the city, affording an excellent panoramic view of San Juan.

Panama

During the latter part of 1999, I had a note passed to me from the Pan Am sales division secretary, Vicki. It was from Jose Montero, the director of the Systems Operations Control Center for Compañía Panameña de Aviación, S.A. (Copa Airlines, or COPA), to speak with Pan Am concerning COPA's dispatchers obtaining an FAA aircraft dispatcher certificate. At that time, Pan Am International Flight Academy had no idea what a dispatcher was, and I intervened on behalf of Academics of Flight. Jose flew to Miami on a morning flight, had a meeting with me at the airport, and returned on the afternoon plane to Panama.

I left the airport with the contract that today, more than 10 years later, is still in effect. I saw him last in 2010, when I was at COPA's training center in Panama, and he laughed when remembering how nervous he was giving his approval. Many of his co-workers were against the project, and he wasn't sure Academics of Flight could pull through. If the project were not a success, he would have lost his job. The school did its part, and as of today, more than 52 dispatchers are certified.

The program requires my continual travel for eight straight weeks, after which the dispatchers go to one of Academics of Flight's facilities for a 10-day certification period. A typical week would involve arriving at JFK at 4:00 a.m. for a 6:00 a.m. Monday departure to Panama, a five-hour flight from JFK, and upon arrival in Panama, going directly to the classroom to teach until 5:00 p.m. Tuesdays through Thursdays would be spent in the classroom, and after class on Thursday, it would be off to the airport to catch an 8:30 p.m. departure back to JFK, arriving home Friday at 4:00 a.m.

This schedule left me just enough time in New York to take care of a few business items that materialized while away, do my laundry, and head back to the airport for another week. During one trip, in addition to the normal weekly routine, I had to make an overnight jaunt from Panama to Bogotá, Colombia, to visit and interview the personnel from COPA's newly acquired airline, Aero Republic.

Five days before Christmas in 1989, the United States invaded Panama to oust and extradite Manuel Antonio Noriega, who was once a friend of our country. Many of the Panamanian students I have trained remember the period, and I have been entertained listening to their recollections of the period. None were opposed to the invasion, and one became the proud owner of a new Toyota during the widespread looting. The best story I heard concerning the invasion, of questionable origin, describes how the United States came up with an accurate city street map to use during the occupation. Prior to the invasion, such a map apparently didn't exist, and without one, U.S. troops would be at a distinct disadvantage. To solve the problem, a few U.S. personnel already stationed there who were aware of a future confrontation formed a jogging club. During their morning run, the club members would pick new routes, memorize the street grids and important landmarks, and record the information back at the "clubhouse" after their morning jog.

I feel very much at home in Panama and because of this, I bought an apartment in the city, making the final payment in 2010. The local currency is the U.S. dollar, and without any statistics to back me, I believe there are more English speakers there than in Miami. If you have a passion for gambling, you are in the right spot: there are more casinos than you could possibly venture into.

Of all the many nights and days spent in Panama, I had only one brief encounter that made me momentarily uneasy. Without thinking about Panama's reputation for drug involvement, I wore an embroidered polo shirt with the symbol and letters for the Drug Enforcement Agency (DEA) to dinner at a local restaurant one night. While having my meal, two very rough-looking gentlemen came to my table, not so politely telling me that DEA personnel were not welcome in Panama. I explained the shirt was a gift, didn't wait for dessert, paid my bill, and left rather quickly. I have made sure I've left the shirt in New York on all future trips.

Over the years, I have made numerous friends and consider several of them part of my extended family; my long-term success there could not have been achieved without several. Jairo and his wife Nicole established a branch of the school in Panama. Another, Edgardo, is no longer with COPA but nevertheless remains an inspiration: I wish him the best.

Jose Munoz, the captain on the B-737, and I watched the *ladies of the evening* promenade between the blackjack and roulette tables on many of my trips.

On one trip, Jose and I were sitting at the bar when immigration officers stormed in through all entrances. They were there to check the visa validity of the women; it is a well-known fact that most are from Colombia. Immigration knew what they were doing, since at least 40 young women (including some who were not *so* young) were ushered out to waiting buses for a night of detention.

Jose's wife, Yira, is an immigrations lawyer and I told Jose to tell her that I was very upset with her, since she assisted in taking my friends away from me. He came to New York in 2012, with his daughter, Yira, and son, Jimmy, for a week in hopes that it would snow. They had never seen it, and God was with them, and it snowed. The children also conducted an experiment, since they had never seen water freeze. They put a cup of water in the backyard, and the next morning, they were delighted to see that it had turned to ice. I sincerely hope my association with Panama continues throughout the future years.

13

ACADEMICS OF FLIGHT INTERNATIONAL

MIAMI, FLORIDA, 1997–2012

"Patience is golden," the saying goes and it was demonstrated around 1997, when I received a call from a long-time friend, Frank Berry. I had always wanted to expand the school to Florida. It is the focal point for the aviation markets in Central and South America, in addition to a good portion of the Caribbean. To establish a facility without any guaranteed revenue was too risky; Frank offered the solution. I was selected for a sales position with the Pan Am International Flight Academy in Miami on a 60-day trial period that could be extended.

I made it clear to Pan Am in the beginning that although this was a full-time position, I would not dissolve Academics of Flight and would establish a Miami branch. My stipulation was that the school would not offer courses that conflicted or coincided with those taught at Pan Am. I worked night and day, and the arrangement was advantageous to both schools. After a few years, the new management at Pan Am did not honor the original agreement. It was a good reason for me to terminate the Pan Am contract, since the corporate atmosphere was simply not productive for me and not my business forte. Additionally, by then, I had to focus all my attention on Academics of Flight's New York business and the clientele the school developed from Africa and South America through its association with Pan Am. I realized that the school in New York would suffer to a degree during the first few years with efforts directed to Miami, but in the long run, both locations would benefit.

Frank also found a place for me to stay during the 60-day period that was close to the office; I could walk back and forth, melting from the heat. My temporary living quarters consisted of a room in a house belonging to Jorge Paris, an ex-chief pilot for Lineas Aereas Costarricenses S.A. (LASCA), the national carrier for Costa Rica. He only spent approximately one or two months out of the year in Miami with his family, their main residence being Costa Rica. Jorge was quite a character and a real aviation pioneer in Central America. He and his wife divorced, and he remarried or began living with his housekeeper, Lilliana, who is quite a few years younger. He had his last child at 68 years old.

When it was apparent that the 60 days would be extended indefinitely, I made an arrangement with Jorge. I would do the labor if he would buy the material to repair the house, inside and out. It was neglected for years and looked like the home on the 1970s TV show *Sanford and Son*. After a year of working every possible off minute between Pan Am and Academics of Flight's work schedule, it began to look presentable. I wasn't ashamed to have visitors, as was the situation when I first moved in. The house even won an award from the community for best "yearly home improvement."

Actually, there was an ulterior motive: I wanted to buy the house since it had a lot of potential; of course, you had to use your imagination, but it was there. Lilliana cut off the funds for repairs, and Jorge wouldn't sell it since he wanted to leave it to his sons. Since Karina and her family returned from Madrid to resume work with her company in Miami, we terminated our arrangement with Jorge and left the house in October 2012, 15 years after the original 60-day agreement to live there commenced.

Approximately a year after I arrived in Miami, Karina took a position in Miami in the television industry. She rented a beautiful apartment on Brickell Island. When her position was eliminated sometime later, she moved in with me, and I was delighted to have the company. We were "roomies," and she came to the school to work full-time. Academics of Flight needed her due to the rapid growth of the business. I knew Karina's participation with the school wouldn't last, and I was happy for her when she had the opportunity to return to her own field in communications. Approximately a year after working with me, she joined Telemundo/Universal and moved to an apartment with a lifelong friend from New York, Angie.

I did have another roommate for many years who was a great companion for Karina and me; her name was "Negetta," a Pan Am parking lot cat. Almost nightly when I would leave work, the cat sat on my car hood, and one night, I said, "What the hell, let's take a ride." I never brought her back. Negetta had the affectionate disposition of a dog and was great company. Karina and Negetta were buddies, and although as per Jorge's rules were officially not allowed in the house, rules were meant to be broken. The fastest I ever saw Jorge move was chasing Negetta around the yard. I would be working on my models at the bedroom desk watching television, and she would jump up on the table demanding that I switch my attention to her, just like a woman. Since Karina left, and because I didn't go to Miami as much as I did in the beginning, Negetta understandably wandered off, leaving a few offspring in the area.

Dick Backu handled the airline transport pilot flight checks at his facility in Massachusetts, as previously mentioned. When he moved to Arcadia, Florida, we continued to work together. The candidates would complete their ground and simulator training with Academics of Flight in Miami, and then we drive to Dick's location to complete the flight portion. It was a good three-and-a-half-hour drive each way. You don't realize how flat Florida is until taking a drive through "Alligator Alley," which connects the east and west coasts of the state.

To break the boredom, I would have the passengers count alligators basking in the sun on the other side of the fence that paralleled the highway. Some of them were big, and the others were damn big. Over the course of many trips, I only spotted one that had found a hole in the fence and crossed the road. All in all, the trip broke Miami's daily routine, and it was a pleasant outing, except when a student failed a check ride. It wasn't often, but it did happen occasionally.

Karina took the ride one day for a "father–daughter" outing. When the check rides were completed, Dick took Karina and me flying in his plane. It was a refresher for me, as he cut engines and gave me simulated emergencies. Karina didn't appreciate sitting in the back, especially when Dick rolled the plane into a 60-degree banked turn to show us where he lived.

Unfortunately, Dick was subsequently diagnosed with bone cancer and passed away fairly quickly. He was a towering well-fit man who could have passed for a retired Navy Seal and would scare the hell out of the Nigerian pilots who came to him for a check ride. He was as gentle as a lamb with few words and smiles, but with a stare that could pierce right through steel. I drove up to have lunch with him when he disclosed his health situation. We both knew it would be our last get-together, and it was probably the most traumatic lunch of my life. We were closing the curtain on a 25-year business relationship without ever having a disagreement. We both knew he would pass shortly due to his illness and ended our lunch with a hug. Dick passed away a few weeks later and was given a military funeral with a fly-by with several aircraft. Karina attended the burial with me.

Although Academics of Flight did not train Angolan flight crewmembers in their country, the school did conduct classes for the majority of its airline pilots in Miami for several years. They are a terrific group with their polite and sincere methods of social interaction. Rita would spend endless hours ensuring they were well taken care of during the training periods in Miami. This not only included class-related tasks but extended to arranging living quarters, food, and many trips back and forth to the doctors when a relapse of malaria or other ailment would surface. Rita earned the nickname "Mother Africa." She was the first one they would call for assistance.

Angola had been plagued with civil war since 1975, when it won its independence from Portugal, and the conflict continued until 2002. There were only brief periods of peace during these years, and it became the longest Cold War conflict involving hostilities. The two parties were the Movement for the Liberation of Angola (MPLA) backed by the Soviet Union, utilizing Cuban forces, the majority of which were black, and the National Union for the Total Independence of Angola (UNITA) supported by the United States, through CIA activities.

I knew several of the pilots who flew for the CIA in that region during the conflict and later became instructors for the Pan Am International Flight Academy. Their stories duplicated my Vietnam experiences to the letter. Many of the Angolan pilots we were training flew helicopters during that period. I believe that one of the reasons they took to Rita and me was that they knew I could relate to the conditions they endured. We all agreed that "war" was nothing but destructive for everyone, except for a few who made financial gains paid for with the lives of the average citizen.

One of the crews we were training was on the B-727 and coming in for an approach to Luanda, Angola, when a heat-seeking missile was fired at them. It missed one of the engines by *inches* and went through the tail section without exploding. The crew did not realize what had happened until they got on the ground and saw the hole in the rear of the airplane. At that point, all got down on their knees and kissed the ground; their time was not up.

Several of the pilots that Academics of Flight trained had flown for Executive Outcomes (EO). EO was a very effective South African private military company (PMC) founded in 1989. They were called upon to provide military assistance to Angola's and Sierra Leone's political parties during various civil wars. After they achieved a peace agreement in Angola, they were replaced by UN forces to maintain the peace. Shortly thereafter, Angola returned to war. The company was also active in other world locations and disbanded in December 1998. The purpose of this action was to stop mercenary activities.

On August 24, 2012, the final piece of furniture was removed from the Florida office of Academics of Flight and the school was officially closed on August 30, 2012. Rita agreed with the decision, and it was bittersweet. The Florida location had proven very lucrative for a decade; however, beginning in 2009, the influx of the school's major source of revenue, the clientele from Africa, began to decline. A few companies went bankrupt, and other airlines began to fly aircraft for which the Miami training centers did not have compatible simulators to complement the required training. I felt sorry for Rita, since for the last few years, she was the main force conducting the school's business in that location. I am sure that behind my back she shed a few tears. Two or three companies transferred their non-flight training requirements to Academics of Flight's location in New York.

As a result of Karina and family returning from Madrid to resume work with Telemundo/Universal in Miami, and with Academics of Flight's Miami branch closed, Rita and I terminated our house arrangement with Jorge in October 2012. Ironically, on the final day we were moving the last items from the house, Jorge died.

I was weighing each option with the good and bad points on how to get some boxes containing items from the Miami house and the closed office to New York when my cell phone rang. I couldn't believe the voice on the other end. It was Leslie, who had access to a tractor/trailer. Leslie wanted to repay an old debt he felt owed to me. I explained to him he was not indebted to me but that I would like for him to use his truck to move the items to New York. This size truck has several common names: "18-wheeler," "rig," and "semi."

All arrangements for the trip were completed with Leslie. Karina and I had been shifting boxes from inside the house to the driveway in anticipation of his arrival. We were sitting on the front porch when we heard the noise of the white truck's large diesel engine, prior to seeing it turn the corner to our street. After parking in front of the house, as Leslie was climbing down from the cab, Karina turned to me and said sarcastically, but in a playful manner, after viewing the rig's size, "Daddy, you'll do anything to save a dollar, won't you?"

I was saving a substantial sum by Leslie's generosity; however, the determining factor was that I always wanted to ride in a tractor trailer. The better part of the next hour was devoted to passing boxes back and forth between the three of us, and finally, the last was placed in the driver's compartment. It is absolutely amazing how much freight can be carried in the cab alone. When Leslie first explained to me he wouldn't have the trailer, I felt some items would have to be left behind. I was wrong; everything was on board!

At 4:00 p.m., after giving Karina a goodbye hug, I climbed into the cab, and Leslie fired up the 465-horsepower engine. The noise would have woken any neighbor taking an afternoon siesta. We were on our way, and I must have looked like a little boy taking his first train ride: I was elated. After all those years of wanting to, I was finally going to ride in an 18-wheeler. We maneuvered slowly through the residential area, on to NW 36th Street toward I-95. Once on I-95, we turned north and continued in that direction for the next 29 hours.

Leslie is partially bald and black, with a medium build. He is in his fifties and from Jamaica. Although I had known him for years, he revealed more of his life's story as the semi chewed up the highway to New York. Unfortunately, I could not hear him a good portion of the time over the roar of the engine and grinding gears as well as due to his soft-spoken manner. Leslie moved to Brooklyn with his family as a teenager. His dad was a trucker in Jamaica, and his mom worked for the postal service in their town, which is approximately a half-hour drive from Kingston, the capital of Jamaica. Leslie, like me at that time, was not thrilled with education, but he found his love working on cars and street drag racing. Naturally, this type of racing is illegal on city streets, and more than once, he was confronted by police and paid fines.

As we headed north, his description of a semi driver's life unraveled, and my respect for these people grew as he explained their lifestyle. The truckers pound the pavement during all kinds of weather, day and night, and most have, as is the case with Leslie, driven in all of the contiguous 48 states. I asked Leslie if he ever had an accident and immediately realized I shouldn't have. His reply was, "I flipped one over in Wyoming." Since I asked during the first hour on the road, I knew I was in for a long ride.

When you look down on passing cars from the cab, they seem to be the size of models that could be used in a diorama. Day turned into night as we continued along central Florida's east coast. Leslie keeps the interior of his cab, his "office," in complete disarray, as I do mine at the school. Road receipts, newspapers, and used coffee cups plus empty cigarette boxes lined the floor. Since I had nothing to do, I volunteered to clean and organize the area. I collected the newspapers from the floor and saw a large Bowie knife lying underneath them. Not wanting to ask why it was there, I simply slipped it under my seat. By this time, Rita and Karina had called me, at least twice each, to see how my dream of "trucking" was progressing.

Unfortunately, after a trucker has successfully delivered a load, too often the broker does not pay the driver. The trucker who owns his rig is in the best position to reduce this hazard of nonpayment. They are regulated by law to drive, "wheels spinning," a maximum of 11 straight hours with no more than 14 hours of continuous duty time. At this point, it's time to pull over to the side of the road or into a rest stop for 10 hours of rest. Many truck stops located alongside the interstates have showers and a game room lounge, and some even offer rooms to rent, similar to a motel.

Of course, there is always a restaurant and shopping area. You can purchase food, clothes, and almost any item needed for yourself or your truck. Naturally, gas is at the top of the list. Whereas the gas tank in a car has a capacity of approximately 20 gallons, a truck can hold about 300 gallons. A truck stop is like a downtown shopping area condensed into one building. A trucker will most likely spend his/her sleeping hours in the truck cab, where a bed is located behind the driver and passenger seats. There is a curtain that can be drawn, separating the bed and seats, blocking light for those who sleep during the day. Most drivers prefer to drive at night and rest during the daytime. Some cabs are outfitted with refrigerators, microwaves, televisions, and many other comforts of home: it all depends on what size and furnishings the owner can afford. To many people, the day-to-day life of a trucker appears to be that of a "loner." I prefer to characterize it as "self-sufficient."

By 1:00 a.m., Florida was finally behind us with its heavy rains, and it was good to be surrounded by the savannas of Georgia. At 2:00 a.m., tired and hungry, we pulled into a truck stop off I-95, finding a parking space among what seemed to be at least 1,000 trucks. I am absolutely convinced that "America moves by truck." If rigs stopped, so would the country. After eating in the restaurant, it was back to the cab for a rest period. Although Leslie offered me the bed, I told him he was the captain of this trip; therefore, I declined.

As he disappeared to the bed and drew the curtains, I slept in the passenger seat, leaning my head against the door window, using it as my pillow. Awakening before him, I got out and paced around the truck, making sure I didn't wander from our parking space. I was worried if another trucker saw me hanging around their semi during the wee hours of the morning, they might think I was up to "no good." I've heard that ladies of the evening known as "Lot Lizards" are often seen strolling around the parked trucks; however, we were not paid any such social calls. By 5:00 a.m., Leslie was up, we ate, gassed up the truck, and then it was back on the interstate heading north. The rains from Florida caught up to us, continuing until the last one or two hours of the trip.

I drove large trucks on a couple of occasions in the past (Loring AFB and AirNet), but they were not 18-wheelers. Listening to Leslie's discussion on the rules of the road for trucking, regardless of the size, they are all vulnerable to weight stations or "scales." I told him my experience crossing the border between Maine and Massachusetts, and he said technology affected the procedures when approaching these facilities. These days, there's a small monitor inside the cab that's attached to the windshield, similar to an EZ-Pass tag. Approximately a mile or two from the weight station, there is a plate in the road extending across all lanes that weighs the truck as it crosses. A motorist in a car would not even notice this, since it's buried in the road. By rolling over the plate, the truck's registration and weight are checked. If everything is in order, a green light will appear on the monitor, and the rig continues without having to stop at the station. If it blinks "red," the driver has a problem with either paperwork or weight, or both, and he must pull into the station, in hopes of sorting the problem out.

Often a trucker doesn't see what he is actually hauling. The company will instruct him to drive to a warehouse where the trailer is already loaded and sealed shut prior to the tractor arriving. Paperwork will be exchanged, and the trip begins. Therefore, he can't verify the exact weight of his load.

The trucker who knows that his load is overweight from the beginning tackles the situation the "old-fashioned" way. First, he will call truckers who are currently driving in that area on the CB radio, located in the cab, to determine if the particular weight station is open or closed. Drivers use this radio continuously to advise their fellow truckers of certain road conditions, such as accidents, speed traps, or just plain gossip to stay awake. If the trucker is uncertain as to whether the scales are open or closed, he may simply park the truck alongside the highway, get out, and take a walk up the road to see the station's status. If he thinks it's open, he will attempt to drive a back road around the scale.

Although his haul wasn't overweight, Leslie took back roads several times to avoid paying tolls. This was one of the reasons it took 29 hours to get to New York. Another factor for the trip time was the semi had a governor restricting its speed to 68 mph. Naturally, most truckers don't appreciate this device, since they prefer to drive faster than the monitor allows. Many companies can track their vehicles on radar, as an air traffic controller tracks an aircraft's path through the sky. The advantage to this is by knowing exactly where their trucks are, they can direct the closest rig that is empty to pick up waiting for freight.

As daylight broke with overcast skies, we crossed the North Carolina border, and by this time due to boredom, I was losing my interest in becoming a trucker. Driving through the various states along I-95, it's amazing how differently it's maintained depending on where you are. North Carolina maintains their major highways in excellent condition, whereas when we crossed into southern Virginia, I would give the road a very poor rating. It began to improve the farther north we rode. We arrived in the Washington–Baltimore area prior to the evening rush hour, which allowed us to get through this leg of our journey without delays.

I have made several trips between New York and North Carolina on I-95. It goes through Delaware, connecting to the New Jersey Turnpike, leading to the George Washington Bridge. Leslie took another route to avoid the tolls. This gave me another view of Delaware, and I never realized how flat it is. Everywhere I looked, all I could see was acres upon acres of cornfields.

Darkness overcame us approaching New Jersey, and I called Rita to inform her that we'd likely pull up to the house around 10:00 p.m. We were right on time, and to make it official, I had Leslie give a few blasts on the truck's air horn to let the neighbors know we arrived. When we were turning the corner to our street, someone was walking their dog. Taking a look at the size of the semi, she said we couldn't drive down the street. I guess the 29 hours took their toll on me, and I barked back at her, "Relax, lady, we're making a local delivery!" With that, she continued down the sidewalk without further comment. When the off-loading was completed, we were rewarded with a great home-cooked meal prepared by Rita. After dinner, Leslie fired up the rig, we hugged, and I watched him and the truck disappear down the street. I forgot all about the boredom encountered during the trip and felt emptiness, since I was now being left behind!

14

FLIGHT TALES

"Life is a journey, not a destination."
—Ralph Waldo Emerson, American essayist, lecturer, poet

Taxiing for takeoff on a homebound flight always allows me time to think while staring out the window. It's my moment of solace. "Did I accomplish what I came for? Will I be asked to return for another challenge?" It's 5:15 p.m., March 25, 2010, seat 4A on a Caribbean Airways flight from Piarco Airport, Port of Spain, Trinidad, bound for JFK. As the late afternoon sun filters through the window, and takeoff power is applied, I watch the runway markings flash by. The engines roar, and we become airborne.

"My God, how many times and places have I been through a take-off to fulfill Academics of Flight obligations and then return home? What will I do when it stops?" Over the past 35 or more years, this journey has taken me through Nigeria, Belgium, Morocco, Panama, Guyana, Trinidad, Jamaica, Antigua, and Pakistan, with other less memorable stops along the way. I've visited some of these places many times. Over the past 10 years, there have been at least 80 trips to Panama alone, totaling 160 flights, including round trips.

On this particular flight out of Trinidad, my attention was drawn toward two seats, 3D and 3F, occupied by an Indian couple. Karina and I sat there on one of the first flights to Port of Spain. She is a great traveling partner, and you can expect a humorous moment at any time. By then, Karina had been a world traveler, and this time, it literally caused her to bite off more than she could chew. The flight attendant asked if she wanted hot sauce for her meal.

"Karina, *don't take it*, it's really hot," I intervened.

"Daddy, will you please remember that I have been to Mexico and Pakistan plus many other places, and

I know what hot sauce is?"
"Karina, I am going to say it again, *don't take it!*"
"Yes, thank you, I will have some, please."

I had this type of hot sauce on a previous trip, and it more or less restricted me to the closest bathroom for a significant amount of time. As the flight attendant fulfilled my traveling partner's request, she made sure Karina had her glass filled to the brim with water and gave me a quick wink. Sure enough, no more than 10 minutes later, I glanced over, and Karina's face looked as though she had been on a treadmill nonstop for the previous five hours. She was absolutely covered in sweat. I could only laugh like hell and said, "Now, my little world traveler, would you like me to request more water for you?" You can just imagine her response.

Afternoon-to-night flights are the best. First, the earth goes from light to dark, and then the top of the sky becomes dark, leaving a layer of light between the two. As time goes by, the light gets squeezed between earth and sky, and now it's total darkness with the stars staring in from the other side of the window. Am I flying through *heaven*? Everyone looks up in the sky when they mention the word, but where does it start and end? Is there really such a place? Sitting on the left side of the cabin, the coastal lights of Florida come into view, indicating that in two hours, we will begin our approach to JFK. I have taken this route so many times previously; I know what lights will appear next. Being a pilot and frequent traveler, I could never total the hours spent at altitude, but the sights have been amazing. It was best described by Richard Bach, "Not even to his most beloved can a pilot tell, about the wonders of the sky."

One of the flights on Pakistan International Airlines that I will always remember was between JFK and Karachi, Pakistan. It was a multiple-leg journey that went JFK–Paris, Paris–Frankfurt, Frankfurt–Cairo, Cairo–Dubai, and Dubai–Karachi: 22 hours in total. Captain Saleem Halk brought us to Cairo, and with a strong tailwind, we landed approximately 30 minutes early. The in-flight movie hadn't even ended. He wouldn't let the ground staff open the doors until it finished.

I had an encounter with another passenger after leveling off out of Dubai, headed for the final destination, Karachi. There were only a few of us in first class, and this fellow, probably late twenties or early thirties, kept staring at me and finally came over. At first, I was glad for the company; however, things started going downhill very rapidly.

You have to remember, this was in the mid-eighties, much before 9/11. Apparently, this passenger was a strong fundamentalist and certainly did not like Americans. He began expressing his views toward Westerners and indicated that he believed that Pakistan didn't require my visit. Fair enough, everyone has their own beliefs. However, when he finished by saying that I could get *hurt*, I went straight to the cockpit to discuss the situation with Captain Johnny, who was in command on this leg of the flight. John was, and still is, a very close friend of the family, and it so happens that I was staying with him during my stay in Karachi on this particular trip.

I've never seen a pilot get out of his seat so fast, and before I could turn around, Johnny and my new acquaintance were huddled in a corner of first class with Johnny's finger a couple of inches from the rogue passenger's face, wagging as though it were connected to a metronome. I returned to my seat, and the gentleman never looked at me for the rest of the flight. Somehow we ended up side by side at the baggage belt after landing in Karachi, and he actually smiled at me. Of course, Johnny was right behind me. It's always good to have connections.

It seems Johnny had a remedy for any incident. He was bringing a group of Pakistani soldiers back from Chad where they had been engaged in fighting due to a political situation. As the flight progressed toward Karachi, the soldiers became extremely unruly with the flight attendants. They had a difficult time walking down the aisle without having their bottoms or other parts groped and grabbed by the soldiers. To calm the men down, Johnny simply turned down the cabin pressure from its normal altitude setting of 4,000 feet to approximately 10,000 feet. The brave, battle-weary passengers simply went to sleep due to the decreased oxygen level in the cabin. As the flight approached Karachi, Johnny returned the pressure to its normal setting, and by the time they were fully awake, the plane was on the ground.

Johnny's given name is John Sadiq, and he is one of the true pioneers of aviation history from his era. He wrote a book, *Come Fly with Me—Propellers: An Airline Pilot's Story,* concerning his flying career; it is great reading. The stories are incredible and involve many well-known world diplomats of his time. He was, and I am sure still is, a natural in employing different accents. On one flight, every time he made a position report to the various air traffic controllers, he would imitate a pilot from a different country with an accent, be it German, Arab, or French. At one point, a very confused controller asked, "PIA, how many of you are there? We are showing only one target on radar?" He would come and stay with the family when flying to New York, and in many nights, we would work out plans to save the world over a bottle of scotch at the bar in our family room. It was a good thing nobody had to drive home. On another visit, we went with Rita to see the top movie of the time, *ET*. Johnny and I wept through a couple of scenes, and Rita never let us forget it. Pilots *do* have feelings, just like other people.

On a previous flight to Pakistan, Captain Afaq Rizvi, a senior pilot with Pakistan International Airlines (PIA), arranged for Rita and Karina to travel with me while I gave a group of company pilots an airline pilot ground program. Afaq was the captain on one of the trip legs. Karina, who was about five years old, sat on his lap in the cockpit for most of the flight. At some point, unbeknownst to the crew, she disengaged the autopilot. It wasn't discovered until ATC questioned the pilots as to why the plane was not at the assigned altitude. The airplane was a B-747, and being well taken care of, we had seats in the upper lounge. Karina, being a typical child asked Rita, "Mommy, why are those people sitting in the basement?"

I once took a Nigeria Airways trip from JFK to Lagos, Nigeria, to participate in meetings with several of the country's government personnel. As I had been to Nigeria previously, nothing shocked me, and you simply have to throw away the rule book. Watching people check in at JFK, the entertainment began. If you have anything that won't fit in the overhead rack, such as a VCR or a small appliance, you have to be prepared for a confrontation.

At the check-in counter, you'll generally be told that you can't take the item into the cabin and that it'll have to be checked. If that happens, chances are you'll never see it again. The argument begins and doesn't end till the passenger passes some cash, or "dash," to the check-in clerk at the counter, who quickly pockets it. Is it now safe to say that the item will travel alongside you? Not yet. As soon as the passenger walks through the cabin door, the whole episode is repeated: it means a bit of cash for the flight attendant to get the item on board: At least it didn't go into the cargo hold.

The cabin attendant takes the article to the rear of the plane and places it on top of all the other items that are stacked on the back row of seats. By the time the cabin door is closed, all that can be seen in the back row piled high to the cabin ceiling are small televisions and other electronic components that got there by going through the same process as we did. According to the laws of physics, an object at rest will move forward if a moving object suddenly stops. With my hands covering my head as the plane sped down the runway, I prayed that the takeoff would not be aborted.

Being bald and one of the few white passengers, I stuck out like a light bulb. As the plane taxied to the terminal at Lagos, I prepared myself for a guaranteed *shakedown*. At that time, a passenger going to certain countries had to receive a yellow fever shot one week prior to entering the country. Being unorganized, I got mine the day before. Of course, Nigeria was on the list of places that required this shot. I put $10 and $20 bills in my top pocket, deplaned, and began the walk with the other passengers to immigration. Sure enough, I was not disappointed. I heard, "Sir, welcome to Nigeria, may I please see your shot records?"

"Here we go," I thought to myself. "Oh, sir, we are going to have to quarantine you for six days," the officer said, with a very sad expression accompanied by a make-believe tone implying he really cared about how it would inconvenience me. I was only to be in Lagos for four days. I was then taken to another room that looked like it was the one where they made the movie *Papillon*. The concerned officer began his speech all over, but this time, he ended by saying, "Unless you can help me." Bingo! Out came my $10, which quickly transferred to his hand. His departing words were, "Have a good stay, sir, while you are in my country." I left before he realized he could have had the $20.

On another flight to Lagos, there was no problem entering; however, there was an issue with leaving. I had been on a fact-finding mission for the UN to a Nigerian college that was asking for donations from the United Nations to improve the school. Of course, if given these funds, the upper management of the school would keep it for personal living.

After arriving in the country, due to a team member from Canada arriving a week late for the inspection, my exit stamp was outdated when I checked through immigration to get on the flight home. I wasn't in the mood to do a lot of haggling, and a very pretty young woman immigration officer told me I had to stay for approximately a week to sort out the exit visa problem.

"Fine," I replied. "You will have to take me home, bed me, feed me, and do my laundry, because I have no more money." Apparently shocked, she replied, "I hope you have a pleasant flight home, sir," and passed me through to the boarding gate. I guess I wasn't her type.

I was on a flight to Monrovia, Liberia, on another Nigeria Airways plane. At that time, Academics of Flight was actively accepting foreign students for pilot training. I had been corresponding with a Mrs. Johnson, who resided in Monrovia, and wanted to enroll her son, Alvin, into the program.

I learned that it would be possible to go through Monrovia, spend a day there, and then continue to New York. Contacting Mrs. Johnson, arrangements were made for her to pick me up at the airport. Disembarking and joining the passenger line to clear customs, everything seemed to be going smoothly, until it got to my turn for passport review.

After answering the standard questions such as "Why are you here?" and "What is your occupation," I was told in a not-so-pleasant tone to go sit on a bench. A few more passengers would go through; then the clerk would call me again and go through the same process, telling me to go back to my bench. This was repeated several times, and I began to feel paranoid, especially since Mrs. Johnson had not yet arrived. Other passengers started looking at me, and I felt like saying, "Who, me?"

At this point, a woman with an entourage of bodyguards enters the terminal. You bet: Mrs. Johnson had arrived, barking orders to everyone in sight. After hugging me, Mr. Etchison could not have been treated better. I was laughing to myself, thinking, "How in the hell do I get into these situations?" I was led to a limousine, with another limo in front, flags waving from the fenders, and all of a sudden, I was hot shit. Once settled in my seat, I turned to my hostess and said, "Mrs. Johnson, I don't know who you are or what you do, but I am damn glad you showed up!" To this day, I don't know what her status was and felt it would be better not to research the issue. We headed out of the airport, through the Firestone Rubber Plantation, and on into Monrovia; it reminded me of a small town in Alabama or Mississippi.

One flight in the summer of 2010 allowed me to feel as though I were the CEO of a large company traveling on my own corporate jet, say a B-737/800. I reported to JFK around 4:00 a.m. for my weekly teaching trip to Panama on COPA Airlines. Very infrequently I experienced a delay over the previous 10 years traveling with them; however, that morning, it happened. The departure time was continuously pushed forward to around noon. At that time, it was finally canceled. I knew COPA would sooner or later need the aircraft back in Panama, and since I had my commercial pilot certificate, I was placed on the "general deck" document for immigration purposes as a crewmember. The plane was finally released after repairs around 8:00 p.m. that evening. Off we went, with the full cabin crew to serve me since I was the only passenger.

Another memorable flight was between JFK and Miami, traveling on TWA. I was sitting in economy and was having an ongoing conversation with a Jewish woman sitting next to me. Her husband was seated several rows behind us. At some time during the conversation, I must have told her I was a pilot, and about halfway through the flight, the shit hit the fan due to 30 minutes of turbulence. Passengers were becoming nervous and sick, and my new traveling companion yelled to her husband, "Don't worry, Herbie, I have a pilot next to me."

I am sure she didn't notice how deep my fingernails were buried into the seat, and finally, the plane got back into smooth air once again, becoming stable. As we were disembarking, the captain was standing by the cockpit door and overheard a few of the passengers thanking me. He had an expression of bewilderment on his face, and instead of attempting to explain to him my new popularity, I decided to silently cherish the moment.

I was once on a flight from Miami to LaGuardia, and about an hour from landing, I tried to remember when I first began flying. My dad, being one of the pioneers in commercial aviation with Pan Am, would take me to Idlewild Airport (now JFK) for taxi run-up inspections in the old Constellations (L-049s). I would sit in the cockpit observer's seat, legs not long enough to touch the floor, watching the crew as they would pilot the plane down the runway, reaching take-off speed and then aborting with a grinding noise and the smoking of brakes.

On another trip when I was young, I remember sitting by the open cockpit door watching my dad at work at the flight engineer panel. Those were the days when it was a privilege to fly with passengers wearing sport coats, suits, and ties; even if you were in economy, you were still served a hot meal with real silverware. It was possible to have an alcoholic beverage without paying, and if you smiled at the flight attendant, you could even have a second! It's amazing how things change over time; however, if you are to survive, you have to accept the realities of today instead of always pining for or expecting what life used to be. But no one can make you erase the memories.

In October 2012, I had to make a trip to Miami with my attention on a little girl that was sitting in the window seat, one row in front of me. She couldn't have been more than three or four years old. Her face was pressed against the window, seemingly mesmerized by the wonders of the sky. I started thinking about what kind of window she would be staring from on her travels when she reaches my age.

I always think of a song by Jimmy Buffett, when he says, "It's so damn lonely when you're flying alone." It's very true.

EPILOGUE

I believe a major fear of anyone attempting to write a memoir is that death will overtake them prior to the completion of the task. This uncertainty, in reality, becomes a motivating force to accomplish the undertaking. I started the book several years ago, and I can only thank the many people who encouraged me to finish.

When I began writing, the reasoning behind the effort made sense; however, I really wasn't thoroughly convinced. Although my time on earth has not been boring, I just didn't feel the need or demand, although encouraged by some, to write. Now that the book is complete, I am convinced that the continuous effort to finish it was worth the labor. Not because it has made me more important in life than when I started writing, but simply, because it's a story that will not be buried with me. It will be available to those who are interested, not only when I'm gone but while I'm still living. As an example, my nephew Phil picked up the manuscript not too long ago, and after reading a few pages, he said, "Uncle Jim, I didn't know you went to college to be a farmer."

I think writing a book such as this should be undertaken by everyone, not just the famous. Everyone has a story and it should be told.

I have to laugh at Captain Laird, the helicopter aircraft commander on my last mission in Vietnam. We have a mutual friend who told me he had just completed a book on his ancestry that's over 600 pages long, dating back to the 1700s. Laird's reply when I told him was, "Damn, I can go back further than that with my family's history and give it to you on the back of a napkin." This illustrates how the length of the story isn't important; it's how honest the person is when writing about his own life and those he chose to mention.

Anyone's life cycle can be compared to that of a mountain climber. The person begins ascending toward the crest, which includes the years of maturing and building a future. Once at the peak, our climber reaps the rewards. Then the descent down the mountain begins. This represents the journey toward the person's senior years. As I wrote, I could identify each of the above phases I have traveled through.

I am always reminded of my age by peers and asked the inevitable question as to when I plan to retire from Academics of Flight. My answer is always the same: "Why? I enjoy what I am doing." Henry Ford once commented, "If you like what you do, you haven't worked a day in your life." Although I have worked hard and, at times, felt that I am carrying the world on my shoulders, I understand Ford's statement. Yes, I have slowed down, as our mountain climber does descending from the top, but I cannot imagine completely retiring. I receive too much satisfaction from teaching. As long as my health permits, I plan to remain involved with the school, finding a balance between that and my other endeavors.

At some point in time, Academics of Flight will have to close its doors; it has to happen. However, the benefits realized by the students due to their personal commitment to better themselves will be passed on to future generations. As a result, Academics of Flight will live on in the memories of many.

"Stories live forever, but only if you tell them."

—James Cromwell as Bud Vogel in *Memorial Day* (2012)

INDEX

www.ingramcontent.com/pod-product-compliance
Lightning Source LLC
LaVergne TN
LVHW090559110826
845146LV00001B/194

* 9 7 9 8 9 9 1 2 5 4 7 0 0 *